Christopher

IT'S FUN TO MAKE THINGS FROM SCRAP MATERIALS

(formerly titled: Scrap Fun for Everyone)

BY EVELYN GLANTZ HERSHOFF

B.S. in Ed., M.A.

Illustrated by the author

DOVER PUBLICATIONS, INC., NEW YORK

This Dover edition, first published in 1964, is an unabridged and unaltered republication of the work first published by the Larch Book Company in 1944, under the former title: *Scrap Fun for Everyone*.

Library of Congress Catalog Card Number: 64-25093

Manufactured in the United States of America

Dover Publications, Inc.
180 Varick Street
New York 14, N. Y.

TAKE YOUR CHOICE

JUST FOR FUN

Get a piece of paper, about eight inches square. Fold it from corner to corner to make a triangle. Hold it with the longest edge down. Now fold the right point of the triangle over to the left side of the triangle. Fold the left point of the triangle over to the right side of the triangle. Look at the pic-

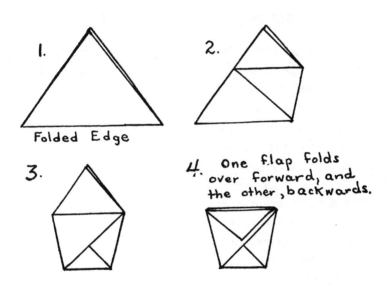

1.

Folded Edge

2.

3.

4. One flap folds over forward, and the other, backwards.

ture on this page. Does your paper look like that? That's fine. Now, at the top of this triangle is a point. Fold this point down, towards the bottom of the triangle, like a little flap. Do the same to the back half of the triangle. You are all finished.

You have just made an easy drinking cup. That wasn't hard to do, was it? If you can make this drinking cup in less than five minutes, then you can make all the things in this book. Some things will take longer than others to make, but all of them will be lots of fun. Except for a little time and energy they will cost practically nothing to make.

Suppose we have some fun with this drinking cup you have just made. Get a small cork or a button. Tie a string to it. The string should be about twelve inches long. Tie the other end of the string to the middle of the top of the cup. Hold the cup in one hand, toss the button or cork into the air, and see if you can catch it in the cup at the first try.

TO MAKE THINGS EASIER

Have a set place to work. Try to work near a window. Put up a bridge table in a corner of the room. That will be your work shop. Have a small box in which to keep a bottle of glue, a jar of paste, a pair of blunt end scissors, for safety, a few pencils, a ruler, clips, fasteners, thumbtacks, needles and thread, paints and brushes, and any other things you might gather when you are making things.

Wear a smock when you work, or an apron, or mother might not like seeing some spots on your clothes. Save some large newspapers to work on. It's much easier to roll up cut scraps in a newspaper that you have worked on than to pick up each little piece separately. A large paper bag is a good wastepaper basket too.

Keep a separate box for scraps of material, colored paper, cardboard, oilcloth, wallpaper, felt, ribbon, spools, pieces of wood, and any odds and ends of material you think you might be able to use.

If more than one of you will be making things, and I suspect Dad and Mother will be trying their hand some times, have a separate box of crayons, paste, scissors, and other things to work with, so that you won't get in each other's way when you work. It would be nice to have an extra box for company.

WHEN YOU ARE PASTING

Put a large clean sheet of paper over the thing you are pasting, and smooth it out with your hands. Then if there is any paint or crayon on your hands it won't get on the things you are pasting, but on this sheet.

If you haven't any paste, here's how to make some. Put half a cup of flour into a small saucepan. Add enough cold water to it to make it creamy and thin. Do this slowly. Boil this for about five minutes. See that the flame is low. While it is boiling, stir it all the time. Now shut the flame. Wait till this cools. If you think it is too thick, add a little cold water. Do you want it to smell nice? Then add a few drops of peppermint oil or wintergreen oil to this mixture. This will make it keep better too.

IS EVERYTHING READY?

You have a place to work in. You have the materials to work with. You have the time and energy to make something. You have over four hundred things to make. I am sure you are headed for a good time, no matter which one of these things you will make. Here's wishing you many happy hours of scrap fun.

AIRPLANES

EACH ONE of these planes will fly. Some of them won't fly very high or very far. Even though they won't ever cross the Atlantic Ocean they'll manage very well in your own back yard. If you make several airplane hangars, as shown in this chapter, you can store your planes safely, and build your own airport. Try making one of these planes right now.

---

1. A QUICKIE PLANE

You will need:

> A clothespin
>
> A piece of paper
>
> Paint, any color

PAINT THE CLOTHESPIN any color. Fold a piece of paper, any size, until it fits into the center space in the clothespin. If the paper feels too thick, then wedge it into the center space with a small piece of cardboard. Make a few of these, but paint each one a different color.

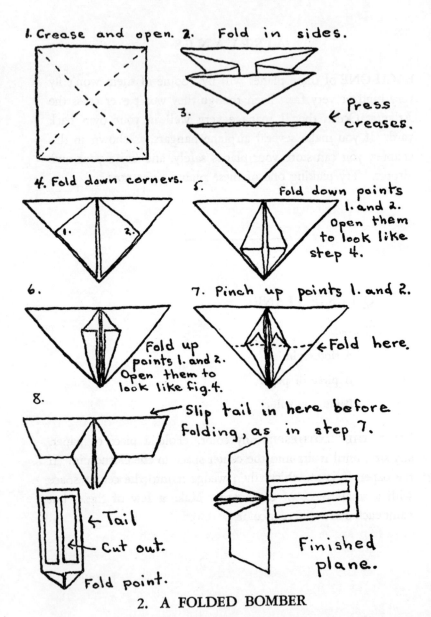

1. Crease and open. 2. Fold in sides.

3. → Press creases.

4. Fold down corners. 5. Fold down points 1. and 2. Open them to look like step 4.

6. Fold up points 1. and 2. Open them to look like fig. 4.

7. Pinch up points 1. and 2. ←Fold here.

8. ← Slip tail in here before folding, as in step 7.

← Tail
← Cut out.
Fold point.

Finished plane.

2. A FOLDED BOMBER

[10]

2. A FOLDED BOMBER

You will need:

> A square piece of paper for the body (6 to 8 inches)
> A strip of paper for the tail

THIS MUST BE FOLDED very carefully and slowly. It will be worth the effort. Fold the square of paper diagonally across until the corners meet. Open it up. Do the same to the opposite corners. Open it up. Push two opposite sides of the paper toward the center and crease the edges so that you will have made a triangle with the point facing down. You will now work with the part of the triangle facing you. Do not touch the back part of the triangle. Bring the left corner and the right corner of the triangle down to the point. Crease the sides. Fold points 1 and 2 to meet at the center. Open it. The idea is to get the crease. This time fold 1 and 2 so that they meet at the center but bring the sides up from the bottom instead of down from the top. Crease and open. Grasp points 1 and 2 in each hand. Pinch them up with your fingers and flatten down all the edges. It will look like 2 horns sticking up from the middle of your paper. Hold these horns between your thumbs and first fingers. Fold the bottom point of your triangle under. Now the points of your triangle have become the motors of your airplane. Press down all creases. Open up this last fold. Slip in the narrow piece of paper which will be the tail. Fold down the top points to form a triangle, before slipping it into your plane. Now refold the last step. This will also fold in the tail holding it securely. Push up the wings a little and fly it. You could cut strips out of the tail of the plane to make it look more complicated. Although this plane may seem hard to make, once you get the trick of it you'll enjoy making it, especially since it will positively fly.

3. CORRUGATED HANGAR

You will need:

> Corrugated paper
> A pair of scissors
> Cellophane tape, pasting paper, or adhesive tape

THE SIZE of your hangar will depend upon the size of the corrugated paper. You can make it as large or as small as you want. Make a curve of corrugated paper. Use another piece as a floor, and fasten the curved piece to the floor with cellophane tape or pasting paper. Make a half circle of the corrugated paper, and fasten it to the curve for the back wall. For the front doors, do the same with a half circle of paper, but cut 2 doors, and fold them back. You may paint this hangar or leave it the color it is which will probably be brown.

4. HIGH FLYER

You will need:

> A lollypop stick or a large match stick
> A piece of paper six inches square
> A pair of scissors

CUT THE SQUARE PIECE of paper diagonally across. Now you will have two perfect triangles. You will only need one of them, so you can save the other one for another flyer. Hold the triangle with the long side up. Fold the left point of the triangle in back until the point touches the point at the bottom

1.

2.

Fold back Fold forward

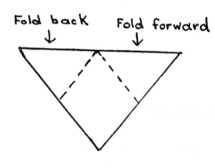

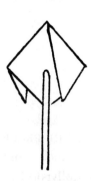

4. HIGH FLYER

of the triangle. Fold the right side of the triangle towards you until the point touches the bottom of the triangle. See if your paper looks like the picture. Make a small split in the top of the lollypop stick or match stick. Stick the point of the triangle in the split end of the stick. The two folded ends will be free of the stick. Now drop it out the window, and watch it twirl down. Be very careful when you watch it twirl that you don't lean too far out of the window, or there won't be any fun in it at all.

---

5. A PROPELLER

You will need:

> A lollypop stick
> A thumb tack
> A tin propeller, cut from an old tin can, and turned as in the picture
> A pair of scissors

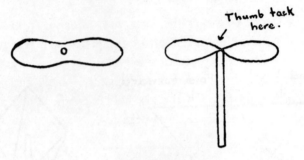

5. A PROPELLER

CUT THE PROPELLER out of an old tin can. Turn it slightly, and punch a tiny hole in the center. Fasten the propeller to the lollypop stick with a thumb tack. Twirl it between the palms of your hands, holding it high, and let it go. It will fly.

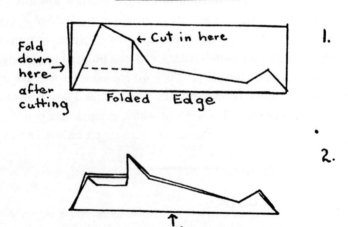

1.

2.

6. A GLIDER — MODEL A

You will need:

A sheet of paper, any size
A pair of scissors, and a pencil

HOLD A SHEET of paper the long way. Fold it in half, the long way. Beginning at the left of the paper, with the folded edge down, draw the shape of the glider you are going to cut out. Draw it as it is drawn in the picture. Now cut it out. To make it skim through the air, hold it in the center at the folded edge, and let it fly. It works too.

---

7. SAILER

You will need:

> A large feather
> A cork
> Glue

GET ANY LARGE FEATHER, as a chicken feather. See that it is clean. Pierce a hole through a cork with a thin nail or needle. Stick the feather through the cork after you have put a little glue at the pointed end of the feather so that it will remain fixed in the cork. It flies nicely through the air. If you have any dye or paint left over from something else, dip the feather in it. It will look nicer as it flies.

---

8. A SIMPLE AIRPLANE

You will need:

> A thin piece of wood, 9 inches long and 3 inches wide
> Another thin piece of wood 4 inches long and 2 inches wide
> A thin piece of wood 8 inches long and 2 inches wide
> Thumb tacks
> Any colored paint
> 2 milk bottle tops

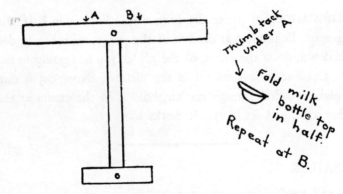

8. A SIMPLE AIRPLANE

USE THE 8 INCH PIECE of wood for the body, the 9 inch
piece of wood for the wings and the smallest piece of wood
for the tail. Fasten them together as shown in the picture,
with thumbtacks. Paint it. When it is dry, fold the milk
bottle tops in half. Thumb tack these tops to the under side
of the plane wings, close to the body so that they will look
like half wheels. The plane can rest on these. A star painted
on each end of the wing will make it look professional.

9. A PARACHUTE

You will need:

> A square handkerchief made of silk or any other thin
> material
> String
> A cork
> A thumbtack

TIE PIECES OF STRING, all the same length to each corner of
the handkerchief. Take the four ends of the string and fasten
them to the cork with the thumbtack. Watch it float from the
window.

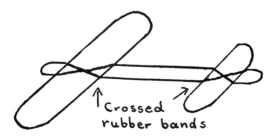

Crossed rubber bands

10. A GLIDER — MODEL B

You will need:

> A piece of cardboard
> A pair of scissors
> 2 rubber bands

CUT THREE PIECES of cardboard so that you have a long, thin strip, about 8 inches by 1 inch, for the body, 6 inches by 2 inches for the wings, and a tail 3 inches by 1 inch. Curve the ends of the wings and tail. Fasten the tail and the wings to the body by criss-crossing rubber bands over them as shown in the picture. Write your name on the under side of it and skim it through the air.

---

11. A TRICKY PLANE

You will need:

> A piece of paper 4 inches by 6 inches
> A pair of scissors

HOLD THE PAPER so that the 6 inch side is at the bottom. Fold the left hand edge over twice, about a half inch each fold. Now fold the paper up in half, through the center. Cut out

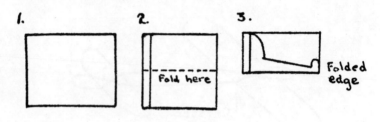

1.   **2.**   **3.**

Fold here

Folded edge

3. This is how your plane will look when it is opened and the wings are folded back.

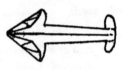

11. A TRICKY PLANE

the plane as it is in the picture. Open out the paper. Fold the tail back. Fold the pointed ends of the wings toward the center of the plane. Now fold it back on itself. Hold it in the center of the body and let it fly. If you will experiment and fold the tail and the wings in different ways, it will fly in different directions.

---

12. BIRD PLANE

You will need:

> A sheet of paper, or thin cardboard
> A pair of scissors
> Crayons
> Paste

FOLD THE PAPER or cardboard in half. Hold the folded edge down. Draw a large bird on it with outstretched wings, as in

[18]

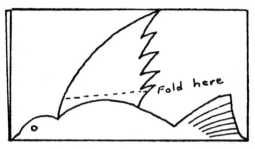

Folded edge

12. BIRD PLANE

the picture. Color the bird. Make it look like a robin or a bluebird. Cut out the bird, but be sure not to cut the folded edge. You will have to color both sides of the bird. Paste the body of the bird together, but leave the wings free. When you think that the paste is dry, fold back the wings. It will skim through the air. Make a few of these and color each one to look like a different bird.

---

13. A FOLDED PLANE

You will need:

One piece of paper, any size

FOLD THE PAPER the long way down the center and open it. Fold the upper left point of the paper until it meets the crease down the center of the paper. Do the same to the right hand side. You will now have three points at the top of the paper. Fold the new point at the left of the paper to the center crease, and do the same to the right side. Thus the paper will have been folded twice over. Now fold the plane in half along the center crease, with the double folded sides on the outside. Hold

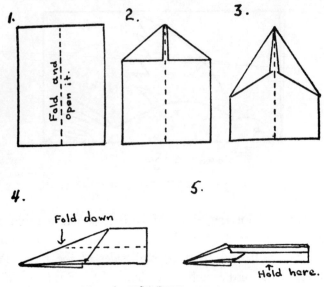

1.

Fold and open it.

2.

3.

4.

Fold down

5.

Hold here.

13. A FOLDED PLANE

it with the point facing your left. With your right hand, fold the right hand point of the paper until it touches the folded edge. Do the same to the other side. These are the wings. Lift these wings up. Hold it in the center of the folded edge and watch it cut through the air.

---

14. AIRPLANE HANGAR

You will need:

> Oatmeal box
> A pair of scissors
> Gray paint
> Paste

CUT AWAY half of the cover of the oatmeal box. Cut down the side of the box until it looks like the picture. Paste the

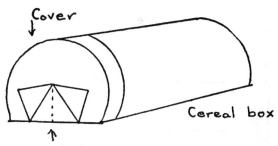

Cover

Cereal box

Cut here and fold back

14. AIRPLANE HANGAR

cut half of the cover, after cutting it into 2 pieces, to the side of the box, to make doors. Paint it all gray. This is good for a small plane.

---

15. CRACKER BOX HANGAR

You will need:

> A large cardboard cracker box
> Paste
> A pair of scissors
> 2 sheets of cardboard
> Cellophane tape, pasting paper, or adhesive tape

HOLD THE BOX with the open side down, after you have removed the cover. Cut out 2 doors, fold them back. For the roof, curve one piece of cardboard and fasten it to the top of the box, as it shows you in the picture, with the cellophane tape. Cut out 2 half circles, to fit the empty space at the top

[21]

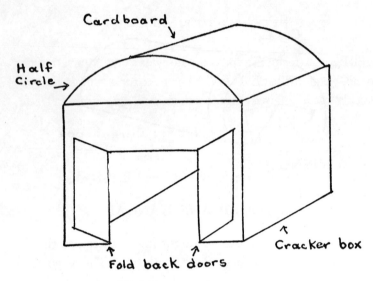

15. CRACKER BOX HANGAR

of the box, and fasten them to the roof with the cellophane tape. Paint it any color you like. This is good for larger planes.

After you have made a few of these planes, and perhaps a hangar or two, why not try to invent planes of your own with other kinds of scrap material that you find around the house? Then you can trade some of them with your friends.

FUN WITH PAPER

HERE are sixteen answers to the rainy day cry, "I have nothing to do," and "What'll I do?" Some of these things are very quickly made and will amuse you and all your friends.

---

16. JUMPING JACK

You will need:

A sheet of cardboard
A pair of scissors
Crayons
String

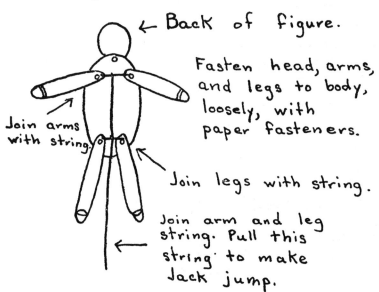

← Back of figure.

Fasten head, arms, and legs to body, loosely, with paper fasteners.

Join arms with string.

Join legs with string.

Join arm and leg string. Pull this string to make Jack jump.

TRACE OR DRAW any figure of a boy or girl or animal or clown.

Fasten the arms and the legs to the figure with paper fasteners. Try to fasten them loosely so that the arms and legs will move easily. Join the arms together at the back of the figure, with a piece of string. Join the legs the same way. Connect the arm string to the leg string at the center with a long string that will hang down. To make the figure move, pull on the long string and the arms and legs will jump.

17. FINGER PICTURES

You will need:

> A sheet of paper
> A pair of scissors
> Crayons
> Paste and a coin

DRAW CIRCLES on the paper by tracing a coin. If you want small pictures use a five cent piece, and if you want large pictures use a quarter. At the side of each circle draw tabs long enough to fit around the tips of your fingers. Draw faces on the circles. Make them funny. Color them. Cut out the circles and be sure to leave the tabs attached to the circles. Now fit them around your fingers. When they fit, paste them by the ends of the tabs. Put them on your fingers so that the faces are upside down to you, but right side up to your audience. Now you can have fun by making the fingers act, or walk around the table. If you change your voice with each face that is "acting," it will make it funnier.

———

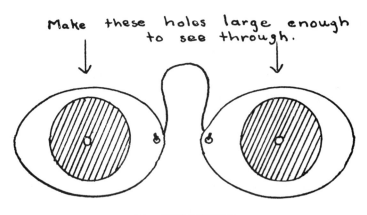

Make these holes large enough to see through.

18. BLINKERS

You will need:

> A piece of thin cardboard
> A pair of scissors
> A hairpin
> Crayons

CUT OUT TWO OVALS, about two inches around, or large enough to cover your eyes. Make a straight piece out of the hairpin. Bend the hairpin to make a nose piece, and attach the two pieces of cardboard to it so that you have a pair of eye-glasses. Color large eyes in the centers of the ovals. Put small holes in the center of the ovals so that you can see through them. To be sure that they don't fall off you may attach a straightened hairpin to the outer edges of the ovals for ear pieces. Suppose you have some fun with these. Color the eyes different colors, or make them cross-eyed, or make the eyes very large. Try all three of these tricks and watch the family laugh.

---

19. FUNNY FACE SCRAP BOOK

You will need:

> An old, partly used notebook or scrapbook
> Lots of pictures of people and animals
> A pair of scissors
> Paste

REMOVE THE USED PAGES from the notebook or scrapbook. Cut off 2 or 3 inches from the top of all the pages in the notebook but leave the cover untouched. Get 2 pictures of people. The funnier the faces the funnier your book will be. Inside the covers paste the faces or the face attached to the person. On the pages of the notebook paste a different person on each page in the center of the page, but see that the head of the picture is cut off, and the edge where you cut off the head just touches the top edge of the paper. When you turn the pages of your book, the heads pasted at the top center inside the cover will remain the same but every page will give the head a different body. If you want to make it really funny, paste a picture of someone in your family inside the cover, and get some funny shaped animals to paste on the pages. You'll all have a good time when you turn the pages.

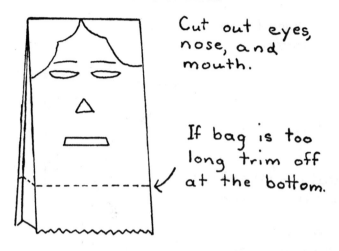

Cut out eyes, nose, and mouth.

If bag is too long trim off at the bottom.

20. PAPER BAG MASKS

You will need:

> Paper bags, large ones
> A pair of scissors
> Crayons

GET A PAPER BAG large enough to slip over your head and to cover your face. Where your eyes, nose, and mouth come, cut out holes large enough to fit your face. Color hair at the top of the bag, eyebrows over the eyes, and a big red mouth where the hole for the mouth is. Trim the bottom of the bag so that it fits comfortably around your neck. Make a few of these to change around.

---

21. FLAT MASKS

You will need:

> A sheet of heavy paper
> A pair of scissors

Paint or crayons
String

Cut all
dark parts
out, without
cutting the
folded edge,
except for
the nose.

Tie
string
here.

↑Folded edge

21. FLAT MASKS

FOLD THE SHEET in half. You will draw whatever design or picture you like on half the paper, and when you cut the picture out, don't cut on the crease, so that when you open the paper the design will have been cut out on both sides. Draw a goblin's, or cat's face on half the paper, holding it with the creased edge or folded edge at your left. Decide where the eyes will be according to your face. Do the same for the nose and the mouth. Color it any way you like. Cut out the eyes and nose and mouth. Cut around the mask. Open it up. Punch holes at the upper edges, right side and left side. Tie a string to each hole, so that you can tie it around your face, with a bow, at the back of your head. If you want to make your mask fancier, cut an extra flap for the nose, color it red, and paste it to the upper edge of the paper near the nose.

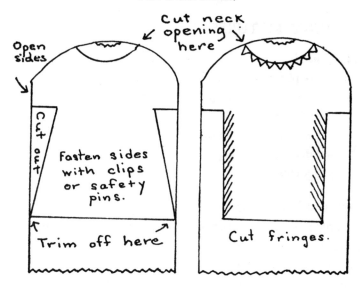

22. PAPER BAG COSTUMES

You will need:

> A large paper bag from the dry cleaner
> A pair of scissors
> Paper clips or staples
> Crayons

WHEN YOU BRING a dress home from the dry cleaner save the large paper bag which is used to cover the clothes. There is an opening at the top of the bag. Cut this a little larger so that it will fit over your head. Shape the sides into sleeves, and cut off some at the bottom so that it won't be too long for you. Fasten the sides together with the paper clips or with a stapler. Don't use pins or you will scratch yourself. Decorate the dress or costume with crayons. A boy can easily make a hunter's or pioneer's jacket for himself out of this. Use your imagination and make any costume you like as this is very quickly made.

[29]

23. FUNNY PICTURES

You will need:

A picture of someone in the family
Used postage stamps or leaves or scraps of material
Glue or paste
A piece of cardboard—a piece of colored paper
Black pasting paper
A clip

MAKE A SURPRISE funny picture for someone in the family and hang it up for everyone to see. Cover the cardboard by pasting the colored paper over it. At the top center, but away from the edge, paste the head from a picture of anyone in your family. Make a body and legs for a boy, but no legs for a girl, and fill in the shape you have drawn (and do make it funny), with the postage stamps, used ones of course, or pasting small leaves or scraps of material. A girl's face, with a huge leaf evening gown with a bustle will certainly make everyone laugh. It'll be all in fun and the one whose picture you are using will enjoy it too. Paste the black pasting paper all around the edges of the cardboard to make a frame. Paste a clip, by slipping a strip of pasting paper through it, to the back of your picture. Hang it up right away.

---

24. PAPER BAG FISHES

You will need:

Paper bags
A sheet of paper

A pair of scissors
Crayons
Paste

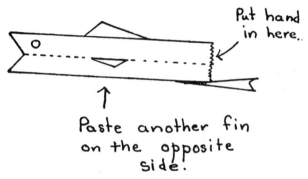

Put hand in here..

Paste another fin on the opposite side!

24. PAPER BAG FISHES

USE THE PAPER BAGS that have creased sides, or gussets. Stick your hand in the bag. Your fingers will find that they can make a fish's mouth at the bottom of the bag. With a crayon make an eye on each side of the bag near the mouth. Cut out three fins and a tail. Color them. Paste a fin on each side of the bag, in the middle of the side piece or gusset. Paste a fin at the middle of the top of the bag. Paste the tail at the bottom end of the bag where your elbow will probably be. When the paste has dried, put your hand in the bag and make the fish "breathe" by opening and closing your fingers in the end of the bag. Make him "swim" through the air.

---

25. FAMILY MOVIES
You will need:

A large square cardboard box, like a hat box
A pair of scissors

Paste
Pictures of the members of your family
A long piece of cardboard

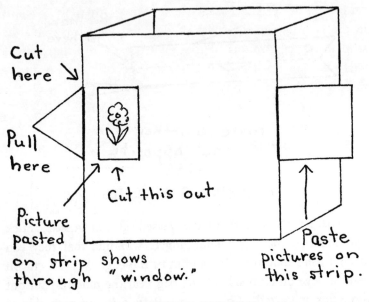

25. FAMILY MOVIES

TAKE THE COVER OFF the box until you have set up your movie. Half way down one side of the box, towards the left edge, cut out a hole, or a square about the size or a little smaller, of the largest picture that you intend to use. At the edge of the box, level with this hole you have cut out, make a cut in the box directly where the cardboard is bent, or rather at the corner. In a line with the hole, and this cut, do the same thing to the right edge. These cuts at each end will be used to slip a piece of cardboard back and forth. Cut the long piece of cardboard wide enough so that it will pass through the cuts in the box. Cut it a little longer than the width of the box, and make the left hand side of the cardboard have a pointed end so that it can be grasped easily for pulling through the slits. Paste the pictures of your family across the middle of this cardboard, at least 2 inches apart. Slip it through the slits in the box, put on the cover of the box, and slowly pull the strip through by means of the pointed end. As the pictures pass the hole you have cut out, everyone will be able to see the people in your family.

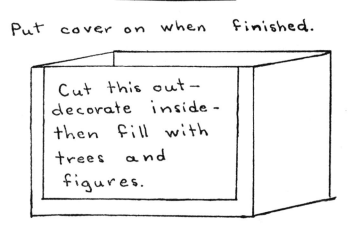

Put cover on when finished.

Cut this out — decorate inside — then fill with trees and figures.

26. THREE DIMENSION PICTURES

You will need:

> A large cracker box or a square hat box
> A pair of scissors
> Crayons or paint
> Pictures of children or animals cut out of magazines
> Paste
> Corks

TAKE THE COVER off the box. Cut out one side of the box,

but leave an inch all around the side and bottom edges. Paint the inside and the outside of the box and the cover any color you like. To make it very interesting, paint trees or houses at the back on the inside of the box. This is the background of your picture. Cut out the pictures you have saved from the magazines. Paste them on the piece of cardboard you have cut out of the box. When the paste is dry trim the edges. Now they are firm enough to use. Make a small cut in the corks. Put the pictures into the cut in the corks. The pictures will stand. Put the mounted pictures inside the box. Put on the cover. Your picture is finished. For variety, make a jungle picture with animals, or a football or baseball picture, or any picture you think might amuse you and your friends.

---

27. FISHBOWL

You will need:

> An oatmeal box
> A piece of cellophane
> A string
> A sheet of paper
> A pair of scissors
> A toothpick
> Paint, any color

CUT A LARGE WINDOW out of the cereal box after you have removed the cover. Paste the cellophane over this window, on the inside of the box. Draw, color, and cut out a paper fish large enough to fit into the box. Tie a string to the fish. Make a small hole in the cover of the box, pass the string through

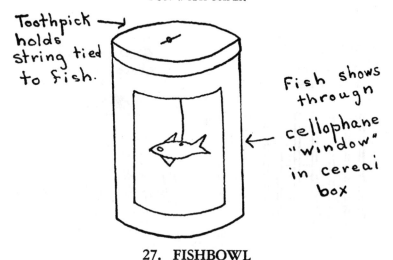

Toothpick holds string tied to fish.

Fish shows through cellophane "window" in cereal box

27. FISHBOWL

this hole, and tie it to the toothpick on the outside of the cover. Be sure that the string is not too long, but just long enough to reach to the middle of the box. Now put the cover on the box. The fish will be suspended from the string into the box. You will be able to see it through the cellophane window. Color the box green or blue. Two fishes would make the bowl more interesting.

___

28. BIRD CAGE

You will need:

> A cracker box cover, or any large cardboard cover with a rim
> A sheet of cardboard
> A pair of scissors
> Crayons
> Paste
> A picture of a bird
> A piece of string

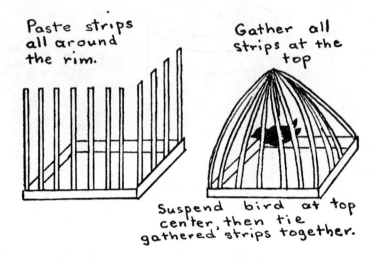

Paste strips all around the rim.

Gather all strips at the top

Suspend bird at top center, then tie gathered strips together.

28. BIRD CAGE

THE COVER WILL be the bottom of your cage. Cut strips from the cardboard about 10 to 12 inches long and one half inch wide. These will be the sides of your cage. Paste these thin strips of cardboard on the inside of the cover 1 inch apart. You may make them closer together if you like. Mount the picture of the bird on cardboard, with paste. When it is dry cut around the edges. Tie a short string through the center of the bird. Very carefully gather up the tops of the strips of cardboard, slip the bird through the strips so that it is suspended in the air in the center of the cage, and tie up the tops of the strips with the end of the string which is attached to the bird. Tie a heavier piece of string to this so that you may hang up your bird cage. Color the cage. If you'd like to, you may color the strips of cardboard and the box before you start to put them together. You might make two birds, but have one hanging a little lower than the other.

29. MR. SNOWMAN

You will need:

A sheet of cardboard
A sheet of paper
A pair of scissors
A few broom straws
A piece of white chalk, black crayon, and red crayon

DRAW A SNOWMAN on the piece of cardboard. See what he looks like in the picture. Color his hat black. Make eyes, nose, and a mouth. Make him smile. Punch a hole in his left hand; one at the top and one at the bottom of the hand. Slip the broom straws through these holes. Make a slit in the middle of the snowman between his hands. Cut out a large hot water bottle big enough to pass through this slit. Color the hot water bottle red. Slip it through the slit in the snowman. Cut out the snowman. Make him stand by pasting a strip of cardboard bent in half, at the back of the snowman. This is nice to make on a snowy afternoon.

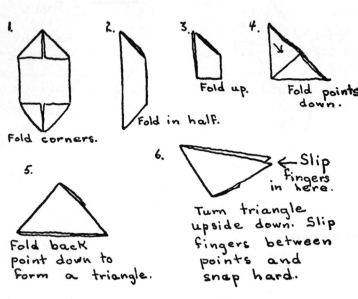

1. Fold corners.

2. Fold in half.

3. Fold up.

4. Fold points down.

5. Fold back point down to form a triangle.

6. Turn triangle upside down. Slip fingers between points and snap hard.

← Slip fingers in here.

30. SNAPPER

You will need:

A sheet of paper
Patience

THE TRICK IN MAKING this is in the folding. Follow the steps in the picture as you make this. Fold the top corners and the bottom corners of the paper toward the center. Fold the paper in half with the folded corners inside. Fold this in half until the points meet. Hold the paper now so that the points are pointing up and to the left. Bring the point facing you down

[38]

until the left edge is even with the bottom folded edge. Do the same to the other point down the same way only this time it will be folded away from you. You will have what will look like a triangle. Hold the top point of the triangle in your left hand. Turn it upside down. Still holding it in your left hand, slip the middle finger of your right hand between the 2 points sticking out at the right of the triangle. Grasp these points with your second and fourth fingers. Your thumb and little finger will be free. You can release your left hand. Raise the snapper in your right hand and bring it down sharply. The paper folded between the wings of your triangle will push out sharply and with a loud snapping sound.

---

31. QUICKIE LANTERN

You will need:

> A paper bag
> Crayons
> A piece of string
> A flashlight

DRAW A FUNNY FACE on both sides of the paper bag. Blow it up or push it out with your hands. Slip it over the top of a flashlight and fasten it all around with the cord. Turn on the flashlight and the lantern will glow. This is fun in a dark room.

Why not have a contest with your friends to see who can make the nicest one of these paper "funnies"? If you make a great many of them it would be a fine gesture to bring them to the local hospital to amuse the children who are ill or who are on the road to recovery. Or bring some of these to the Red Cross who will give them to other children. Don't you think the snowman, or a set of paper fingers would make some little boy happy, and make him want to get better faster?

MAKE YOUR OWN JEWELRY

IF YOU HAVE any string, dental floss, paste, buttons, clothes-pins, macaroni, horse chestnuts, acorns, old magazines, paper, melon seeds, or shells, you can make a whole boxful of jewelry nice enough to wear yourself if you are a girl, or nice enough to give away as a gift if you are a boy.

---

32. BUTTON JEWELRY

You will need:

> Mother's button bag
> A needle
> String

BUTTONS make lovely necklaces, bracelets, belts, and lapel ornaments. For lapel ornaments choose very large bright buttons. Put string or wool through the holes, and tie a safety pin at the end of the string in the back for pinning on. If you are making a belt, sew differently colored buttons across the belt. If you are making necklaces, thread as many buttons as you like on strong string and tie it with a bow in the back. Make a bracelet to match. Wooden buttons are nice to work with.

---

33. LAPEL PIN

You will need:

> A small picture, of any subject
> A piece of dental floss
> A small safety pin

Paste
A small piece of cardboard, or thin wood
Shellac
A pair of scissors

Before pasting picture.

33. LAPEL PIN

DECIDE what picture you would like to pin on your lapel. A magazine picture would be fine. A very attractive one would be a picture of you, anyone in your family, or of your favorite movie actress or actor, or favorite baseball player. Cut the picture out very carefully. Cut the cardboard a little bit larger than the picture. If you are using the thin wood, sandpaper the edges. Put two small holes in the middle of the cardboard or wood. Thread the dental floss through these holes, and then tie the ends of the thread to the safety pin. This will enable you to pin it to your lapel. On the side of the cardboard or wood, which hasn't got the safety pin, paste your picture, over the holes and the little bit of dental floss showing. When it is dry, if you are using the cardboard, cut around the edge of the picture. Shellac it carefully. Use 2 coats of shellac to make it last longer.

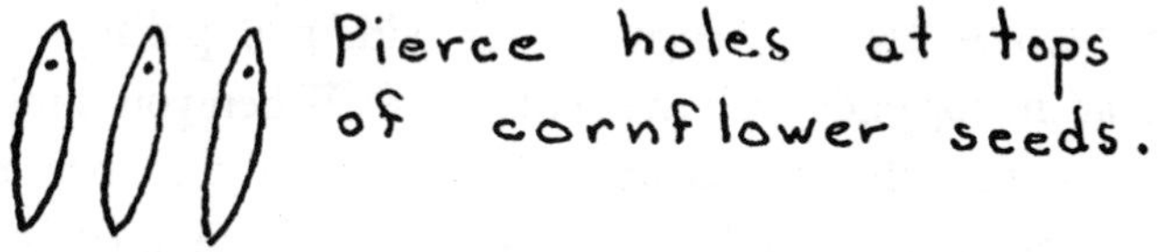

Pierce holes at tops of cornflower seeds.

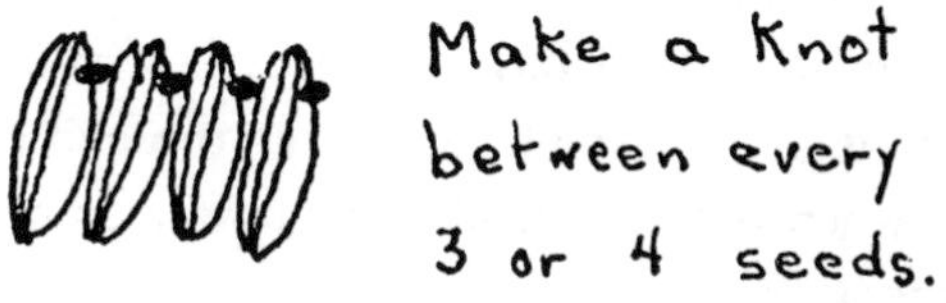

Make a knot between every 3 or 4 seeds.

34. CORNFLOWER SEED NECKLACE AND BRACELET

You will need:

    Cornflower seeds
    Green wool yarn
    A needle

THE NATURAL COLOR of cornflower seeds, which is black and white look very attractive when strung on green wool. String them near the top corner of each seed. Put a knot between every 3 or 4 seeds. Leave a piece long enough at the end to tie a bow, with the green wool yarn. Make a shorter string for a bracelet, leaving enough yarn to make a bow around the wrist. Any other colored wool would be nice to use too.

---

35. PEANUT BEADS

You will need:

    Peanuts
    Nail polish
    Dental floss
    Wool yarn

[43]

PAINT BOTH ENDS of each peanut with nail polish. String them at the top ends with the dental floss. When you think that you have enough peanuts on your string, make a knot in the dental floss at each end of your string, tie a piece of colored wool yarn to the end of the dental floss and leave the wool long enough to make a bow at the back of your neck. As an extra trimming, tie a small peanut at the end of the wool yarn so that when you have made your bow, a small peanut will dangle in the back.

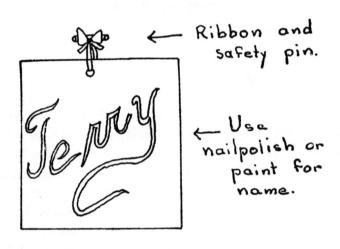

Ribbon and safety pin.

Use nailpolish or paint for name.

36. NAME PIN

You will need:

A piece of beaverboard or thin wood about 2 inches by 2 inches

Sandpaper

Shellac

Nail polish

A piece of ribbon and a safety pin

SANDPAPER the thin piece of wood or beaverboard all around the edges. Shellac it on both sides. Make a hole in the top center. Do this with a nail held in a pair of pliers and heated on the stove. Be careful that you don't burn yourself with the nail. With the nail polish write your name or initials across one side of the wood. Tie a small piece of ribbon through the hole, and fasten the safety pin at the back of the bow so that you can pin it to your blouse or coat.

---

37. CLOTHESPIN NECKLACE

You will need:

> 2 dozen toy clothespins
> A nail
> A pair of pliers
> A ribbon or colored wool yarn
> Paint or nail polish

GET THE CLOTHESPINS in the dime store or toy store. They are small, about 1½ inches long. Hold the nail in the pliers, and heat it on the stove. With this nail, make holes through the top of each clothespin. Paint the clothespins any color you like with paint or nail polish. Yellow or green are nice. When they are dry, string them on the ribbon or wool. Tie it in the back with a small bow. These are very pretty in a bracelet to match.

If you have a few clothespins left over, they would look grand tied to the window shades, as window shade pulls.

38. MELON SEED BEADS

You will need:

>A bunch of melon seeds
>A needle and thread
>Paint

WHENEVER MOTHER is serving melons ask her for the seeds. Wash them in a dish and dry them on newspaper. When you have quite a bit collected, with a needle and thread, string them into a necklace as long as you like. Tie a bow in the back. If you have some paint left over dip the melon beads into the paint and hang them up with a safety pin on the line to dry. If you make two necklaces, one red and one white, and wind them around each other before you make the bows in the back to tie them, it will be an unusual necklace. Another variation would be to use heavier colored string to string the seeds, and make a knot every 5 or 6 seeds. You will probably think of other combinations yourself.

---

39. PAPER BEADS

You will need:

>A pair of scissors
>Any comic pages of the newspapers, colored preferred
>A toothpick
>Paste
>Shellac or paint

SAVE THE SUNDAY colored comics. Cut out triangles four inches long and from ½ to 1½ inches wide at the bottom of the

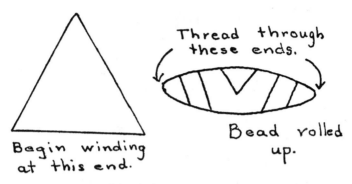

39. PAPER BEADS

triangle. When you have a number of these triangles cut out, do this to each one. Cover one side of the triangle with paste. Roll it tightly on the toothpick, beginning at the wide end of the triangle. You could use a thin knitting needle instead of the toothpick if it will be easier for you. When it is tightly rolled, slip out the toothpick. When you have made a number of these beads, thread them on a string or wool, and tie them with a bow in the back. If you want them to last longer paint them with shellac. If you want to vary it, paint some of the beads in the string different colors. They look nicest when they are shellaced because the comics are brightly colored.

---

40. PAPER BELT

You will need:

>   Heavy colored mounting paper (or Christmas wrapping
>   paper)
>   A pair of scissors
>   A small piece of ribbon

CUT THE CARDBOARD to measure 5 inches long and 2½ inches

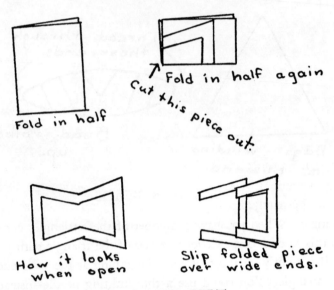

Fold in half

Cut this piece out.

Fold in half again

How it looks when open

Slip folded piece over wide ends.

40. PAPER BELT

wide. Fold this cardboard in half, until it measures 2½ by 2½. This will be your pattern. Trace the design of the pattern as it is in the picture. Using this model trace the design on the colored paper. Make as many pieces as you think you will need. For a larger person you will need more pieces. When you have a number cut out, slip one over the other as in the picture. When it is long enough, use a straight piece of paper to close the belt, punch a hole in the ends of the straight piece of paper, and join the ends with the piece of ribbon. Oilcloth or felt would also be good to use instead of paper.

41. "NUTTY" BEADS

You will need:

A bunch of horse chestnuts

A bunch of acorns
Dental floss
A heavy needle
A pair of pliers

JUST AS YOU MADE holes in the toy clothespins, do the same
with the acorns and horse chestnuts. Carefully hold the needle
in the pliers, heat it over a flame on the stove, and pierce holes
through the nuts. String them on the dental floss. Here are
some variations. Use all horse chestnuts, or all acorns. Or use
them alternately, first a chestnut, and then an acorn, until your
necklace is long enough. You might like to color them with
paint or nail polish, or leave them their original color and just
shellac them to make them shine.

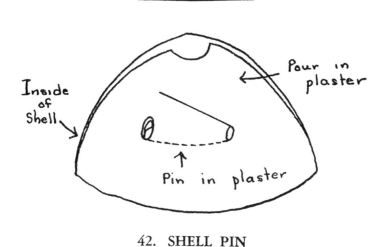

42. SHELL PIN

You will need:

Small shells, any size, color or shape
Small safety pins

    Plaster of Paris
    Water
    Paint
    A cup

TRY TO GET naturally nicely colored shells as they look nicer than when they are painted. Mix a quarter of a cup of plaster of Paris with sufficient water to make it creamy. See that the shell is washed and dried. Be sure to do this on a newspaper. Pour the plaster mixture, carefully and slowly into the shell. When it is almost filled,.let it set for about ten to twenty minutes. (To be sure that the plaster stays in the shell it would be a good idea to "rough" up the inside of the shell with a piece of sandpaper.) Meanwhile wash out the cup so that no plaster sticks to it in case you would like to use the cup again. When the plaster is half "set," gently push in the safety pin sidewards, and tilted, so that the end which opens up is toward you. When the plaster will be completely "set" or hardened you will be able to pin the shell on you with the safety pin which will be firmly encased in the plaster. Cover the shell with shellac when it is finished. A pink shell is very attractive. A good size to remember to use is a shell about 2½ inches long. If it is too large it will be too heavy to wear.

---

43. MACARONI NECKLACE

You will need:

    A package of star or elbow macaroni
    String
    Nail polish or paint, any color
    A needle

WITH A NEEDLE, make holes through the centers of the macaroni pieces. Do this to as many pieces as you think will be enough to make a fairly long necklace. Use less for a short necklace. String the pieces unpainted if you like a white necklace. If you want to paint it, cover the pieces with nail polish or several shades of paint. Dry them on a newspaper. When dry, string them on strong string or thread. A bracelet to match would make a nice set.

---

44. A SAFETY PIN BRACELET

You will need:

> A bunch of safety pins
> 2 colored beads or buttons
> Nail polish
> Colored wool yarn

THE ONE INCH safety pins are a good size to use. Color the both ends of the safety pins with nail polish. When they are dry, string them on the colored wool, long enough to fit around the wrist of the person for whom you are making it. Tie a colored button or bead at the ends of the string. You are all finished. When you tie on the bracelet, make a bow. A nice color combination would be red nail polish, and blue or yellow wool.

---

45. WISHBONE PIN

You will need:

> A wishbone

Nail polish
Ribbon
A safety pin

THE NEXT TIME mother has chicken for dinner save the wishbone. Wash it and let it dry. Paint it with nail polish or wind colored ribbon all around the wishbone, and just paint the head of it. Tie a ribbon bow at the tip, stick a safety pin in the back of the bow, and pin it on your favorite dress or coat. Make some for your friends.

Although there are only fourteen ideas presented here you most likely could interchange them and make twice as many bracelets, beads, belts and necklaces. Try using tiny corks instead of buttons. Two peach pits, cleaned and dried, a hole bored through the center, and tied on a ribbon, for a pin is another idea. Artificial flowers tied to a bobby pin would look nice in anyone's hair. A club insignia pasted on a large flat button, tied to a string and safety pin would be an odd club badge. Burn your name in a small piece of wood with a heated nail held in pliers, and screw in a tiny screw eye in the corner, and add it to your key chain. These are only a few extra ideas to start you off on at least a hundred of your own. You'll have a grand time making your own jewelry using your own ideas.

INDIAN CRAFT

EVERY boy or girl at some time or another would like to play "Indians." Here are many ideas on how to make costumes and equipment. There are Indian head bands, hats, masks, canoes, tents, shirts, and many others. Choose the ones you would like best to make.

46. FEATHER HEAD DRESS

You will need:

> A dozen chicken feathers
> A strip of material
> A needle and thread
> A pair of scissors
> Paint

CUT A STRIP of material 2½ to 3 inches wide and long enough to fit around your head, and with the ends long enough to hang down about a foot after the knot will be tied around your head. See that the feathers are clean. Dip them in any left over paint that you may have. The next step is tricky. Fold the long strip of material, which could be any scrap mother may have left over, so that it is in half, the long way. Now the strip is about 1¼ inches wide. Hold it with the folded edge down. Take each feather separately. Slip the pointed end of the feather into the folded material. With the needle and thread make several stitches through the material and around the feather. This will hold the feathers securely. Sew the feathers in the center of the material so that you have two pieces evenly matched to tie around your head. At the ends of the material sew two smaller feathers to hang over your shoulder when the head dress is on your head. Use your own color combinations when you dip the feathers. A good trick would be to dip the ends of the feathers only.

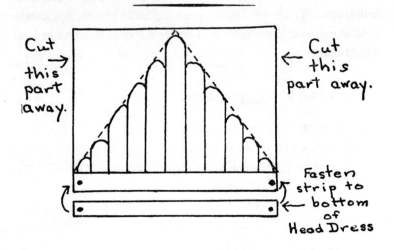

47. HEAD DRESS

You will need:

> A sheet of drawing paper
> Some fasteners
> A ruler
> Crayons
> A pair of scissors

HOLD the drawing paper the long way. Draw a line across the bottom of the paper one inch up. Do this again. Now you have two lines at the bottom of the paper. Cut off the bottom strip. Save it. Lightly draw a triangle from the one inch line to the top center of the paper. Draw 1½ inch lines from the bottom of the paper to the sides of the triangle. Round out the tops as in the picture. Color each feather a different color. Color the one inch strip at the bottom brown. Color the one inch piece you cut off before, brown. With your scissors, cut out the feathers. Be sure to leave them attached to the head band. Attach the one inch strip of paper to each side of the head band with fasteners. Make it larger or smaller to fit your head. Paint would be good to use instead of crayons.

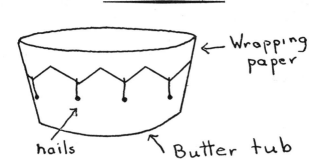

Wrapping paper

nails

Butter tub

48. TOM TOM

You will need:

A butter tub
Brown wrapping paper
Paint
Heavy string
Small nails

WASH the butter tub very well so that there is no grease in it. When it is dry, tie the heavy wrapping paper to it with heavy string, and attach the string to the nails placed half way down and around the tub. Paint the tub with Indian designs. Try to keep wrinkles out of the paper. If you can't get a butter tub get a nail keg or small pickle barrel.

[55]

49. TOM TOM DRUMSTICK

You will need:

> A branch of a tree or a small stick
> Old rubber ball
> An old clean sock
> A pair of scissors
> A piece of string

FIND a straight branch of a tree, about 1½ feet long. Make a slit in a rubber ball and stick it onto the end of the stick. To fasten the ball securely to the stick, slip the toe end of a clean sock over the ball and tie it to the stick with a string. You could paint the whole stick and the covered ball with paint left over from the tom tom.

50. HEAD BAND

You will need:

> A strip of material 3 inches wide, and 2 feet long
> Colored buttons
> 4 feathers
> A needle and thread

JUST AS YOU DID in the other feather head dress, fold the strip of material in half the long way. This time sew only two feathers firmly to the center of the head band. Sew colored buttons all along the strip until you have covered it completely. Sew a feather at each end. Tie it around your head so that the feathers are at the right or left side of your head over your ear. This is very effective if you make the center feathers a bright red.

51. BOW AND ARROW

You will need:

> A thin pliable branch about 4 feet long
> Another branch less than 3 feet long
> Strong string

FIND a thin branch that will bend slightly but will not break. Trim off any rough twigs. Tie a strong piece of twine or string to one end of the branch and tie the other end of the string to the other end of the branch, but pulling the string until the branch curves into a bow. Tie the string very firmly. To make the arrow, trim off any twigs on the smaller branch. Make a small cut at one end of the twig. Slip the cut end of the branch to the center of the string, pull the branch and string back until the smaller branch end just touches the bow, and release the arrow and string at once. If you want to, you could slip a feather into the slit end of the arrow. Make a few arrows in case you lose one.

---

52. TOMAHAWK

You will need:

> A triangle shaped flat stone
> A stick about a foot long
> Strong cord
> 2 or 3 feathers

LOOK UNTIL YOU find a flat triangle shaped stone, large enough to be the size of the tomahawk that you want. Split the end of the stick very carefully. Tie the ends of the stick in two

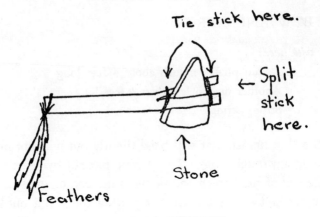

52. TOMAHAWK

places, after you have wedged in the stone in the split end. Tie
it as it is done in the picture. At the end of the stick tie the two
feathers. Paint the feathers if you like.

---

53. INDIAN MASKS

You will need:

> A large paper bag
> A sheet of paper
> Paste
> A pair of scissors
> Crayons or paint

SEE THAT THE BAG can slip over your head. Cut off the bottom if it is too long. Cut out holes for the eyes and nose and
mouth where they fit over your own eyes, nose and mouth.
Color brown eyebrows over the eye holes and a thin red mouth
over the mouth hole. Draw long feathers on the sheet of
paper. Cut them out after you have colored them bright col-

ors. Paste these feathers all around the top of the bag. It will look like a real Indian head dress when you slip the bag over your head.

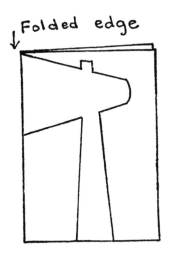

Folded edge

Trace tomahawk first, then cut it out.

54. CARDBOARD TOMAHAWK

You will need:

> A large sheet of cardboard
> Crayons
> A pair of scissors

FOLD THE CARDBOARD in half. Draw a tomahawk as it is shown in the picture. When you cut out the tomahawk be sure not to cut along the folded edge. Color the tomahawk brown or any color you like. If you care to, with string tie a feather to each side of the tomahawk. This is very quickly made.

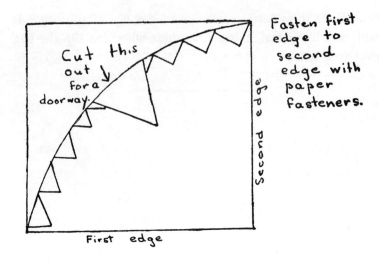

55. INDIAN TENT

You will need:

> Several sheets of heavy wrapping paper
> Paper fasteners
> Crayons or paint
> A pair of scissors
> Paste

IF YOU WOULD LIKE to make a tent large enough to creep into, use many sheets of wrapping paper. If you would like to make a small tent, use only one sheet of wrapping paper. Paste the sheets of wrapping paper to each other until you have one very large sheet. You will have to do this on the floor or back porch so as to have plenty of room. As in the picture, draw a large half circle across the paper. In the center of the circle make a V for the doorway. Along the bottom of the circle draw triangles. Color these triangles different colors. Cut out the half circle and the doorway. Join the two sides of the circle to each other with paper fasteners. If you want to be comfortable when you creep into the tent, spread a small blanket on the floor first and then place the tent over it. Be sure to make the doorway large enough to crawl through.

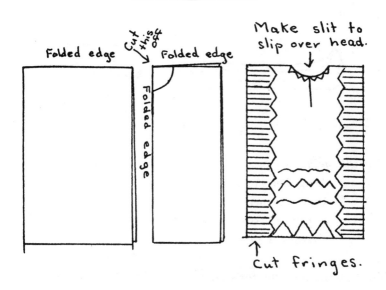

56. INDIAN JACKET

You will need:

> A large sheet of wrapping paper or newspapers
> A pair of scissors
> Safety pins or paper fasteners

FOLD THE SHEET of wrapping paper in half. Cut a half circle at the top or folded edge for the head opening. From the top to the bottom at both sides, 2 to 3 inches in, cut fringes. Color Indian designs around the neck, sides and bottom. Fasten it together with the pins or fasteners after it is slipped on.

[61]

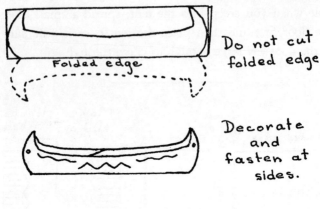

Folded edge

Do not cut folded edge

Decorate and fasten at sides.

57. CANOE

You will need:

Long sheets of cardboard
Paper fasteners
A pair of scissors
Crayons or paint

THESE WILL BE USED for scenic effects. Fold the long sheet of cardboard in half. Trace the shape of the canoe, holding the folded edge down, as it is in the picture. Carefully cut around the canoe, but do not cut the folded edge. Fasten the sides of the canoe to each other with the fasteners. It would be wise to paint or crayon Indian designs around the canoe before you fasten the sides together. Shellac it if you want it to last longer. Make it as long as you like, depending upon how large a piece of cardboard you can get. If you would like to make small canoes, use the same pattern, but fasten the sides together with toothpicks. A few of these canoes around your Indian campfire will make it look very realistic.

58. INDIAN SHIELD

You will need:

> The top of a bushel basket from the vegetable store, or
> Heavy cardboard
> Some chicken feathers
> Paint
> String
> A pair of scissors
> A strip of material

IF YOU ARE USING the top of the bushel basket see that it is smooth all around so that you won't get any splinters. Paint it a bright color. Put an Indian symbol in the center. With the string on the underside tie the strip of material across so that you can hold the shield comfortably. At each side of the shield, in the front, tie the chicken feathers.

If you are using the cardboard, draw a large circle on it and cut it out. Color it the same as the wooden shield, attach the handle strip in the back, and tie the feathers securely to the sides. A set of these would make any boy's "Indian Tribe" a huge success.

---

59. INDIAN BREECH CLOUT

You will need:

> A strip of cloth or oilcloth about 2 inches wide
> A piece of dark material 7 inches wide and about a yard
> long

THIS IS VERY easily made. Tie the narrow strip of cloth around your waist. Or if you would like to, use your own belt. Loop

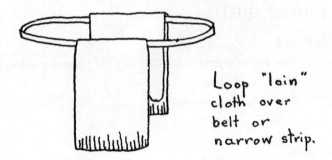

Loop "loin" cloth over belt or narrow strip.

59. INDIAN BREECH CLOUT

the wider piece of material under the front of your belt so that a little apron hangs down. Slip the other end of the cloth between your legs, bring it out through the back, and loop the other end through the back of your belt making a little apron in the back. If you want to decorate it pin paper fringes to the ends of the cloth, or feathers at the corners.

---

60. INDIAN CRADLE AND BABY

You will need:

>Cardboard
>A pair of scissors
>Paste
>Crayons or paint
>String

YOU WILL WANT to have Indian Squaws in your tribe when you are playing. Indian Squaws will be glad to have a papoose cradle on their backs. Use a piece of cardboard large enough to fit over the back of the person who will carry the papoose. Follow the pattern in the picture and cut out the cradle. Fasten

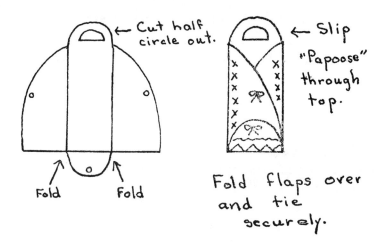

60. INDIAN CRADLE AND BABY

the flaps of the cradle to each other with string. Slip in any doll for the papoose. If you have no doll, draw a face out of the scraps of cardboard, color it and paste it to the back of the cradle. Tie it around the shoulders and across the front of the "Squaw" with heavier string or ribbon. Any girl would be delighted to have one of these.

61. LEG FRINGES

You will need:

>Wrapping paper or newspaper
>A pair of scissors
>Safety pins
>Crayons

CUT STRIPS of wrapping paper 3 inches wide and long enough to reach down the sides of your legs. Cut fringes, but leave a half inch along the side of the paper so that you may be able to pin it on. Color the fringes. Fasten them to your trousers and stockings with the safety pins. Make them match the fringes on the jacket you have already made.

When you have gathered your tribe, and made your costumes and canoes, and other scenic effects, why not have an Indian Pow Wow in your back yard? Invite all the other boys and girls in the neighborhood for a real Indian "get-together." An Indian Club would appreciate some of these Indian Crafts.

BOXES ARE HANDY

HOW MANY TIMES have you reluctantly thrown away a good box with the feeling that you hated to part with it, but you just didn't know what to do with it? Here are some suggestions, that will no doubt give you more ideas of your own on what to do with that old cracker box, or cereal box, or shoe box, orange box, or egg box. Make a few of these the next time you have a few hours to spare.

---

62. BANK

You will need:

> A candy box
> A picture from a magazine
> A pair of scissors
> Crayons or paint

GET THE KIND of candy box that has a deep cover on it that covers the whole box. Paint or crayon it a bright color. Paste the picture on the top of the cover. Carefully make a 1½ inch slit in the center of the cover, for the coins to slip through. To make the box stronger give it a coat of shellac. This makes a nice birthday or Christmas gift. Be sure to put a coin in it for good luck.

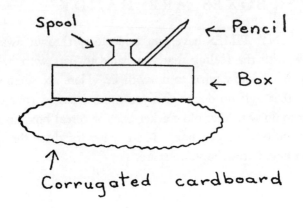

63. BOX TANK

You will need:

> Any small cardboard box, as a candy box
> Brown or gray paint
> Paper fasteners
> Corrugated paper
> An empty thread spool
> Glue

MAKE A FLAT ROLL of the corrugated paper larger than the length of the box. Fasten the box to the top of this flat roll. If the box is too heavy and seems to sink the roll, double the corrugated paper before you roll it. Use paper fasteners for this. Glue the empty spool to the top center of the box. Paint the tank brown or gray. Make a few of these. If you'd like to make the tank look realistic stick a pencil slantwise through the top of the box near the spool, to look like an anti-tank gun.

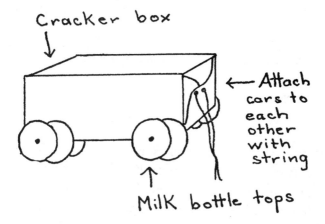

Cracker box

← Attach cars to each other with string

Milk bottle tops

64. DOUBLE WHEELED CAR

You will need:

> A small empty cracker box or milk container—the quart size
>
> 8 milk bottle tops
>
> 8 paper fasteners
>
> String
>
> Paint

FASTEN THE MILK BOTTLE tops to the bottom corners of the box, doubled, as they are in the picture, after you have painted the box the color you like. If you want to use it as a single car then tie a string to the front top of the box to pull the car. If you want to make a row of box cars as in a freight yard, make a few of these and tie them to each other in a row by punching 2 small holes in the front and back of each car and connecting them with string drawn through the holes. Then you can decorate the sides of the boxes with different names to represent fruit and cattle cars.

65. BOWLING GAME

You will need:

>9 small milk containers—the half pint size
>Paint, any color
>White paint
>A ball

WASH OUT the milk containers until they are thoroughly cleaned. Paint them any color you like. If you have no paint you might cover them with colored paper, or material or oil-cloth. On one side of the containers paint a large number in white paint, going from one to nine. When the containers are dry, you will be ready to play. You may play this indoors or outdoors. Set the containers up as in a bowling game, or in any fashion you prefer. Stand about 10 to 15 feet away from them and mark a line where the players are to stand. Roll the ball and see how many "pins" you can knock over. Add the numbers of the boxes you throw over and the one who gets the highest score wins. Take turns with your friends at rolling the ball and setting up the boxes.

---

66. ANIMAL CAGE

You will need:

>A shoe box
>Cellophane tape or adhesive tape
>A pair of scissors
>Paint
>4 milk bottle tops or spools and 4 fasteners
>Glue

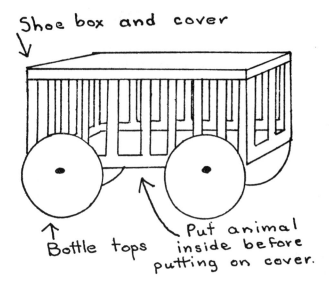

Shoe box and cover

Bottle tops

Put animal inside before putting on cover.

66. ANIMAL CAGE

REMOVE THE COVER from the box. Cut narrow bars down from the edge of the box almost to the bottom of the box. Carefully cut away every other strip so that you have bars left, as in a cage. Try not to bend the bars as you do this. Attach the milk bottle tops to the corners of the box with the paper fasteners, to represent wheels. If you are using spools, then glue the spools to the corners of the box. Cut an animal out of a magazine if you like, paste it on cardboard to stand up, slip it into the slit top of a cork to make it stand, and put this animal in the center of the box. Now put the cover of the box on and if you want it to be on permanently fasten the cover down with cellophane tape or pasting paper. Paint the box the color you like. If you prefer you may paint the box before you put the wheels on. Make a few of these and put a different animal in each cage and you will have your own circus.

67. MAGAZINE AND NEWSPAPER BASKET

You will need:

>A large cardboard cracker box
>A piece of rope about 2 feet long
>4 large magazine pictures
>A pair of scissors
>Paste
>Shellac

GET A CRACKER BOX from the grocer's. Shake out all the crumbs thoroughly. Cut out 4 pictures from a magazine large enough to cover the sides of the box. Paste these very carefully around the box. At opposite sides of the box, 2 inches down from the top make a hole large enough to slip through the rope. Slip each end of the rope through the holes, and make a knot on the inside so that the rope won't come out. Shellac the outside and inside of the basket. If you are making this for someone, try to get pictures that will interest that person or show his hobbies.

---

68. A BOAT

You will need:

>A shoe box
>A sheet of thin cardboard
>A pair of scissors
>A sheet of white paper
>Paste
>Paint

KEEP THE COVER on the box. Make three holes in the cover

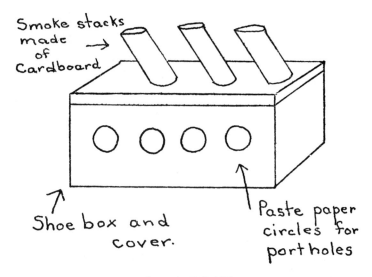

Smoke stacks made of Cardboard →

Shoe box and cover.

Paste paper circles for portholes

68. A BOAT

in a straight line along the center. Cut three pieces of cardboard, roll them into small enough rolls to fit into the holes. These are the stacks or chimneys on the ship. Slant them a little, all in the same direction. Around the sides of the box, along the middle, paste white paper circles for portholes, after you have painted your ship. Use a round small glass to trace the circles. Paint the ship blue or gray. If you want to make your ship more interesting, paint it various colors to camouflage it. Make a fleet of ships to play with on a rainy day.

---

69. A JEWELRY BOX

You will need:

> A wooden cigar box
> Glue
> Paint
> Shellac

[73]

SEE THAT THE BOX is thoroughly cleaned and aired so that it doesn't have that tobacco odor. Paint the box a bright color. If you want to make it fancy, paste a picture on the top of it. Shellac the box inside and outside. A good trimming idea would be to nail a satin bow to the cover with a small nail. Or glue a small empty thread spool to the front center of the cover to use as a lifter.

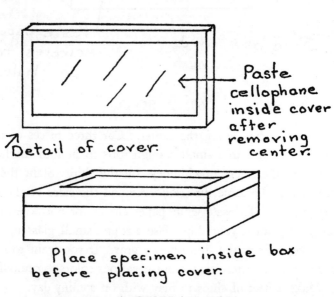

Detail of cover.

Paste cellophane inside cover after removing center.

Place specimen inside box before placing cover.

70. A DISPLAY BOX

You will need:

> A cardboard box with a cover, any size
> Absorbent cotton
> A sheet of cellophane
> Cellophane tape
> A pair of scissors

EVERY BOY AND GIRL likes to collect things. Many of us like to collect leaves, or stones or insects or other specimens of nature. Here is a good way to display your finds and keep them clean and protected at the same time. Cut the inside of the cover of the box away, but leave a small edge all around. It will look like a window frame. Paste the cellophane to the inside of the cover with cellophane tape or pasting paper. See that there are no wrinkles in the cellophane. You will have to cut the cellophane to fit the cover. Fill the inside of the box with the absorbent cotton. Place your specimen in the box and cover it. It will show through the cellophane window. You might paint the box if you like. A set of these would look nice in any home museum.

---

71. STRAW HOLDER

You will need:

> An empty quart size milk container
> Shellac and paint or
> Colored cellophane
> Paper fasteners

CUT OFF the top of the milk container 2 or 3 inches down, so that it will be short enough to allow the straws to stick out. Paint the box. Shellac it when it is dry. It would be more colorful if you cover the box with colored cellophane fastened to the box with paper fasteners. This will look nice on any table. A cereal box could be used instead.

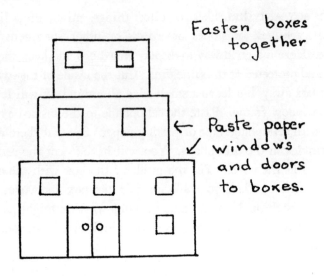

Fasten boxes together

← Paste paper windows and doors to boxes.

72. APARTMENT HOUSE

You will need:

3 or 4 cardboard boxes of different sizes
Red paint
White paper
Colored paper
Paste

PLACE THE BOXES one on top of the other so that the largest box is on the bottom and the smallest box is on the top. Fasten them to each other with paper fasteners by taking off the cover, fastening the bottom of one box to the cover of the box underneath it. When all the boxes are fastened to each other, and look like a building, paint the whole thing red. When it is dry, cut out white paper squares and paste them around the sides of the boxes to look like windows. Make a large door at the bottom. This could be of brown or black paper. Now you can have some fun by cutting colored triangles and pasting them to the windows to look like curtains. You could then cut out small pictures of people and paste them over the windows to look like people who are looking out. How about putting a doorman at the door?

---

73. WOOL HOLDER

You will need:

> A round cereal box with a cover
> Colored pictures
> Paste
> Shellac
> A pair of scissors

IF YOU DO NOT have a round cereal box try to get a 2 quart milk container. See that both or either box is clean. Paste colored pictures all around the box and on the cover. Trim any rough edges with the pair of scissors. Shellac the box. Punch a hole in the cover with a pencil. Put the wool in the box, and bring the end of the wool up through the cover. Then the wool won't get dirty or roll on the floor while the knitter is working.

---

74. A DOLL'S HOUSE

You will need:

> 2 orange boxes or egg boxes
> Red, yellow or blue paint
> Wallpaper
> A few nails and a hammer
> Paste
> White paper or cellophane

[77]

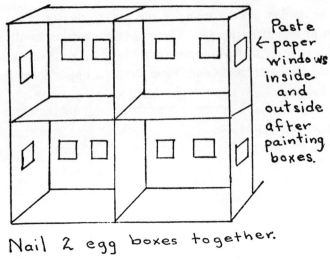

Paste ← paper windows inside and outside after painting boxes.

Nail 2 egg boxes together.

74. A DOLL'S HOUSE

PLACE THE BOXES one on top of the other so that you have 4 spaces, 2 on top and 2 on the bottom. Nail them to each other. Paint the outside of the boxes any one of the three colors suggested. On the outside of the boxes paste white paper squares for windows. Paste colored paper over them for curtains. Cover the insides of the boxes with left over wallpaper. Be careful that you make the corners neat. Paste white paper windows inside the boxes to match the outside, or use cellophane for the windows. Cover the floors with scraps of material for carpets, and some rainy day help any little girl to make spool furniture for the house.

---

75. NAPKIN RING
You will need:

> Empty pill boxes
> Colored wool
> Glue

WHEN YOU HAVE gathered a few pill boxes, enough for every one in the family, carefully remove the tops and bottoms of the boxes, by pushing them out of the rims. This will leave two rings for each box, the box ring and the cover ring. Glue these two rings into each other to strengthen them, and wind the colored wool around the ring. Tie the ends of the wool with a knot. Use a different colored wool for each ring, so that each one in the family will know which one is his or hers.

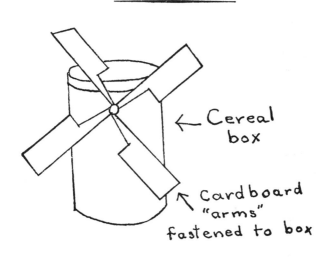

← Cereal box

← Cardboard "arms" fastened to box

76. A WINDMILL

You will need:

> An oatmeal box or round salt box
> A sheet of thin cardboard
> A pair of scissors
> A paper fastener
> A sheet of white paper

REMOVE THE COVER of the box until you have put on the windmill arms. Cut out 4 cardboard arms as in the picture. Fasten them to the top center of the box. Put the cover on. You might now paint the box, and paste paper windows and a door on it, cut out from the white sheet of paper. How about pasting a little Dutch girl on the box near the door?

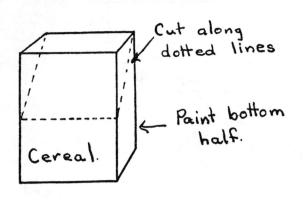

77. LETTER TRAY

You will need:

     A cereal box
     A pair of scissors
     Paint

CUT AWAY the cereal box as it is shown in the picture. Paint the box any color you like. Put it on your desk. That's all there is to it. It is very convenient for holding letters or notes.

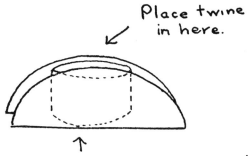

Place twine in here.

Half of a cereal box pasted between 2 cardboard half circles.

78. TWINE HOLDER

You will need:

    An oatmeal box
    A small sheet of cardboard
    Glue
    A pair of scissors
    2 small pictures
    Crayon or paint or colored paper

CUT THE CEREAL BOX in half. It should be a round box. Cut 2 half circles from the sheet of cardboard, large enough to cover the sides of the box. You might make one large circle and then cut it in half. Fasten the 2 half circles on each side of the box with the straight edge down, the curved edge up. This will hide the box. Paint the box and the half circles. If you do not want to use paint, cover the box with colored paper, and the half circles with colored paper, and then fasten them to the box with paper fasteners. Now paste a small picture on each half circle. You may shellac it if you like. Put your ball of twine in the box. This will look nice on any desk or table.

79. HAT STAND

You will need:

>An oatmeal box
>A few small stones
>Paste
>Magazine pictures
>Shellac
>Pasting paper or adhesive tape

PASTE THE COVER of the box to the box with cellophane tape, or pasting paper. Put the stones in before you cover the box. This will prevent the box from tipping over. Paste the pretty pictures all around the box. Paint the box if you want to instead of using the magazine pictures. Shellac the box. A set of three of these hat holders will decorate any closet.

If you use your imagination you can make other things with all kinds of boxes, as apple boxes, pear boxes, peach baskets, and cardboard egg boxes. How about making a footstool from a small wooden box, padded on the top and painted all around? Why not make a child's work table or bookcase from an orange box? You'll soon think of many others to add to this list just as fascinating to make as all the things explained so far.

SCRAPS OF OILCLOTH

SAVE THAT OLD worn out oilcloth tablecloth. Trim off the worn out edges and you'll have plenty of it left to make many nice things. Or you could go to the dime store and buy a yard or two of new printed or solid colored oilcloth if you have no oilcloth scraps at home. Here are a few oilcloth suggestions.

---

80. SCRAP BOOK

You will need:

> A piece of oilcloth 16 inches long and 10 inches wide
> A needle
> Wool yarn
> 6 pieces of cloth 15 inches long and 9 inches wide

MAKE POINTS all around the piece of oilcloth with your scissors so that it looks as if you have cut little v's all around the edges. Place the 6 pieces of cloth together evenly and then place the 6 pieces of cloth in the exact center of the oilcloth, with the oilcloth side outside. Fold it in half. Through the center about 2 inches apart sew the yarn through, coming out on the outside of the oilcloth and tie the 2 ends into a bow. This is a nice scrapbook into which to paste pictures for a small child. The book is washable and the pages won't tear easily.

81. DOILIES, TABLE RUNNERS AND PLACE MATS

You will need:

>Oilcloth, large pieces of it
>Needle
>Wool yarn
>Nail polish
>Large pot covers

WHEN YOU ARE making the doilies, trace circles on the oilcloth with the pot covers. Sew an overcasting stitch all around with the needle and wool. Leave a small end of the wool when you start to sew so that you can knot it with the end of the wool when you come back to the beginning of your sewing. With the nail polish paint a design or your name or initials in the center or around the doily. If you are making a table runner cut it as long and as wide as the table or dresser you are going to cover. Sew around the edges and use the nail polish for trimming as you did with the doilies. For place mats make them 9 inches wide, and 14 inches long. Trim and decorate them the same as the doilies. Your initial in the left hand corner is very attractive. Put it on with the nail polish. A set of these will decorate any luncheon table.

82. A BIB FOR BABY

You will need:

>A piece of oilcloth large enough to cover baby
>A pair of scissors
>Colored wool yarn

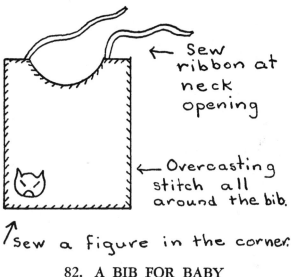

← Sew ribbon at neck opening

← Overcasting stitch all around the bib.

↑ Sew a figure in the corner.

82. A BIB FOR BABY

A needle
2 pieces of ribbon from a candy box

CUT OUT a square of oilcloth less than twelve inches on each side, or large enough to cover the front of the baby. Cut a half circle out of the top to make an opening for the baby's neck. Sew an overcasting stitch all around the edges with the needle and wool. Sew the 2 pieces of ribbon at the neck points as it is shown in the picture. Now you can make a nice bow at the back when you tie on the bib. Sew a felt or cloth bunny or face in each corner of the bib. This is very easy to keep clean.

---

83. SPACE SAVING CHECKERBOARD

You will need:

Checked oilcloth
An old broomstick or bottle tops

A saw
A pair of scissors
Paint

GET SOME OILCLOTH at the dime store. If you can't get oilcloth that has large squares already on it, then paint squares yourself. Cut 24 pieces from the broomstick for the checkers. Paint 12 of them one color and 12 another. If you haven't a broomstick then paint 24 bottle tops. This checkerboard can be folded up when not in use.

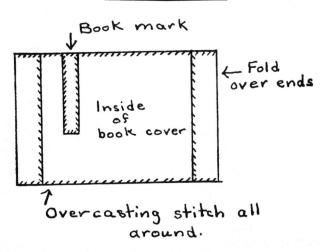

84. BOOK COVER

You will need:

A piece of oilcloth
Wool yarn
Paper clips
A needle
A pair of scissors
A pencil

THIS BOOK COVER will have its book mark attached if you make it right. You will have to decide how large a book you want covered. To do this take an average sized book, open it in the center, and place it on the piece of oilcloth. Draw lines around the book as close to the top and the bottom as you can with a pencil. But at the sides of the book allow 2½ inches wider than the book. These will be folded in for pockets to hold the covers of the book. Cut a piece of oilcloth 1 inch wide and 6 inches long. This will be your book mark. With your needle and wool make an overcasting stitch all around the book mark. Make an overcasting stitch at the ends of the oilcloth, the ends where the covers of the book were resting. Now fold over the 2½ inches at each side, so that the pattern of your oilcloth will be on the outside of your book when you are finished, and the pockets will be on the inside. So that these foldovers won't slip while you are sewing, use paper clips to hold them down. Clip the book mark an inch away from the folded edge. With the same overcasting stitch go all around the book cover, over the folded ends, and over the book mark. Keep your favorite book in this and it will always be protected. Why not make a cover for this book right now?

---

85. KITCHEN SET

You will need:

>Quite a lot of oilcloth if you are making this for more than 1 chair
>Clean rags
>A pair of scissors
>Wool yarn and a needle
>Tape or ribbon

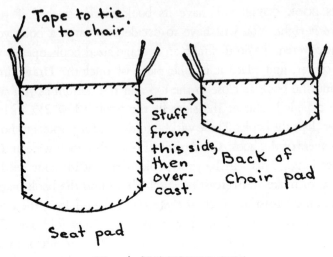

Tape to tie to chair

Stuff from this side, then overcast.

Back of chair pad

Seat pad

85. A KITCHEN SET

Suppose we make one seatpad and seatback. Then if we are successful we can make a set for all the kitchen chairs. Measure the seat of your kitchen chair. Cut out two pieces of oilcloth as large as the seat. Sew 3 sides with an overcasting stitch with the needle and wool. Stuff it with the clean rags which you have cut into little pieces. Close the pad with an overcasting stitch at the open end. At two corners sew a piece of tape or ribbon in the center so that you have 2 ends. Tie these two ends around the back of the chair with a bow. For the seat back, measure the width of your chair and cut out 2 pieces of oilcloth as wide as the back of the chair but only half as long as the back of the chair. Sew it and stuff it as you did the seat pad. Sew the tape or ribbons in the 2 corners, and tie this to the back of the chair. Use oilcloth and wool which will match the kitchen. I'm sure that once you have made one set it will be very easy to make a set for every chair in the kitchen. These would also be nice on the porch chairs.

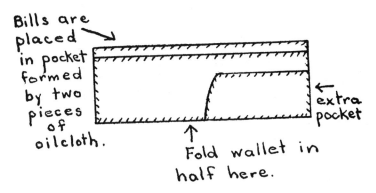

Bills are placed in pocket formed by two pieces of oilcloth.

extra pocket

Fold wallet in half here.

86. A WALLET

You will need:

A piece of oilcloth
Wool yarn
A needle
A pair of scissors

PLACE A DOLLAR BILL on the oilcloth, and cut out two pieces ¾ of an inch larger all around. Make one piece ½ inch narrower. Put the 2 pieces together with the left sides of the oilcloth facing each other. The narrower piece will be the inside of the wallet when you fold it in half. Sew the top edges with an overcasting stitch. Sew the 3 sides together with the needle and wool with an overcasting stitch. Leave the top side open to slip in the dollar bills. If you would like to make an extra little pocket in which to put a card with your name on it, cut a small piece of oilcloth half as large as the wallet, and clip it to the inside of the wallet so it won't slip while you sew. When you reach this little pocket while you are sewing you will be going through 3 pieces of oilcloth. Be sure to overcast the inside edge of this little pocket. If you feel very ambitious you could even make a little pocket on the other side inside of the wallet.

[89]

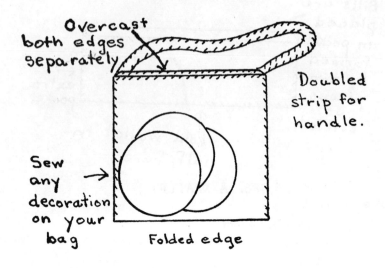

Overcast both edges separately

Doubled strip for handle.

Sew any decoration on your bag

Folded edge

87. SHOPPING BAG

You will need:

> A fairly large piece of oilcloth
> A needle and wool yarn
> A pair of scissors

AFTER MAKING the travel cushion and kitchen seat pads this will be very easy. Cut a piece of oilcloth 14 inches wide and 30 inches long. Fold it in half so that it is 14 inches wide and 15 inches long, doubled. At both sides sew the overcasting stitch. At the top sew this stitch around both edges, but do not sew them together or you won't be able to put anything into your bag. Cut a strip of oilcloth 18 inches long and 3 inches wide. Fold it in half so that it is 1½ inches wide. Sew the overcasting stitch all around it. Sew it to each corner at the top of your bag, for a handle. Sew any felt or oilcloth decoration on your bag, or write your name on it with nail polish.

[90]

Cut 2 forms this way.

← Sew ear with wool yarn

Put them together, right side out.

Sew buttons for eyes.

Leave opening here to stuff it - then join.

88. STUFFED TOYS

You will need:

> A piece of oilcloth
> A pair of scissors
> A needle
> A hole puncher
> Wool yarn
> Clean rags or old clean socks
> A paper pattern of the thing that you want to make
> Some paper clips

TRACE A PATTERN of a dog or cat or rabbit on wrapping paper and cut it out. Trace this pattern on the back of a piece of oilcloth. Make 2 tracings as they will be sewed together. Be careful that when you make the second tracing that you turn it around or you will have 2 right pieces and won't be able to sew them together. When the pieces are cut out, put them together, and see that the edges match. Hold them together with paper clips. You can remove them as you sew. With an overcasting stitch sew with the wool all around but leave a space at the bottom for the stuffing. Cut clean rags or old clean socks into small pieces, and stuff the toy. Close the opening with the overcasting stitch. If you want to make it easier to sew, punch holes all around with a paper puncher. If your toy has eyes, sew buttons on for eyes, and use wool to make a mouth and a nose. A big white oilcloth bunny with pink button eyes would make any little girl and boy perfectly happy.

---

89. TOY CHEST

You will need:

> A wooden butter tub or a fruit box
> A large piece of oilcloth
> Thumbtacks
> 4 metal chair slides

IF YOU ARE GOING to use a butter tub wash it well several times with hot water so that there will be no grease in it. Whether you use the butter tub or the fruit box, line the inside first with oilcloth. Fasten the oilcloth down evenly, with no wrinkles, with the thumbtacks. Try to use the same colored thumbtacks as the color of the oilcloth. Cover the outside of the box with oilcloth too. Cut the oilcloth larger than the outside of the box so that a piece will lap over into the box and under the box. Turn cut edges under a little so that the oilcloth doesn't ravel. When the box is completely covered, turn it bottom side up and nail the 4 chair slides to the bottom. Then it won't scratch the floor. This is very convenient for the youngsters because the box is washable and is easily moved from room to room.

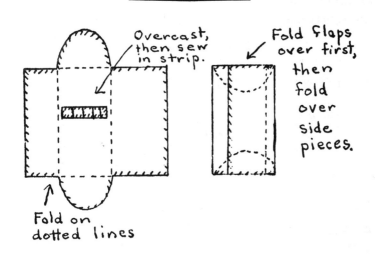

Overcast, then sew in strip.

Fold flaps over first, then fold over side pieces.

Fold on dotted lines

90. A PENCIL CASE

You will need:

A piece of oilcloth
A pair of scissors
Wool yarn
A needle

CUT OUT the oilcloth as it is shown in the picture. Make it 13 inches long at the longest part, and 9 inches wide at the shortest part. Make it 13 inches wide. Round the top and bottom flaps. When the case will be closed, the left hand flap will be 4 inches wide, folded over a 4 inch center, and the right hand or final closing flap will be 5 inches wide. With the needle and wool overcast all around the case. On the left side in the center, sew a strip of oilcloth one inch wide and 4 inches long. Overcast this strip before you sew it in. Make a little stitch in a few places a pencil's width away from each other, to slip in pencils. This could hold about a half dozen pencils, and is very easy to carry.

91. FLOWER BASKET

You will need:

> A piece of cardboard 14 inches by 14 inches
> 2 pieces of oilcloth 14½ inches by 14½ inches
> A needle and wool yarn
> A piece of ribbon

MAKE A SANDWICH of the oilcloth and the cardboard. The cardboard will be in the middle. With the wool yarn and the needle sew an overcasting stitch all around the 4 sides. Curl this up by lifting 2 opposite corners. Join the corners with the ribbon. To carry flowers in this basket slip your hand through it under the ribbon bow, and place the flowers inside. This is easy to make, handy to carry, and nice to look at.

92. TRAVEL CUSHION

You will need:

> A large piece of oilcloth
> A needle

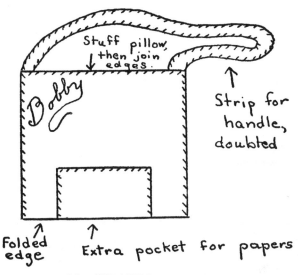

Stuff pillow, then join edges.

Strip for handle, doubled

Dobby

Folded edge

Extra pocket for papers

92. TRAVEL CUSHION

Wool yarn
A pair of scissors
Clean rags

CUT A PIECE of oilcloth 28 inches long and 14 inches wide. Fold it in half. Sew your name in the corner with the wool. With an overcasting stitch sew along the two sides, but leave the top open. Cut the clean rags into small pieces and stuff them into this pocket you have made. When you think it is padded enough, sew the top edges together with the overcasting stitch. Double a 3 inch strip of oilcloth, about 20 inches long. Sew an overcasting stitch all around this strip. Sew the ends of it to the top corners of the pillow. This will be a convenient handle. If you want to make an extra pocket to hold a newspaper while you are carrying the cushion, sew a small narrow piece of oilcloth 5 inches wide and 7 inches long to the bottom of the pillow before you stuff it. This is a handy pillow to take on a train trip or to the beach.

[95]

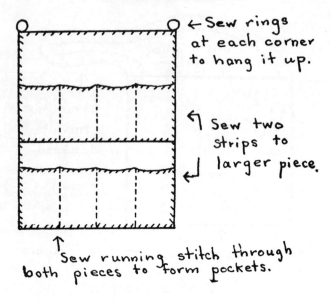

← Sew rings at each corner to hang it up.

Sew two strips to larger piece.

↑ Sew running stitch through both pieces to form pockets.

93. A SHOE BAG

You will need:

A large piece of oilcloth
A needle and wool yarn
2 rings
A pair of scissors

CUT ONE PIECE of oilcloth 20 inches wide or wider if your closet door is wider, and 24 inches long. Cut 2 strips of oil-cloth as wide as the first piece but only ten inches long. Sew an overcasting stitch along the tops and bottoms of the 2 strips. Clip them to the larger piece as it is shown in the picture. Have them an inch or two apart. Sew an overcasting stitch all around. Sew a running stitch six inches apart along the strips to make pockets for the shoes. Sew a ring at the top in each corner to hang it up on the inside of your closet.

94. POTHOLDERS

You will need:

Not much oilcloth
A few small clean cloths
Wool yarn and a needle

CUT 2 PIECES of oilcloth 7 inches square. Cut 2 or 3 pieces of cloth the same size. If you have an old blanket, that would be fine. Put the pieces together so that the cloths are in the middle and the oilcloth is on the outside right sides out. Clip them together so that they won't slip while you are sewing. Make an overcasting stitch all around. Sew a little ring or tape loop in the corner, so that mother can hang it up. This takes only a short time to make and is very useful.

———————————

Most of these will suggest another idea to you. Make an apron for yourself or for mother, or for dad. Make a tool kit out of oilcloth. You can invent a garden carrying case or a dish powder can cover. Jot these things down and then you won't feel you are wasting something when mother decides to discard that old oilcloth tablecloth.

MATERIAL FROM THE MENDING BOX

DID YOU KNOW that boys can sew as well if not better than girls? Did you ever stop to think who are our best tailors? Here are a few things to make from scrap material that require some sewing. Both boys and girls can make these and really feel pride in accomplishing something when they have completed any one of the things explained in this chapter. They are all lots of fun to make.

---

95. PIN CUSHION

You will need:

> A small piece of heavy material
> A needle and thread
> Clean sand
> A metal ring

DECIDE UPON THE SHAPE of the pin cushion. It could be a circle, or square, or long and narrow, or heart shaped. Cut 2 pieces of material the shape you like but not too large, about as big as your hand. Sew the edges with small stitches, all around with the right sides facing each other, and the stitching on the left side. Leave an opening about $1\frac{1}{2}$ inches. Turn the material right side out. Fill it with clean sand. Tuck in the edges of the opening and sew them together with a small overcasting stitch. Sew a ring or a tape loop in the corner so that you can hang it up. This will not only keep your needles in place but will keep them clean and sharp.

Thumb fits in here.

Stuff head and fasten on dotted line.

Sew around all edges. Leave bottom open.

pinky fits in here.

Slip hand in here.

96. FINGER PUPPETS

You will need:

> A piece of material for the body of the puppet
> Scraps of material for the head of the puppet
> Cotton
> A needle and thread
> A pair of scissors

CUT A PATTERN from a piece of wrapping paper as it is shown in the picture. Sew around the edges. Leave the bottom open so that you can slip your hand into the puppet. Sew scraps at the top for a face. Stuff the face with cotton and fasten the material securely under the face. Slip your hand into the puppet. Your thumb and pinky will fit into the fingers of the puppet. Make the puppet act by moving your fingers, and talk in a disguised voice. To make your puppet funnier you could make the face look like a monkey or a cat. Make 2 or 3 of them and put one on each hand and have an extra one for a friend.

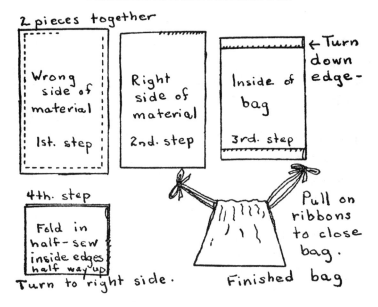

97. DRAW STRING BAG

You will need:

> A piece of any material (to match an outfit) 10 inches by 20 inches
>
> A piece of material the same size for a lining
>
> A pair of scissors
>
> A needle and thread
>
> 2 pieces of ribbon, 20 inches long

THIS BAG IS NICE to have when you have some material left over from an outfit, as a dress, or skirt, or coat. A matching bag of the same material will make the outfit complete and very chic.

Hold the two pieces of material together so that the right sides are facing each other and the long sides match. Sew the long sides together less than ½ inch from the edge. Sew one of the short sides together, and only ½ of the other short sides together. Turn the bag inside out to the right side. Tuck in the half side you did not sew, until it is even all along the edge, and sew that with an overcasting stitch. Now you will have a piece of material, doubled, sewed all around, and ready to be made into your bag. Turn each end down one inch, with the folded end on the left side or what will be the inside of your bag. With little stitches sew this down, leaving an opening at each end, or making a little tunnel. Do this to the other end. Fold the material in half, the sewed ends or tunnels matching, the lining or left side, outside. With an overcasting stitch, beginning at the bottom, sew half way up. End it securely. Turn it right side out. All you have to do now is draw in the ribbon, and your bag is finished. With a safety pin tied to the end of one piece of ribbon, slip it through both tunnels, until you come out to where you started. Join the 2 ends with a bow. Do the same with the other ribbon, but be sure to start drawing the ribbon through from the opposite side. Tie a bow. Pull both bows, and your bag will be drawn together. To open it pull the ends of the bag. This is very attractive in corduroy or velveteen.

---

98. MUSLIN AND CRAYONS

You will need:

> Unbleached muslin
> A pair of scissors
> Crayons
> A pin

WE'LL BEGIN with a book mark. Cut a piece of muslin 9

inches long and 2 inches wide. With the pin pick off threads all around the material until you have made fringes ½ inch all around. Draw a design or your initials on one side of the material. Color it with the crayons. The next step will make the crayon stay on permanently. Put a newspaper on the ironing board. Place the book mark on the newspaper, crayon side down. Go over the book mark with a hot iron. The colors will melt slightly into each other and will become fixed in the cloth. The newspaper will keep the ironing board clean.

Here's a very nice thing to make. Take a square yard of unbleached muslin. Fringe the edges all around. If you are a good sewer, turn in the edges and hem them all around so that the material will be even all around. Draw a design all over the cloth. The more designs on it the nicer it will be. Use the same kind of pattern that is used on floor linoleum, or use fruit and flower designs. Color it with crayon, and press it on newspaper, on the wrong side as you did with the book mark. This makes a lovely bridge table cloth.

You can make table scarfs, dresser sets, handkerchief cases, and many other things out of unbleached muslin and crayon in the same way.

---

99. DOOR STOP

You will need:

> A brick
> A needle and thread
> A medium sized piece of heavy cloth

TRY TO GET a piece of material that will match or harmonize with the door which you want to keep open. Place the brick on the material. Wrap it around the brick until you have 4 sides covered. Cut the material to measure this distance around the brick, but leave an extra half inch to sew on. Trim the sides of the material near the sides of the brick. You will use separate pieces for this. With a small overcasting stitch join the material after wrapping it around the brick securely. Turn the edge in a little so there will be no rough ends on the material. When you have finished sewing this you will still have to cover the ends of the brick. Cut out two pieces of material ½ inch wider all around than the sides of the brick. Fold the material ½ inch around the edges. Place the material at the sides of the brick with the folded edges inside. Join it to the material around the brick with a small overcasting stitch. Do this to the other side too. This doorstep will look nice and cost next to nothing to make. Make one for each door in the house.

---

100. CLOTHESPIN BAG

You will need:

> A piece of heavy material 13 inches wide and 26 inches long
> A needle and thread
> A metal or wire hanger

FOLD THE MATERIAL in half with the left side out, so that it measures 13 inches by 13 inches. Sew the 2 sides together. The bottom will already be finished. Fold the sides of the metal hanger until the hanger is less than 13 inches wide. Cut a 7 inch slit down the middle of one side of the bag. Turn the edges in and sew that on the left side. This will enable you

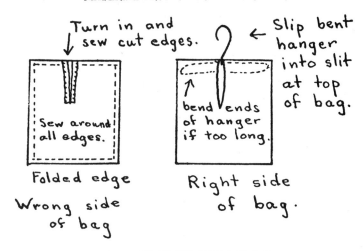

Turn in and sew cut edges.

Sew around all edges.

Folded edge

Wrong side of bag

Slip bent hanger into slit at top of bag.

bend ends of hanger if too long.

Right side of bag.

100. CLOTHESPIN BAG

to put your hand in to get the clothespins. Now sew the top edges of the bag together on the left side. Turn the bag inside out so that it will be on the right side. Through the slit you have made, slip in the hanger. Now you can put the bag on the line and take it off very easily when mother has finished hanging out the clothes.

---

101. BOOK COVER

You will need:

> A piece of heavy material, as cretonne
> A needle and thread
> A pair of scissors

MEASURE THE MATERIAL on an average sized book. Cut it out ½ inch longer than the top and bottom of the book, and 2½ inches wider than the width of the book when it is opened. Turn in ½ inch at top and bottom and sew this edge down on

101. BOOK COVER

the left side. Sew ½ inch in at each end. Then turn in each end 2 inches to make a little pocket for the covers of the book to slip into. Slip the book into the cover. Cut 2 strips of material 12 inches long and 1½ inches wide. Fold these strips in half the long way, turn in a little edge on the left side, for a smooth edge and sew the edges together. This will make a doubled handle. Sew the 2 handles to the book cover at the folded edges. Now you can carry your book comfortably. If you want to decorate it, print your name in the corner in indelible ink.

---

102. BED BAG

You will need:

> A piece of heavy material 9 inches wide by 18 inches long
>
> A needle and thread
>
> A thin piece of wood 8 inches by 12 inches
>
> Paint
>
> A few thumbtacks

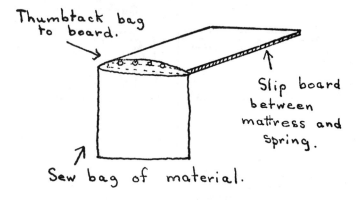

Thumbtack bag to board.

Slip board between mattress and spring.

Sew bag of material.

102. BED BAG

FOLD THE MATERIAL in half. Sew the 2 sides together. Turn in the top edges on the left side and sew them down. You have just made a pocket. Paint the board or piece of wood. Thumbtack the pocket to the narrower side of the wood. Leave one edge unattached. Slip the board between the mattress and the spring of the bed. The pocket will hang down at the side. The board will prevent it from falling down. This is nice for an invalid to hold a book or glasses or extra handkerchiefs. If you slip a paper bag into it it will become a handy wastepaper basket that can be easily discarded.

103. DIRNDL SKIRT

You will need:

> 1½ yards of any cotton material
> A needle and thread
> A pair of scissors

THIS IS REALLY something for a girl to make. But I am sure

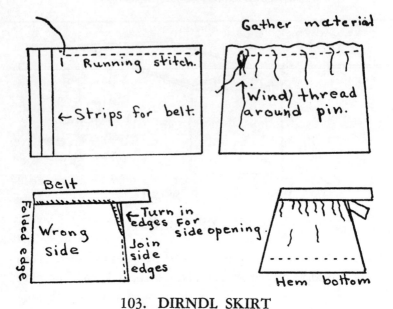

103. DIRNDL SKIRT

that any girl would be pleased and of course surprised if she got one of these skirts made by her brother.

Cut off two 4 inch strips of material from the width. These strips will be used for the belt. Hold the material so that it is width side up. Take a piece of thread 1½ times longer than the waistline of the person for whom the skirt is being made. About ½ inch down from the edge make a little running stitch all along the edge. When you get to the end, place a pin and wind the thread around this pin, after you have gathered in the material. Join the 2 ends of the material at the side on the left side, but leave it open 7 inches from the top. This will be the side opening. Turn in the edges of this opening on the left side and sew it with a small stitch. When you are sure that the skirt is gathered enough to fit around the waist of the person who will wear it, remove the pin, and make a few stitches over each other to hold the thread firmly. Adjust the gathers so that they aren't all bunched together. The belt is the next step. You will only need one strip of material for a slim person. The other strip will have to be joined to the first strip if it is for a stouter person. We'll assume this is for a slim person. Hold the right side of the strip to the top of the right side of the skirt where the gathers are. Sew them together. Turn the strip over to the left side of the skirt, when you have finished that; turn in an edge, and sew the strip to the left side of the skirt with a small stitch. Turn in the ends of the strip. You will have 2 ends left with which to make a knot when the skirt is on. Turn up a hem at the bottom the length the wearer likes. This skirt takes about 2 hours to make and looks fine with any kind of blouse.

---

104. SHOPPING BAG OR SCHOOL BAG

You will need:

> An old discarded awning
> A pair of scissors
> 2 rulers
> A needle and thread

TRY TO GET an old discarded awning. When you do, remove the canvas from the frame and wash and iron the canvas. Cut a piece of canvas 13 inches wide and 26 inches long. Turn in the ends of the canvas at the 13 inch sides, a little more than one inch. Use a small stitch to sew this. When this is finished, slip the rulers into these "tunnels" that you have made. Fold the material in half, ruler touching ruler, and sew the sides together on the left sides about ½ inch in from the bottom until you get to about 4 inches from the rulers. Turn in the edges that remain of both sides, at each side of the bag about a half inch and sew with a small stitch. These will be side openings so that it will be easier to take things out or put things into the bag. Cut two 3 inch wide strips of canvas, about 18 inches long. Fold these in half right side out, turn the edges in a little so that no rough edges show, and join these edges with an overcasting stitch. These are the handles. Sew them to the corners at each side of the bag. The rulers in the bag will always keep it firm and easy to carry.

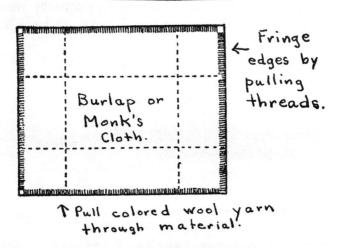

105. BURLAP AND WOOL

You will need:

> Burlap, any color, or Monk's cloth
> Wool yarn
> A pair of scissors
> A blunt pointed needle

DECIDE UPON what you would like to make out of the burlap.

You could make a table cloth, or table scarf or a small doily or a pillow top. Let's see how a small scarf is made, and all the other things are made the same way except that they will be cut larger or smaller.

Cut a piece of burlap or Monk's cloth 14 inches square. Fringe the edges all around for about ¾ of an inch by pulling the threads away. Then, pull a thread out in the width of the material an inch apart. Do the same in the length. You will now have spaces in the material forming one inch boxes. We will replace these pulled threads with the colored wool. With the blunt needle, and the wool, sew under and over the spaces of the pulled threads, first doing it in the width, then doing it in the length. This will make very pretty colored lines every inch. If you do not want to pull so many threads, then only pull one an inch away from the fringe. Use brignt, colored wool, in 2 colors for contrast.

---

106. PATCHWORK

You will need:

>Scraps of material
>A needle and thread
>A pair of scissors
>A good imagination

WHEN MOTHER OR SISTER is sewing, ask her for the scraps of material she has left over. When you have quite a few collected, cut them into 6 inch squares. Sew these squares together on the left side, into long strips. Then sew these strips together on the left side. You will then have made patchwork material. When you have 2 or 3 yards of this material made

you can make many things with it. You can make a dirndl skirt
as previously described. You can make 6 yards of it, and make
a bed cover by cutting the 6 yards into 2 three yard pieces, and
joining them on the left side and turning in the edges all
around. You can make window drapes, a dressing table skirt,
lingerie bags, laundry bags, and many other things to dress up
a girl's room. Start saving those scraps now.

----

107. LAUNDRY OR MENDING BAG

You will need:

> A fairly large piece of material
> A needle and thread
> A pair of scissors
> Heavy cord

THE LARGER the piece of material the larger the bag. The
smaller the piece of material the smaller the bag. Fold the
material in half. Sew one side all the way on the left side of
the material. Sew the other side half way up. Turn in the
edges of the two parts not sewed all the way up and sew that
on the left side. At the top, turn down ¼ of an inch of the
material, then turn it down again for one inch. Sew this on
the wrong side. This will make a "tunnel" for the draw string.
Get a heavy cord. If it is not heavy enough then braid 3 cords
together. With a safety pin tied to the end of the cord, slip
it through the one end of the "tunnel" and bring it out the
other end. Use a cord about ¾ of a yard long. Join the two
ends of the cord with a double knot. Your bag is finished.
You could decorate it by embroidering your name across the
middle of it.

108. BANDANNA

You will need:

> An old printed tablecloth
> A pair of scissors
> A needle and thread or a pin

USUALLY a tablecloth gets worn and faded around the edges. Ask mother for one of her old tablecloths. Cut out the center into a 2½ foot square. If you don't want to sew the edges under all around with a needle and thread, then using the pin to pull threads, make a one inch fringe around all four sides. This is very good to wear as a bandanna on your hair, especially at the beach, or as a neckerchief over your favorite sweater.

Weren't some of these things really easy to make? I have seen 6-year old boys have a fine time sewing laundry bags for their mothers. Of course the stitches weren't perfect or very small, but they had a grand time making them and the family had a grander time getting them.

ALL KINDS OF BASKETS

MANY OF THESE baskets may be used when you are having a party. They can also be used on holidays, such as Christmas or Hallowe'en. All of them are made of boxes or scrap paper and only require a little time, effort, and lots of enthusiasm to make. You will surely enjoy making some of these right now.

---

109. WALLPAPER BASKET

You will need:

> A round cereal box
> A piece of wallpaper
> Paste
> A pair of scissors
> A piece of ribbon

CUT DOWN the top of the basket or box about one third. Measure a piece of wallpaper to fit around the box. Paste this to the box. When it is dry, one half inch down from the top edge of the basket make two small holes with the end of a pencil, opposite each other for the handle. Use a piece of ribbon about 12 inches long. Slip it through the holes towards the inside of the box and make a knot at each end of the ribbon, so that it won't slip out. Put a glass of flowers in the basket and hang it up. It will look nice on the porch or in the kitchen.

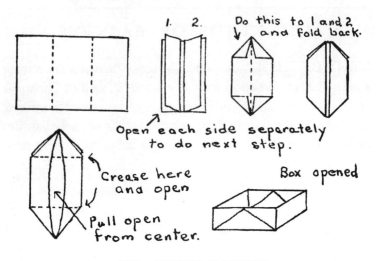

1. 2. Do this to 1 and 2 and fold back.

Open each side separately to do next step.

Crease here and open

Box opened

Pull open from center.

110. TRICK BASKET

You will need:

A sheet of paper 9 inches by 6 inches, and that is all

THE TRICK in making this basket or box is in the folding. You will not need any paste or any scissors. Follow the steps in the picture. Fold the paper in thirds, very evenly, so that you have 3 boxes, each 3 inches wide. Open up the paper, and fold the outer boxes or thirds, in half towards the outside. The folded edges will meet in the center of the paper. Start with the left half of the paper. Fold down both corners, at the top and at the bottom, to meet at the crease, into small triangles. Refold it. Do the same thing to the right part of the paper, folding the corner triangles, and closing the fold. You will now have a point at the top and at the bottom of the paper. Fold the points toward each other and crease the paper. Grasp the paper on the inside of these points and pull open the basket. Straighten the bottom folds of the box or basket all around on the outside. How do you like this box that you have made? It may seem complicated at first. Do it two or three times, and then see how easy it is to make. Use colored paper to start with and you won't have to paint or decorate it.

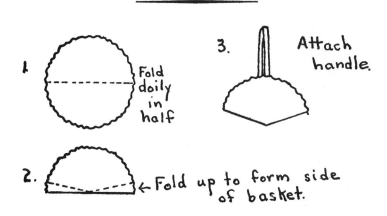

111. PAPER LACE DOILY BASKET

You will need:

A lace paper doily
Colored paper
A piece of colored ribbon
2 paper fasteners

THIS WOULD LOOK very nice for a birthday party. Fold the paper doily in half. Be sure to use a circular lace doily. Paste colored paper on the inside of the doily before you fold it in half. The colors will show through the cutout work in the doily. Make a triangular fold at the bottom of the folded doily at each side. Open the basket and push this fold into the center of the basket. It will form a little side wedge or gusset in the basket. At the top centers attach a piece of colored ribbon with the paper fasteners (or you could use safety pins) long enough to make a handle. Red paper lining against the white doilies is very attractive.

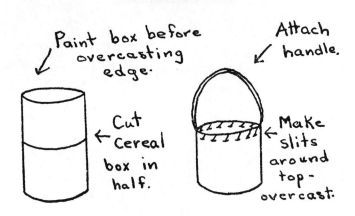

Paint box before overcasting edge.

Cut Cereal box in half.

Attach handle.

Make slits around top - overcast.

112. CEREAL BOX BASKET

You will need:

> A round cereal box
> Wool yarn
> A needle
> A pair of scissors
> Paint

CUT THE BOX in half. If you fasten the cover to the box with pasting paper or cellophane tape you can make two baskets from the one box. Paint the box any color that you may have. When it is dry, carefully cut slits around the top of the basket with the end of the scissors, about ½ inch from the top of the basket. With the needle and wool make an overcasting stitch through the slits. You could use colored ribbon or colored tape instead of the wool. In that case you would have to push the ribbon or tape through the slits with the end of the scissors. Make a handle of the ribbon or tape, or braided wool. Attach it to the sides of the box, through one of the slits, and with a knot on the inside of the box, so the handle won't slip off.

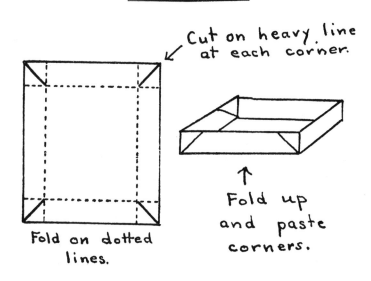

Cut on heavy line at each corner.

Fold on dotted lines.

Fold up and paste corners.

113. PAPER BOX BASKET

You will need:

A sheet of paper
A pair of scissors
Paste

HOLD THE PAPER the way it is in the picture. It could be the same size as a sheet of notebook paper. Fold each edge down about 1½ inches. Be sure each edge is the same width. Open up the paper. You will have a small box in each corner formed by the creases. Make a cut with your scissors from the corner of the paper diagonally across to the opposite corner of the little box, just as it is in the picture. Fold up the sides to make a box, and paste the cut corners, one triangle of paper inside the box, and one outside the box at each corner. Use colored paper to start with and you won't have to decorate the box.

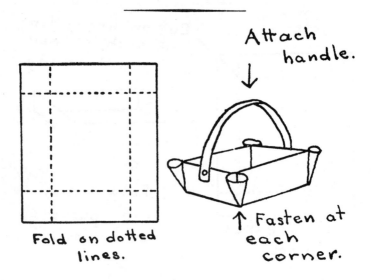

Attach handle.

Fold on dotted lines.

Fasten at each corner.

114. PASTELESS BASKET

You will need:

    A sheet of colored paper about 9 inches square
    A strip of paper 7 inches long and 3/4 inch wide
    6 paper fasteners

FOLD DOWN each side of the paper 2 inches. This will make a small box at each corner of the paper, formed by the creases. Pinch up each corner of the paper, joining the sides of these little boxes, leaving a circular triangle sticking out at each corner of the box, and hold it together with the paper fastener. You could also use a paper clip or a small safety pin. Do this to each corner. Attach a handle to opposite sides of the box, using the narrow strip of paper and the paper fasteners. If you haven't any colored paper, use crayons before you begin to fold the basket.

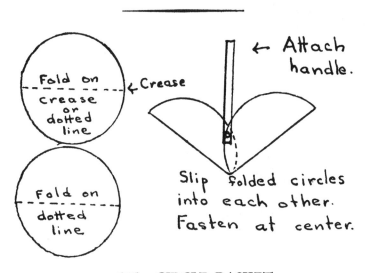

115. CIRCLE BASKET

You will need:

> A sheet of drawing paper or any colored paper
> A pair of scissors
> Crayons
> 2 paper fasteners
> A saucer

USE THE SAUCER to trace two circles on the drawing paper. Cut the circles out carefully. Fold the circles in half. Decorate them on the outside with the crayons. Cut a paper strip for a handle. Double it to make it stronger. Decorate the handle too. The whole trick of this basket is in putting it together. Hold the circles in each hand at the folded edge. Slip the left hand circle into the right hand circle until you have a point at the bottom and a heart shape at the top. Look at the picture. Does your basket look like that? Where the circles meet at the top, fasten the handle there, through the two circles with the paper fastener. Do this to the other side too. Wasn't that easy and tricky to do?

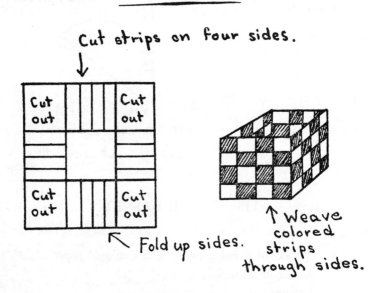

Cut strips on four sides.

Cut out

Cut out

Cut out

Cut out

Fold up sides.

Weave colored strips through sides.

116. WOVEN PAPER BASKET

You will need:

A sheet of drawing paper about 9 inches by 12 inches, or smaller

A sheet of colored paper

Paste
A ruler
A pair of scissors
A pencil

DO EACH STEP carefully and slowly, and watch it grow under your fingers. Measure 4 inches from each edge of the paper. Draw a line where you have measured. You will have 4 square boxes at each corner, made by the crossed lines. Cut these boxes out. The 4 pieces that will now be sticking out are the pieces you will work with. Cut into these pieces of paper from the outer edge to the line you have drawn 4 inches in, making the cuts an inch apart. You will then have 4 strips of paper on each side, attached to a center piece. Fold these strips up to form the sides of the basket. Now you are going to weave on these strips. Cut strips of the colored paper one inch wide and about 17 inches long. If necessary paste two strips together to make them long enough. Beginning at the bottom corner of the basket, weave in and out with the paper strips, and paste the ends together when you get to the start of your weaving. Do this around the basket 4 times, until you have reached the top. Make the weaving have a box effect by putting the second row under the strips where you have put the first row over the strips. This is very attractive if you make the body of the basket blue and the weaving paper red.

---

117. TRIANGLE BASKET

You will need:

A sheet of drawing paper or colored paper
A pair of scissors

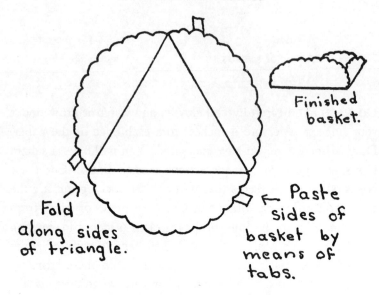

Finished basket.

Fold along sides of triangle.

← Paste sides of basket by means of tabs.

117. TRIANGLE BASKET

Paste
Crayons
A ruler

YOU CAN MAKE this large or small, depending upon what you will need it for. In the center of the paper draw a triangle with your ruler, each side of the triangle measuring 3 inches. This will be the bottom of your basket. On each side of the triangle draw a scalloped edge, as it is in the picture. Draw a little tab on one side of each side of the basket. Carefully cut out the basket but do not cut off the tabs. Fold along the triangle. When the sides are up paste them to each other with the little tabs on the inside. You might tie the sides together with a ribbon if you prefer. This basket is pretty enough to use without a handle. Before you paste or tie the sides together decorate the basket with the crayons.

[124]

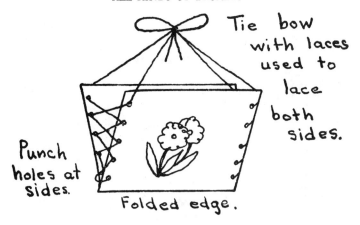

Tie bow with laces used to lace both sides.

Punch holes at sides.

Folded edge.

118. SHOELACE BASKET

You will need:

> A sheet of colored paper 9 inches by 6 inches, or larger
> A hole puncher or a pencil to make the holes
> 2 brightly colored shoe laces

FOLD THE SHEET of paper in half. With the hole puncher or the pointed end of a pencil make holes at the side of the paper ½ inch from the edge and about ½ inch apart. Try to get brightly colored or plaid shoe laces. Lace up the sides of the basket just as you would lace a pair of shoes. Use one lace for each side of the basket. When you have finished lacing the sides make a bow at the top with the ends. Paste a little picture at the sides of your basket to dress it up.

---

119. PETAL BASKET

You will need:

> A round cereal box
> A pair of scissors
> Paint or colored paper

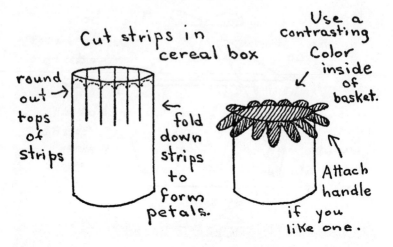

Cut strips in cereal box

round out tops of strips →

← fold down strips to form petals.

Use a contrasting Color inside of basket.

Attach handle if you like one.

119. PETAL BASKET

CUT OFF about one third of the box. Paint the outside and the inside of the box. To make it very interesting paint the box a different color on the inside. If you have no paint you could use colored paper pasted on the outside of the box. Draw a circle around the outside of the box, one third of the way down. Make lines from the top edge of the box to this circle you have drawn, ¾ of an inch apart. Cut these lines to the circle. Carefully bend back these strips you have made, until they look like petals on a flower. With your scissors round out the ends of each strip. If you like you may put a handle on this basket. If you don't want to use a handle, put it on the table and use it as a vase for flowers or just as a decoration.

120. BOTTLE COVER BASKET

You will need:

> Some crepe paper

A stapler or paste
Milk bottle covers
Small pictures

SAVE THE CUP-LIKE covers that are placed over the tops of milk bottles. When you have a few of them make a set to decorate the table, to hold nuts or raisins or candies. Cut strips of crepe paper a little wider than the cup and long enough to fit around the cup. Use a stapler to fasten the crepe paper to the cup. If you haven't got a stapler, use paste or a paper fastener. With your fingers flute the edges of the crepe paper by pulling along the edge of the paper. This will make little scallops. Paste a small picture at the side of the cup or tie a colored ribbon around it. It only takes a few minutes to make one of these.

———————————

Sometimes when you are just in the mood to make a basket which requires a round cereal box, and if you just don't seem to have any, don't let that stop you. A square cereal box will do just as well. Any size or shaped box will do to make an interesting basket. They are always gratifying to make because they always look so nice when they are finished.

PARTY IDEAS

EVERYONE LIKES TO GO to a party. Everyone likes to give a party. Here are some ideas that will make your parties interesting, different and more enjoyable.

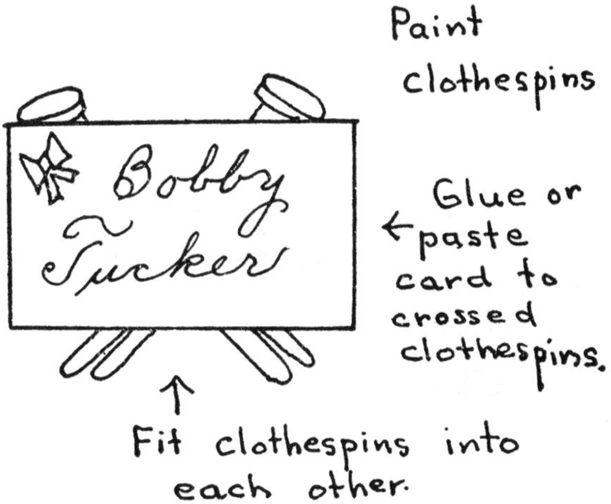

Paint clothespins

Glue or
←paste
card to
crossed
clothespins.

Fit clothespins into each other.

121. PLACE CARDS

You will need:

>2 clothespins for each place card
>A card measuring 4 inches by 2½ inches for each card
>Paint or crayons
>Glue

PAINT THE CLOTHESPINS any color. Paint the heads of the clothespins a different color. If you want to have some fun make a person's face and head at the top of each clothespin. Try to make the face or head look like the person for whom you are making the place card. When the clothespins are dry, if you are painting them, slide them into each other, and slant them away from each other at the heads, the prongs being crossed. Print the name of the person across the card, or write it clearly in crayon, and glue it across the middle of the crossed clothespins. They make nice souvenirs to take home.

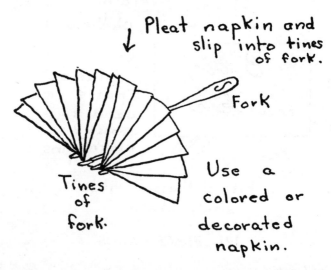

Pleat napkin and slip into tines of fork.

Fork

Tines of fork.

Use a colored or decorated napkin.

122. BUTTERFLY NAPKINS

You will need:

A fancy paper napkin
A fork
A minute or two

THIS IS very quickly and easily made, and makes any party

table very festive looking. Use colored, or printed paper napkins. If your napkin is large, fold it in half, the long way. If
the napkin is small, open it up. Fold one edge one inch over.
Now fold it back on itself. Keep folding the napkin, every
inch, first over, then back on itself like an accordion, until you
have come to the end of the napkin. It will look like a stick.
Carefully, so as not to tear it, slip the folded napkin at the center into the end space of a fork, with the napkin sticking toward
you. Slip the other part of the napkin under the back of the
fork and through the last space of the tines of the fork. The
folded napkin will open up like a butterfly, and will stay that
way while the fork is resting on the table, tines up. If you use
paper forks the children could take these home as souvenirs.

---

123. INVITATIONS

You will need:

> Sheets of colored paper
> A pair of scissors
> Crayons
> Bits of ribbon

THE KIND of invitation you will send will depend upon the
kind of party you are going to have. Whatever party you are
giving, use differently colored paper for each invitation. Cut
them twice as large in the length as the envelopes you will use.
Fold the paper in half, the long way. Draw a picture simply to
give a clue as to the kind of party, and with the crayons print
the time, place and the kind of party. Tie a little bow with a
scrap of ribbon, in the corner.

Here are some suggestions:

> A large cup and saucer for a tea party
> A large pumpkin for Hallowe'en
> A clown's face for a child's party
> A large flag for a 4th of July party
> A big birthday cake with candles for a birthday party
> Shape the paper into a house for a housewarming party
> A large bell for a bride's shower
> Paste a picture of a man blowing a trumpet for a welcome home party

You could probably find many more ideas for lots of interesting party invitations.

---

124. NEWSPAPER HATS

You will need:

> A single sheet of newspaper
> Paste
> Tiny flags or strips of colored paper
> Paper fasteners, stapler or small safety pins
> A pair of scissors

THESE HATS are best made by the children themselves, for themselves, at the party while it is in progress.

Fold the sheet of newspaper in half. Fold each corner down toward the center until they meet at the center. Fold up a cuff at the bottom in the front and the back of your hat. Fold over the ends of the cuff and fasten them with a stapler, or paper

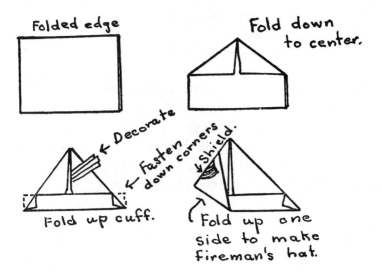

Folded edge

Fold down to center.

← Decorate

← Fasten down corners

↓ Shield.

Fold up cuff.

Fold up one side to make Fireman's hat.

124. NEWSPAPER HATS

fastener or paste or a small safety pin. Stick a tiny flag in the cuff of the hat. Or slip in a few strips of colored paper and fasten them down. If you really want to have a hat with zip to it, make it look like a fireman's hat. Fold the hat in half until the ends of the cuffs meet. Fold one half of the hat up, and back on itself. In the center of this folded up half, pin a large red circle or shield. Now open up the hat, and put it on so that the shield is in the front and wear it straight on your head.

---

125. QUICKIE PLACE CARDS

You will need:

>Heavy colored paper 4 inches by 6 inches for each place card
>
>A crayon

> Flower pictures, small ones
> Glue or paste
> Scraps of ribbon

FOLD THE HEAVY PAPER in half so that it measures 4 inches by 3 inches. Hold it with the folded edge up. The open edges will rest on the table. In the left hand corner, at the top, paste a small flower picture. Some dime stores have packages of these flower pictures all ready to paste on by just wetting the back of the picture. Make two little holes next to each other under the flower. Slip through a scrap of ribbon and make a bow. Write the person's name across the middle of the card. The card will stand up by itself. If you want to have some fun, paste funny little pictures in the corner instead of the flower pictures.

---

126. CIRCLE PARTY HAT

You will need:

> A sheet of cardboard for each hat
> Colored paper
> Colored crepe paper
> Ribbon
> Paste
> A pair of scissors
> A saucer

PASTE THE COLORED PAPER on the cardboard. Use a saucer to trace circles. Cut these circles out. At the center, and on top of these circles paste little bunches of flowers bought in the dime store, or made out of colored crepe paper. To make the flowers out of crepe paper, make small circles by tracing them with a glass or small bottle. Bunch these up in the center, tie them with a string at the middle, and use about a dozen of these in different colors to make a bouquet at the top of your hat. Make 2 small holes near the center, slip a piece of ribbon through these holes, and tie on this decorative party hat at your next gay party.

---

127. FLAG HOLDER FOR TABLE DECORATION

You will need:

> As many small flower pots as necessary
> A bucket of clean sand
> As many small flags as necessary
> Any left over paint and a brush

PAINT THE FLOWER POTS any color you would like. Red or white or blue would be attractive. When the pots are dry, plug up the little holes at the bottom of the pots with paper. Fill the pots with clean sand. Stick the little flags in the center. They will dress up any patriotic party table.

---

128. DRINKING CUP HATS

You will need:

> A paper drinking cup for each hat
> String
> A pair of scissors
> Colored crepe paper
> A stapler or paste or paper fasteners

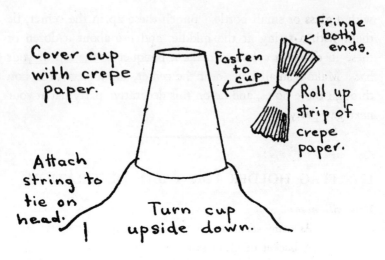

Cover cup with crepe paper.

Fasten to cup

Fringe both ends.

Roll up strip of crepe paper.

Attach string to tie on head.

Turn cup upside down.

128. DRINKING CUP HATS

COVER THE DRINKING CUP with colored crepe paper. Fasten it to the cup with a stapler or fastener or paste. Make a pompom for the front of the cup by taking a strip of crepe paper 12 inches long and 3 or 4 inches wide. Roll it up, tie it around the middle with colored string, and with your scissors, fringe half of it down to the string. Tie this to the cup with a piece of string, or a fastener or paste. Make a tiny hole at the rim of the cup on opposite sides. Tie a piece of string through this hole. This will be to tie it around your head, as a chin strap. Turn the cup upside down, pompom on top, and wear it at your next party.

---

129. CLOTHESPIN NAPKIN HOLDERS

You will need:

    A clothespin for each napkin
    Paint

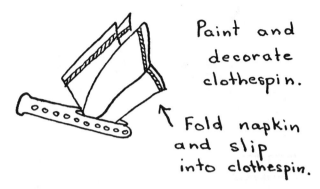

Paint and decorate clothespin.

↑ Fold napkin and slip into clothespin.

129. CLOTHESPIN NAPKIN HOLDERS

DECORATE CLOTHESPINS to look like people. Make the 2 prongs look like legs. Make the top of the clothespin look like a face. For fun you could paste a paper hat on the clothespin. Paint a blouse or dress on the clothespin. Decorate it any way you like. When the clothespin is dry, fold a napkin in half and then in half again. Slip this into the clothespin, and put it beside the plate on the table. A set of these, using a different face and decoration on each clothespin will make your party table very different. Try a row of painted black buttons down the front of your clothespin. Be sure to use paper napkins, as they will slip in easier.

---

130. GUMDROP CANDLESTICKS

You will need:

Large gumdrops, many colored ones
Birthday cake candles, as many as the gumdrops
A few rolls of candy Life Savers

USE A DIFFERENT colored candle for each gumdrop. Make a small cut at the top center of each gumdrop. Slip in a birth-

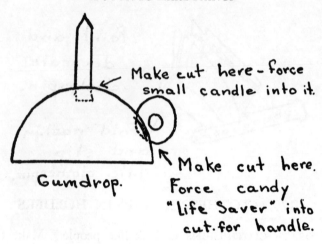

Make cut here - force small candle into it.

Gumdrop.

Make cut here. Force candy "Life Saver" into cut. for handle.

130. GUMDROP CANDLESTICKS

day cake candle in this cut. At one side of the gumdrop make a cut. Force a candy Life Saver into this cut. This will be the handle of your candlestick. If the children want to take these home as souvenirs of the party, try not to light the candles. Yellow gumdrops, green candles, and red Life Savers make a fine combination.

131. PAPER BAG HAT

You will need:

> A small brown paper bag for each hat
> A pair of scissors
> String
> Crayons or paint

CUT THE PAPER BAG in half so that you can use the bottom half for a hat. Tie a string to the bottom edge of the hat on each side. This will be to tie on the hat. With your paint and crayons decorate the hat any way you like. For fun write the names across the hat of the people who are coming to your party so that each one will have a hat ready for him, and then it might be taken home as a souvenir.

Force candle into cut at top.

Fasten candy "Life Saver" to marshmellow with ribbon.

132. MARSHMALLOW CANDLESTICKS

You will need:

    A package of marshmallows
    Birthday cake candles—red or yellow ones
    A package of peppermint Life Savers
    Very narrow red ribbon

MAKE A SMALL CUT at the top center of each marshmallow. Slip in the birthday cake candle. Around the center or middle of the marshmallow, tie the narrow red ribbon, and at the same time slip a peppermint Life Saver onto the ribbon so that it will be tied to the marshmallow. Make a small bow at the side. The Life Saver will be the handle of your candlestick. You could use other colors for the candles and the ribbon.

133. GRAB BAG HATS

You will need:

> As many large paper bags as there will be people at the party
> As many old hats as there are bags—the older the better
> Safety pins
> Scraps, odds and ends from the kitchen or trimming box
> A sense of humor and loads of imagination

IF THIS IS DONE the right way a very hilarious time is guaranteed. These must be prepared in advance of the party. If you have a small group coming to the party, then each one may prepare a hat, in another room, one at a time, and add it to the pile for exchange. The idea is to trim these old styled hats with any kitchen gadgets or knickknacks you might have. There is nothing funnier than an old fedora or bonnet decked out with a toothbrush or tea strainer, or dish cloth, or pot holder, or screwdriver or a bottle brush, or any 101 things from the kitchen drawer. Fasten these around the hat with the safety pins so that they can be removed after the party is over. When each hat is trimmed, put it in a paper bag, and close it. During the party, pass out these paper bags. When each one has a bag, shut the lights at a given signal, and have each one put on his or her hat. Turn on the lights and if you don't laugh until you cry then I am certainly surprised. The funnier you can make the hats the more you will laugh.

---

134. TISSUE PAPER CURTAINS

You will need:

> Doubled colored sheets of tissue paper

Scalloped tops are fastened over curtains.

Pleat curtains and thumb-tack to window.

134. TISSUE PAPER CURTAINS

A pair of scissors
Thumbtacks
Pins

THESE ARE NICE for any windows, not only at a party but in any room. Be sure the tissue paper is doubled. See that it is long enough to cover the bottom part of your window. They need not go all across the window. You could make 2 halves, one on each side of the window. Make pleats on the tissue paper, by folding in the paper. Pin these pleats at the top so that they won't open. Take a different colored sheet of tissue paper, fold it in half, and in half again. Cut scallops, about 5 inches wide. This strip will go across the top of the curtain. Fasten the curtain and the scalloped strip on top of it to the window with the thumbtacks. A nice color combination is pink tissue paper curtains and brown scallops, or blue tissue paper curtains and brown scallops. You could use any color combination you like.

135. NAME TABLECLOTHS

You will need:

>	Unbleached muslin large enough to cover your table
>	A needle and thread
>	A box of crayons

MAKE A TABLECLOTH for the party table by using enough un-bleached muslin to cover the table. Sew an edge under, all around with small stitches so that the edges won't ravel. Cover the table. Even though you have your favors and food on the table you can still do the next step. When all your friends are at the party, clear away some of the things around the edges of the table, and give each one a crayon. Let each one write his or her name across the tablecloth. When the party is over, write the date in the center of the tablecloth. Put a newspaper on the ironing board, and iron the tablecloth, crayon side down. This will make it permanent, the crayon won't wash out, and you will have a grand souvenir of the friends who were at your party.

---

136. MARSHMALLOW FACES

You will need:

>	Marshmallows
>	A few toothpicks
>	A square of chocolate

MELT THE CHOCOLATE by putting it in a cup and placing the cup in a saucepan of hot water. When the chocolate is melted, dip the end of the toothpick into the chocolate. This will be your pencil. Draw eyes and nose and a mouth on the marshmallow with the toothpick dipped in the chocolate. Or instead of making faces on the marshmallow you could write some-one's name across the marshmallow with the same toothpick. Set them in a cool place to make the chocolate become firm again. Make more than enough for everyone at your party. They'll make a hit.

---

137. FISH GAME

You will need:

> Thin writing paper
> A pair of scissors
> A bunch of paper straws

DRAW FISHES on the paper. Make them about 2½ inches long. Color them if you want to. Put them in a dish. Have a dish for each one playing the game. Have another glass dish next to it to represent a fish bowl. Give each player a paper straw. At a given signal the player will pick up a fish by drawing it up to the straw and releasing it into the fishbowl. The one who puts the most fish into the bowl wins the game.

---

138. CREPE PAPER APRONS

You will need:

> Several rolls of wide crepe paper
> A pair of scissors
> A needle and thread
> Paste

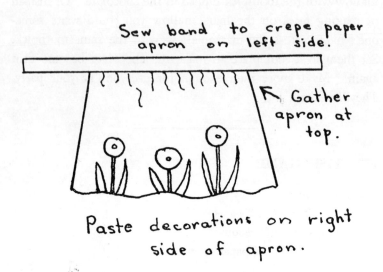

Sew band to crepe paper apron on left side.

Gather apron at top.

Paste decorations on right side of apron.

THE CHILDREN at the party might make their own aprons to take home after the party. Or you might make them the day before. Cut a piece of crepe paper, any color, 16 inches by 24 inches. Cut out flowers by making red crepe paper circles and yellow crepe paper circles. Make green crepe paper stems and green crepe paper leaves. Paste these across the bottom of your apron. Cut a strip of crepe paper about 30 inches long and 4 inches wide. Make little folds in the top of your crepe paper apron to form gathers when you sew on the band. On the left side of your apron sew on the band by joining the center edges of the band to the top edge of the apron. Sew on the side where you do not have any flowers pasted. These will tie around any little boy or girl. If you would like them for a boy, paste a picture from a magazine at the bottom corner of the apron, and make the apron of blue crepe paper.

139. APPLE CANDLE HOLDERS

You will need:

> Large firm round red apples
> A small saucer
> A small colored candle

POLISH THE APPLES until they shine. Cut a small, round, deep hole into each apple at the stem end. Fit the candle into this hole. Place the apple in the saucer. These look very gay when you light the candles at the party table. They are especially nice at a Hallowe'en party.

---

140. PATRIOTIC CUP CAKES

You will need:

> Several cupcakes
> Narrow red, white and blue ribbon
> Tiny flags

TIE A SMALL RIBBON bow around each flag. Stick a single flag into the center of each cup cake. Place them around the table at your next patriotic party. They'll be a huge success.

Any one of these ideas, or a combination of these ideas will insure a successful party. All your friends will want to do the same. It will make you proud to have your friends say what a nice time they had at your party, because it was so different and novel. It will be worth the little time and effort you have put into it in making these party ideas, when you hear people say, "Didn't we have a good time at John's or Mary's party?"

GIFTS FOR MOTHER

EVERY BOY AND GIRL likes to make his or her mother happy. The nicest way to do this is to give your mother a small gift made all by yourself. She'll treasure this more than if you bought her an expensive article in any store, because you were thoughtful enough to put your time and effort into making something especially for her. Any one of the gifts described here will please even the most exacting mother. Of course you could make a gift for someone else's mother too.

---

141. BUTTON BOOK

You will need:

      Heavy colored paper
      Buttons
      A needle and thread

MOST MOTHERS save buttons. Ask mother for her button jar. Draw designs on the colored paper. Sew buttons on the paper following the designs. Sew the buttons once and fasten them with a knot in the back. When the design is finished paste another sheet of paper to the back of the paper with the buttons. When mother needs a button she can cut it off. The other buttons won't fall off as the paper in the back will hold them. Make several button sheets and fasten them together to look like a book. This is a delightful gift to make and to receive.

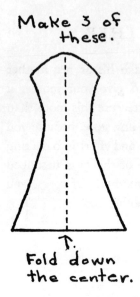

Make 3 of these.

Fold down the center.

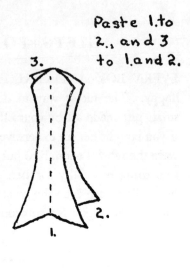

Paste 1.to 2., and 3 to 1.and 2.

142. HAT STAND

You will need:

       A medium sized piece of cardboard

       A pair of scissors

       Glue or paste

       Wallpaper or colored paper or crayons or paint

PASTE THE WALLPAPER or colored paper over the cardboard. If you have none of these use crayons. When it is dry, cut 3 pieces of cardboard shaped like the pattern in the picture. Make it 9 inches long, 4 inches at the bottom, and taper it up to 3 inches at the top. Very carefully fold these 3 pieces down the center, with the wallpaper inside. Open them up. These will now be pasted together. Paste one half of one piece to one half of the second piece, on the left sides. Then paste the free half of the second piece to one half of the third piece. Now paste the free half of the third piece to the free half of the first piece. All pasting will be on the side that has no decorations. When all the pieces are pasted together, they will stand. When it is dry, put it on mother's closet shelf, and it will hold any one of her hats.

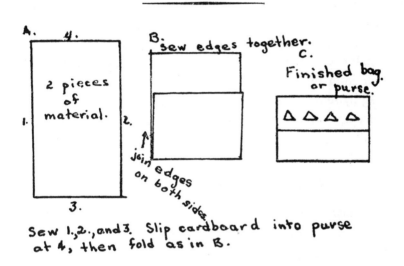

Sew 1., 2., and 3. Slip cardboard into purse at 4, then fold as in B.

143. PURSE

You will need:

> A piece of heavy material 12 inches wide and 20 inches long
>
> A thinner piece of material for a lining, the same size
>
> A needle and thread
>
> An old felt hat or scraps of felt
>
> A piece of cardboard slightly smaller than the pieces of material

HOLD THE 2 PIECES of material so that the right sides are facing each other. Along the side edges, with a small stitch sew both sides. Sew the bottom edges. You have now made a long pocket. Turn this pocket inside out so that the material is on the right side. Slip the piece of cardboard into this pocket. This will make your pocketbook firm. Fold up the bottom of the pocketbook until it is 7 inches up. Fold down the top of the purse to make a flap. Tuck in the open edges of the flap and make a small overcasting stitch to finish the edge. Join the sides of the purse, 7 inches on each side, with the same kind of small overcasting stitch. Cut out little shapes or designs of the felt from the old felt hats, and trim the flap or cover of your bag by sewing these felt cutouts along the edges. It will be a very attractive purse. Try to make it match one of mother's outfits.

---

144. APRON

You will need:

> A yard of unbleached muslin
> Crayons
> A needle and thread
> 2 buttons
> A pair of scissors
> A small piece of tape

CUT 2 STRIPS from the ends of the material, 2 inches wide. These are the straps of your apron. Turn in the edges of the 2 strips with a small stitch. Turn in the edges all around the piece of muslin you have left, after cutting off the strips. Hold the apron so that there is a point on top and on bottom. Turn down the top point about 6 inches to make a little bib. Sew a strip on the left side at the top fold of the apron on each side of the bib. Sew a button on the front of the apron 2 inches or

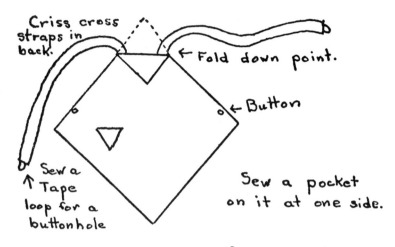

Criss cross straps in back.

← Fold down point.

← Button

↑ Sew a Tape loop for a buttonhole

Sew a pocket on it at one side.

Cut off two strips for apron bands.

144. APRON

more above each side point. At the ends of the strips of material sew a loop of tape for a button hole. You will have to decide where the loop of tape is to be sewed by measuring it first on the person who is going to wear the apron. Draw a design all around the edges of the apron on the right side with crayons. Put a sheet of newspaper on the ironing board. Place the apron crayon side down on the ironing board, and iron it with a hot iron. This will make the design permanent. If you have a scrap of muslin left over from something else you could sew a pocket at the right side of the apron.

---

145. KNITTING NEEDLE CASE

You will need:

A mailing tube
Glue

[151]

Cellophane tape, pasting paper, or adhesive tape
Wallpaper
A pair of scissors
A piece of cardboard

EARLIER IN THIS BOOK you learned how to make a case for holding wool. Here's a handy case for holding mother's knitting needles. Cut down the mailing tube, (the kind which is made of cardboard and is used to mail large posters), until it measures about 14 inches long, or as long as mother's longest pair of knitting needles. See that it has a bottom. If it doesn't, make a circle as large as the bottom of the mailing tube, and attach it to the tube with pasting paper or cellophane tape. Cover the outside of the tube with wallpaper. If you'd like to you may paint it instead. When it is dry, make a cover for it. Cut a strip of cardboard 2 inches wide and long enough to go around the tube, and a half inch over. Paste this to fit around the tube. See that it will slip off easily. Make a top to the cover the same way that you made a bottom to the tube, with a circle of cardboard and pasting paper. Cover this with wallpaper or paint. Now the cover can come off. Mother will be able to keep all her needles for knitting and crocheting in this box, and not worry about losing them any longer.

---

146. SEWING BOX

You will need:

An empty cigar box
Wallpaper or colored paper or paint
Glue
Shellac
2 knitting needles
2 small corks

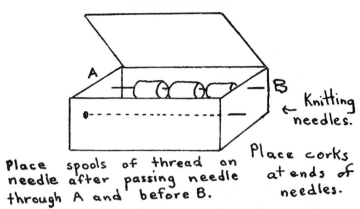

Place spools of thread on needle after passing needle through A and before B.

Place corks at ends of needles.

← Knitting needles.

146. SEWING BOX

SEE THAT THE BOX is thoroughly clean. Decorate the box with colored paper or paste wallpaper on the outside and inside of the box. For a quicker finish paint the box inside and outside. When the box is dry, bore 2 holes on each side of the box, in the center of the sides, 2 inches apart. An easy way to do this is to hold a nail in a pair of pliers, heat it over the flame on the stove and burn the hole in the box. Be very careful that you do not touch the nail with your fingers or you will burn yourself. Slip a knitting needle through one hole, but before you bring it out through the opposite side of the box, put a few spools of thread on the needle, then bring it out through the hole on the opposite side of the box. Do the same thing with the other knitting needle, through the other holes. This will give you 2 rows of spools of thread. To prevent the needles from slipping out, push a small cork on the outside of the box onto the pointed end of each needle. Mother can then always find any color thread she needs by just lifting the lid of her sewing box. A nice finishing touch would be to write mother's name across the cover of the box.

147. DUST CLOTH BOX

You will need:

>   An empty coffee can or an old spice can
>   Paint
>   A small picture from a magazine
>   Glue
>   An empty spool of thread—a small one

IT IS ALWAYS SAFER to keep dust cloths in a covered box, especially if the cloths have any oil on them. Clean the can thoroughly. Paint the can on the outside, and do the same to the cover. When it is dry, paste pictures around the outside. Shellac it if you like. Glue a small spool to the center of the cover to form a handle. An empty spice can, the kind mother uses for flour or sugar can be fixed up the same way. If you have an old drawer knob you could use that instead of the spool. This will be nice enough to keep out on the shelf.

---

148. HANDKERCHIEF CASE

You will need:

>   A piece of material about ¾ of a yard long, or less
>   A needle and thread
>   A piece of tape
>   A piece of ribbon

TRY TO USE a pretty piece of cotton material or fancy satin left over from a dress mother has made. Cut it out like the picture. Make the center square 8 or 9 inches square. The triangle pieces should be long enough to meet at the center.

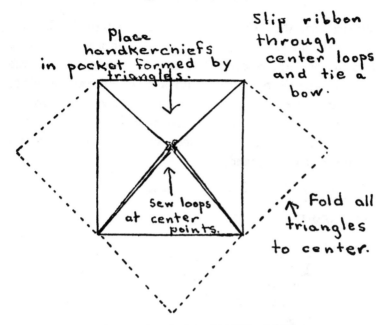

148. HANDKERCHIEF CASE

Turn a little edge in on the left side and sew it down all around
the edges. Sew tape into small loops at each point of the triangle. Slip the ribbon through the loops, bring the points of
the triangle together, and tie it with a bow. Put a sachet in the
pocket you have formed, and let mother keep her hankies here.

---

149. KNEELING PAD

You will need:

> A piece of canvas 20 inches long and 26 inches wide
> A needle and thread
> Old clean rags

MAKE A POCKET of the canvas by folding it in half so that
it measures 20 inches by 13 inches. Fold it so that it is on the

left side. Sew the 2 sides together with a small stitch. Sew one half of the top side. Turn it inside out. Stuff it with the clean rags cut into little pieces. Tuck in the remaining edges at the top and sew them together with a small overcasting stitch. Don't stuff it too much, just enough to make it comfortable when mother uses it to kneel on in the garden. Sew a piece of tape in one corner to make a loop so that it can be hung up when it is not being used.

---

150. SEWING TRAY

You will need:

> A square piece of wood from the end of an orange box or egg box
> A piece of sandpaper
> Paint
> A few nails
> A hammer
> A large cork or an empty typewriter ribbon box

SANDPAPER THE EDGES of the piece of wood so that it will be smooth all around. Paint the wood on one side with the color you like best. When it is dry paint the other side and the sides. With the hammer put long thin nails around the top of the piece of wood not too close to the edge. Slip spools of thread onto these nails. In the center of the wood nail a large cork for a pincushion. If you have an empty typewriter ribbon box or any other small tin box with a cover, paint the outside of the box. When it is dry, nail the bottom part of the box to the board next to the cork. This is handy for holding pins. This makes a convenient sewing tray that can easily be slipped away when not in use.

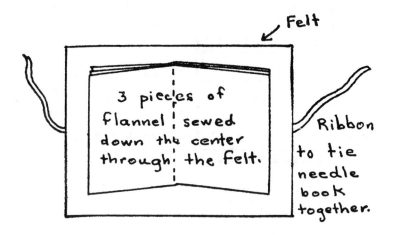

Felt

3 pieces of flannel sewed down the center through the felt.

Ribbon to tie needle book together.

151. NEEDLE BOOK

You will need:

    A piece of flannel
    A piece of felt from an old hat
    A small piece of ribbon
    A needle and thread
    A pair of scissors

CUT 3 PIECES of flannel 7 inches by 4 inches. Place one over the other. Cut a piece of felt 8 inches by 5 inches. Place the flannel pieces directly in the center of the felt piece. There will be a half inch of felt showing all around. With a small stitch carefully sew down all four pieces, 3 of flannel and one of felt, through the center. Fold it in half to form a book. Pin the needles through the flannel and also use it for pins. Sew a piece of ribbon about 6 inches long, in the middle edge of each side of the felt cover. Tie a bow to close the needle book.

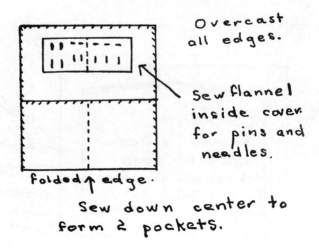

Overcast all edges.

Sew flannel inside cover for pins and needles.

Folded ↑ edge.

Sew down center to form 2 pockets.

152. NEEDLE CASE

You will need:

> A piece of material 8 inches long and 5 inches wide
> A needle and thread
> A small piece of flannel or other thick soft material 3 inches wide and 2 inches long
> Wool

MAKE A LITTLE PURSE of the material by folding it into a pocket with a flap cover. The pocket should measure 2½ inches up, so that 5 inches of material will be used. That will leave a 3-inch flap. Sew all around the outside of the little pocket and the flap with the wool with an overcasting stitch. Sew a little stitch down the center of the pocket. In one side you can put a thimble and in the other side a spool of thread. Sew the soft piece of flannel with a little stitch down the center, to the inside center of the flap. Put some needles in this. Even though the cover is wider than the width of the bag it will not be longer as the flannel sewed to the cover takes this up when you fold over the flap. Two or three of these will be appreciated by **any** mother.

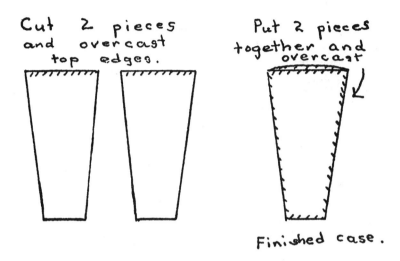

Cut 2 pieces and overcast top edges.

Put 2 pieces together and overcast

Finished case.

153. SCISSORS CASE

You will need:

> A piece of chamois or an old felt hat
> A pair of scissors
> Wool
> A needle

GET A SMALL CHAMOIS SKIN in the dime store, or use an old felt hat. Place the scissors for which you are making the case on the chamois or felt and cut 2 triangles a little bit larger than the scissors. Make the top and the bottom of the triangle flat. With the wool and the needle, sew an overcasting stitch across the wide end of the material. Put the 2 pieces together to match and sew the sides and the small bottom with the overcasting stitch. The scissors will slip in easily, pointed ends down and will not get dull because it will always be clean and covered. A case for each pair of scissors won't take long to make and will certainly make mother happy.

---

154. RECIPE BOX

You will need:

> A small empty wooden cheese box
> Paint
> A package of filing cards from the dime store
> A picture

ASK YOUR GROCER to save you one of those small wooden cheese boxes that cream cheese usually comes in. Paint this box inside and outside. Paste a picture of fruits or vegetables or any food on the outside of the box. Put a package of filing cards in the box. When mother isn't home make this as a surprise for her, and leave it on the table for her to find when she comes in.

This group of ideas is a good start for making mother happy. Add your own and see how delighted she will be when she gets any of them made all by yourself.

GIFTS FOR FATHER

JUST as mother will be pleased, so will Dad be pleased when he receives a gift made for him all by yourself. He'll be so proud of it that he'll probably show it off to all his friends and all the neighbors. Try making one right away.

---

155. A PICTURE CALENDAR

You will need:

> 12 sheets of colored paper
> Paste
> A pair of scissors
> 12 pictures from a magazine
> A small piece of ribbon
> A calendar of the 12 months of the year

YOU CAN GET a calendar, unattached, in the dime store or from an advertisement. Separate the leaves of the calendar. Try to have the 12 sheets of paper different colors. At the top of each sheet of colored paper paste an interesting picture that you have cut from a magazine. At the bottom of each sheet, under the picture, paste a month from the calendar. When you have all 12 pasted, put them together in the correct order according to the months of the year, and punch 2 holes a half inch from the top edge of the papers, and in the center. Slip the ribbon through the holes, and make a bow so that Dad can hang up the calendar when you give it to him. The nicer the pictures the more attractive your calendar will be.

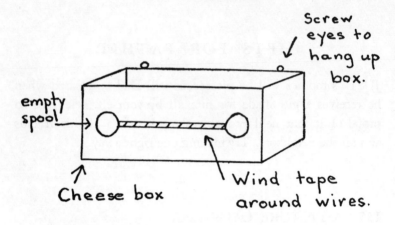

Screw eyes to hang up box.

empty spool!

Cheese box

Wind tape around wires.

156. TIE RACK

You will need:

> A small wooden cheese box
> A piece of wire
> Ribbon, tape, or crepe paper
> 2 screw eyes
> 2 empty spools of thread
> Paint

PAINT THE CHEESE BOX inside and outside. When it is dry, on the outside of one of the longer sides, towards the bottom edge, paste or glue 2 empty spools. If you can do so nail them on to make them firmer. Nail them near the corners. Wind a piece of wire around one spool, bring the wire over to the other spool, wind it around the other spool, and repeat this 2 or 3 times so that you have enough wire between the spools. Paint the spools. Cover the wire by winding tape or ribbon or even strips of crepe paper around it. If you use crepe paper, shellac it so it won't ravel. Screw the screw eyes to the back top corners of the box so that Dad can hang it inside his closet door. He can put his ties over the covered wire, and his belts and small things inside the box. A nice picture pasted on the outside of the box will make it look more professional.

---

157. CHECKERBOARD GAME

You will need:

> A piece of cardboard 13 inches by 13 inches
> A red crayon and a black crayon
> A ruler and a pencil
> Bottle tops—24 of them
> Black paint and red paint

DRAW A LINE on each side ½ inch from the edge. From each line you have drawn measure and draw boxes 1½ inches wide and 1½ inches long. Color the outside edge black or red. Color the boxes red and black, alternating, first black, then red. Paint would be more durable than crayon. You should have 64 boxes when you are finished, 8 in a row, and 8 rows. Make the checkers by painting the tops of 12 bottle tops red and the other 12 black. If you want to make your checkerboard different, paint it other colors, as blue and orange and paint the bottle tops the same. This is made very quickly.

---

158. ASH TRAY
You will need:

> A large shell
> Plaster of Paris
> Vaseline
> A saucepan

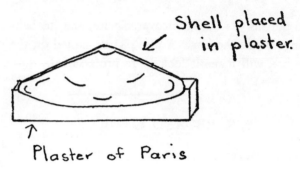

Shell placed in plaster.

Plaster of Paris

Paint when thoroughly "set."

158. ASH TRAY

WHEN YOU GO to the beach, look for a large sea shell. Clean it. Make a plaster of Paris mixture with water until it is of the same consistency as heavy cream. Line a saucepan with vaseline or cold cream. Pour the plaster of Paris mixture into the saucepan for about an inch or a little over. The grease prevents the plaster from sticking to the pan. Let the plaster harden for about 10 to 20 minutes. Carefully place the rounded side of the shell in the center of the saucepan into the plaster. It will become firmly imbedded in the plaster. Let it set for 2 or 3 hours, or until you are sure it is hard. The plaster encased shell will then slip out of the saucepan. You may have to tap the sides of the pan to help it come out. Wipe off the grease from the outside of your ashtray. You might like to paint it, or just paint the plaster and leave the shell its natural color.

---

159. SMOKING SET

You will need:

> A coffee can cover
>
> A small vegetable can

            Paper fasteners
            A small tuna fish can
            A hammer and a nail

SEE THAT THE CANS and the coffee can cover are clean. Smooth the edges of the cans. If they have been opened with a mechanical opener they won't have to be smoothed. Paint all the pieces. Punch a hole in the center of the 2 cans with the nail. Remove the nail. Place the 2 cans on the cover and see where the holes of the can come to. Make 2 holes in the cover to match the holes in the cans. Fasten the cans to the cover with the paper fasteners. The cover will be a tray, the vegetable can will be for cigarettes and the tuna fish can will be for ashes. Paint it Dad's favorite color.

---

160. MATCH SCRATCHER

You will need:

            A piece of cardboard 8 inches by 5 inches
            A piece of colored paper the same size
            A piece of sandpaper
            Glue
            A pair of scissors
            A small piece of ribbon or string

PASTE THE COLORED PAPER over the cardboard. Cut out the sandpaper into any shape you like, as a tree or a boat or a dog. Paste this cutout on the center of the paper. Punch 2 little holes next to each other at the top edge of the paper. Slip the piece

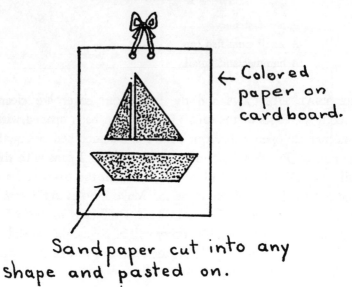

← Colored paper on cardboard.

Sandpaper cut into any shape and pasted on.

160. MATCH SCRATCHER

of ribbon through and make a bow, so that Dad can hang it up and have it ready to use whenever he likes.

---

161. CIGARETTE BOX

You will need:

> A tin used for cigarettes, called "Flat Fifties"
> Paint
> A picture
> Shellac

CLEAN THE TIN BOX thoroughly. You could use any other tin box that has a cover, instead of this box. Paint it on the outside in your favorite color. Paste an attractive picture on the cover. Shellac it. It will look nice on any table, and Dad will certainly enjoy using it.

Cut this out

← Paste to back of frame to make picture stand.

Paste picture right side out to back of frame.

162. PICTURE FRAME

You will need:

A piece of cardboard 8 inches by 6 inches
A piece of colored paper the same size
Crayons
A picture
Paste
A pair of scissors
A pencil
A ruler

PASTE THE COLORED PAPER over the cardboard. Measure an inch and a half from each edge on the wrong side of the cardboard and draw lines. Cut out this box that you have made. Turn it over on the right side and draw a design all around the center edges to make your picture look more attractive. Put some glue or paste around the front edges of your picture and paste it to the back of your frame so that the picture shows out on the right side. Decide whether this picture will be hung up or will stand up. If you are going to hang it up make 2 holes ½ inch from the top edge in the center. Slip a small piece of ribbon or string through these holes and make a bow. If you want the picture to stand up, cut a piece of cardboard 6 inches long and 2 inches wide. Fold down one inch. Paste this piece of cardboard a little above the center of the back by putting glue on the one inch piece you have folded. This will form a leg on which the picture will lean. It will look nice either way.

---

163. BOOK ENDS

You will need:

> 2 bricks
> Paint
> An old felt hat
> Glue
> A pair of scissors

THIS IS THE EASIEST PAIR of bookends to make. Get 2 clean bricks. Paint them any color. You could decorate them if you like. Paste felt on the bottoms of both bricks. Set them up the long way or the short way. There are your bookends. Wasn't that easy?

---

164. DESK BLOTTER

You will need:

> A piece of heavy cardboard 19 inches by 12 inches

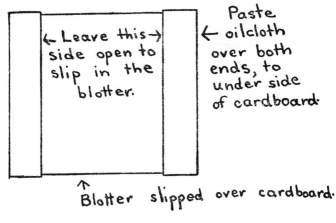

← Leave this → side open to slip in the blotter.

Paste ← oilcloth over both ends, to under side of cardboard.

↑ Blotter slipped over cardboard.

164. DESK BLOTTER

2 strips of oilcloth 2½ inches wide and 13 inches long
Glue
A blotter as large as the cardboard

PASTE THE STRIPS of oilcloth over both short ends of the cardboard. This will make a pocket at each end. Press the edges of the oilcloth firmly and smoothly on the underside of the cardboard so that there are no wrinkles. Slip the blotter into these pockets. That didn't take long, did it?

---

165. FILING SET

You will need:

A few heavy used envelopes, all the same size
A few pictures
A pair of scissors and paste
A piece of ribbon
A crayon

SAVE THE ENVELOPES as you get them in the mail. When you

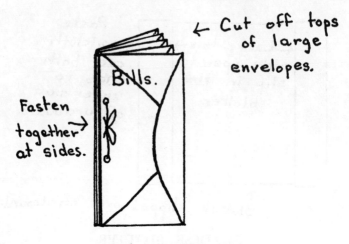

Fasten together at sides. →

← Cut off tops of large envelopes.

Bills.

165. FILING SET

have about 6 or more, cut off the narrow ends of them. Put them together. Punch holes at one side of them. Paste a picture on each envelope over the name and address. Label them according to the bills they will hold, as Gas, Electric, Insurance, etc. Fasten them together with a ribbon. These will hold many important papers and will take up very little space.

---

166. TOOL RACK
You will need:

> A piece of wood about 16 inches long, 8 inches wide and ¾ to 1 inch thick
> Paint
> A pair of scissors
> Small nails and a hammer
> An old felt hat or an old leather bag
> Sandpaper

WITH THE SANDPAPER smooth the board on all sides. Paint it any color you like, on both sides. Bore holes at each top end.

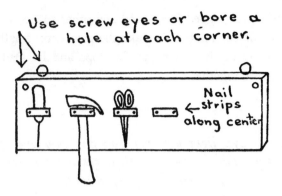

Use screw eyes or bore a hole at each corner.

Nail strips along center →

166. TOOL RACK

Put a piece of strong cord through these holes so that you can hang up the rack. You could use 2 screw eyes instead. Cut strips of the felt or leather from the bag so that they measure one inch in width. Make them 2 or 3 inches long depending upon the size of the tools you are going to put on the rack. Nail these strips of leather or felt across the center of the board, and allow a little slack, so that the tool can slip into the loops. Nail as many strips as you have tools. Hang it up in Dad's workshop.

---

167. JIG SAW PUZZLE

You will need:

>A large picture from a magazine
>Glue
>A piece of cardboard
>A pair of scissors

TRY TO FIND a very colorful picture with a lot of action in it. Paste this picture on a piece of cardboard. Trim the edges. Cut out different shapes until the picture is all cut up. Make squares, triangles, jagged pieces and any other shapes you like. When it is all cut up (don't make the pieces too small), put it in a fancy candy box or heavy envelope and let Dad try to put the picture together.

———————

Watch Dad's eyes light up when you give him one of these things that you have just made. He'll get as big a kick out of getting one as you got out of making these things.

SISTER WOULD LIKE THESE

ANY ONE of the things described in this chapter will please the fancy of even the most critical sister. She'll love the powder puff lapel ornament. And when you show her how to make her own bonnet in a jiffy, watch how happy she'll be. Of course a gift for sister could mean someone else's sister too.

Use an old felt hat to make this.

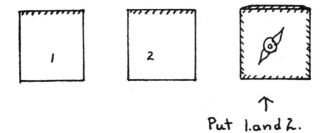

Put 1 and 2.
together.

168. COMPACT CASE

You will need:

> A piece of felt from an old hat
> A needle and wool
> A pair of scissors

CUT 2 PIECES of colored felt from an old hat so that they measure 4½ inches by 4½ inches. With the wool overcast one edge of each piece. Hold the 2 pieces together so that the overcast edges are together. This is the opening of your case. Sew around the 2 sides and the bottom with the overcasting stitch. These 3 sides will be sewed right through both pieces. You will now have a pocket into which to slip your compact so that it won't be scratched by the other things in your bag. If you want to decorate it, cut out a flower of another colored felt and sew it on, or embroider your name across one side, or embroider a face, or a flower, or anything you would think would dress up the case. Make one for each compact that you have.

---

169. HANDKERCHIEF BOX

You will need:

> A flat wooden cigar box
> Glue
> A pair of scissors
> A needle and thread
> Paint
> A piece of printed material

SEE THAT THE BOX is thoroughly clean. Paint the inside of the box only. Cut out pieces of material a little larger than the outside of the box, but not the bottom of the box. Fold in edges on the left side of the material all around and carefully glue the material right side out to the 4 sides of the box. Cut out a piece of material a little larger than the cover. Fold in an edge all around on the left side, and glue this material right side out to the cover of the box. To finish the box, make a tab of material by folding a piece 1½ inches long and 1 inch wide, over twice, sewing it all around the edges and then sewing it to the edge of the material at the center of the cover. Put a sachet in the box, and see if sister won't be surprised when she gets it.

Wool yarn for hair may be braided or plain.

Fasten wool yarn here.

Fasten here →

← Fasten here.

↑ Powder Puff

170. POWDER PUFF LAPEL ORNAMENT

You will need:

> A large powder puff, but not too large
> A needle
> Colored wool yarn
> A pencil
> A large safety pin

DRAW A FACE on one side of the powder puff. Draw eyes, a nose (2 dots will do for that), and a smiling mouth. Leave space on the top for the hair. With blue wool cover the eyes, use black or yellow wool for the nose, and red wool for the mouth. Take several strands of wool, black, or brown or yellow, and make 2 separate braids. This is for the hair. Place them joined at the top center of the powder puff. Fasten them with a needle and the same colored wool as the braid. Now separate them and bring these 2 braids around the top edges of the puff so that they look like hair. Fasten them down in 2 or 3 places. Leave about an inch hanging down. Tie a little bow at the end of each braid to hold the wool and prevent it from opening, if you'd like. Pin the safety pin on the back of the puff so that it can be pinned on to a coat. You could make a few of these using different colors for the hair on each powder puff.

———————

171. COVERED HANGERS

You will need:

>Several wooden or metal hangers
>Glue
>Strips of material or ribbon or crepe paper
>A needle and thread
>Shellac
>Small pieces of ribbon

WHETHER YOU USE the wooden or metal hangers you can cover them the same way. If you are going to use ribbon or strips of material for the covering, wind the strips all around the parts of the hangers, even the tops of the hangers. Wind the strips evenly and tightly. When the hangers are completely covered, join the end of the strip to the beginning where you started to wind, with a few stitches with your needle and thread. If you are covering the hangers with crepe paper, cut stripe of crepe paper one inch wide, and wind it around the hangers. Instead of finishing it with a few stitches use paste or glue to join the last ends. For the crepe paper covering, you will have to shellac the finished hangers. When they are dry, with a small piece of ribbon make a small bow at the top of each hanger. Make a set of 6 to trim up sister's closet.

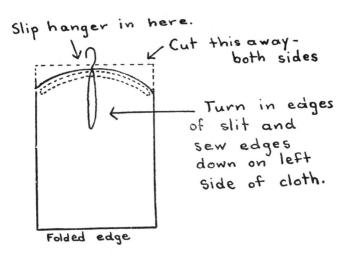

Slip hanger in here.

Cut this away - both sides

Turn in edges of slit and sew edges down on left side of cloth.

Folded edge

172. HANGER LAUNDRY BAG

You will need:

>A wooden hanger
>A piece of material a little wider than the hanger, and 20 in. long
>A needle and thread
>A pair of scissors
>A pencil

FOLD THE MATERIAL in half. Place the hanger at the top of the material opposite the folded edge, which will be at the bottom. With a pencil trace the curve of the hanger. Cut across this curve. If you fold the material right side in you won't have to worry about sewing it on the incorrect side. Sew the 2 curved edges together with small stitches, about ½ inch from the edge. Make a slit on one piece or side of the material from the curved edge at the center 7 inches down. Turn the edges of this slit toward the left side of the material and sew these edges down with small stitches. Sew the two sides with a small stitch about a half inch from the edge. Turn the material inside out, or to the right side, through the slit opening that you made. Straighten out the bag, and slip in the wooden hanger. It will fit in the curve you have sewed, and you can hang it up on the back of any closet door.

---

173. FANCY SHOES

You will need:

> An old pair of sneakers
> Paint
> Wool yarn
> A needle and thread
> Buttons

GET ANY OLD PAIR of sneakers that sister thinks are too shabby to wear. Wash them so that they are clean. When they are dry, paint them a bright color. Use canvas paint if you have it. Around the top edges of the sneakers make an overcasting stitch all around with colored wool. Do this to the tongues of the sneakers too. To trim them up, sew small colored buttons all over the sneakers. These will certainly be fun to wear.

Any boy could do the same to his sneakers, and if he sewed

fringes of felt all around the top edges of his sneakers he could wear them as Indian moccasins.

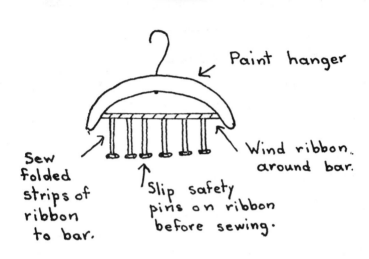

Paint hanger

Wind ribbon around bar.

Sew folded strips of ribbon to bar.

Slip safety pins on ribbon before sewing.

174. STOCKING DRYER

You will need:

    A wooden hanger used for men's coats
    Paint
    Ribbon
    A needle and thread
    6 safety pins

PAINT the hanger. When it is dry, cover the rod at the bottom of the hanger by winding ribbon around the bar. Sew the end down with a few stitches so that the ribbon won't unwind. Cut 6 pieces of ribbon 4 inches long. Fold these pieces in half. Slip a safety pin on each piece of ribbon, then sew each folded piece to the covered bar. When the 6 folded pieces of ribbon are sewed across the bar, or to the bar, your stocking dryer is complete. When sister washes stockings all she has to do is pin them to the hanging safety pins and hang the hanger up and the stockings can be dried in any room of the house.

---

175. FANCY SHOE STRINGS

You will need:

> A pair of white shoe laces
> Colored wool
> A needle

WITH A SMALL STITCH make a line down each shoe lace with the needle and wool. Tie a bead or button to the end of each shoe lace after you have put the lace in your shoe. Make a knot at the end of the lace so that the head or button won't fall off. This will dress up any pair of drab oxfords. You could use any color combinations you might like.

---

176. RAIN CAPE

You will need:

> An old shower sheet
> A pair of scissors
> A needle and thread
> 2 pieces of ribbon

STRETCH THE OLD shower sheet out on the floor. Cut as large a circle as you can around the shower sheet. Cut from any point on the circle into the center, for an opening. Cut a smaller circle in the center for a neck opening. Turn in all

Turn in and sew all
edges after cutting

Cut out
↓ for neck
opening

1 . 2.

← Cut to center
of circle.

↑
Cut circle from
old shower sheet.

Sew ribbon at
1. and 2.

176. RAIN CAPE

edges for a half inch and sew it with small stitches on the left
side. At the top sew 2 pieces of ribbon at the neck opening so
that sister can tie her rain cape securely when she goes out into
the rain.

---

177. SLIPPERS

You will need:

> Old felt hats
> A pair of scissors
> A needle and thread

HAVE SISTER put her foot or both feet on any old felt that
you have from old felt hats. Draw around the shape of her
feet. Cut out the 2 pieces. Measure across her instep to see how
long a strip you will need. Cut 4 strips an inch wide and long
enough to go across her instep. Cross 2 strips across each felt

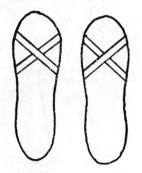

Cross strips of felt and fasten to sides.

Trace pattern by placing feet on felt and draw outline.

177. SLIPPERS

piece you have cut out, and fasten these to the foot soles or slipper bottoms. Then, to wear the slippers, all sister has to do is slip her feet under the crossed strips. These are very handy for travelling as they take up very little space in a valise.

---

178. FOLDED BONNET

You will need:

> A square yard of any material
>
> A few minutes of your time

THE WHOLE TRICK in making this bonnet is in the folding. You don't need any needle or thread to make it. Fold the material in half. Hold it with the folded edge down. Fold back the top half on itself until the top edge touches the folded edge at the bottom. Grasp the material at each bottom corner, and turn it up and over so that the folded half is now underneath and the folded edge is on top. Now bring both top corners towards the bottom center to form a triangle.

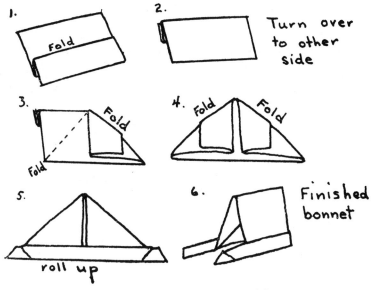

178. FOLDED BONNET

Roll up the bottom edge until you cover the loose ends you have just folded down. When you have rolled it up a little way, pick up your bonnet by the roll and put it on. It can be tied under the chin with the ends of the roll. If you are afraid that the bonnet might open, put a little safety pin at the back where you have rolled the material. Look at the pictures and see if you have followed each step. It doesn't take more than a few minutes to make.

---

179. COSMETIC CASE

You will need:

> A piece of material or oilcloth 13 inches by 6 inches
> A needle
> Wool yarn

WITH THE WOOL and the needle make an overcasting stitch at the shorter ends of the material. Fold it one third up so that you have a flap to bend over. Make the same overcasting stitch on both sides, thus forming a pocket. Any girl would like to have one of these to keep her cosmetics from being lost in her purse.

———————————

Can you add any more ideas to these? ...Of course you can. Just look around the house for any odds and ends ready to be discarded, and presto, make something of them.

BROTHER WOULD LIKE THESE

SHOW ME any boy who would refuse one of these sure fire fun-makers. Any brother would be "tickled pink" to get any one of the things described in this chapter. Make one of them right away and give it to brother as fast as you can, unless you'd like to try some first for yourself. It'll be tempting to keep them so better make 2 of each to be sure both of you have a good time.

---

180. DART GAME

You will need:

> A piece of cardboard 20 inches by 20 inches
> 6 chicken feathers
> 6 corks
> 6 phonograph needles or small sewing needles
> Crayons

DRAW 3 OR 4 circles on the cardboard, from the center to the edge. Use pot covers or different sized plates to trace the circles. Color the circles different colors. Put a number in each circle, like 10 for the outer one, 20 for the next, 30 for the next and 40 for the center circle, so that you can keep score. Pin this square of cardboard, with a thumbtack, to any outside wall of the house or fence or garage. To make the darts which you will try to throw into the circles, make a hole through the center of each cork. Glue a feather into the top center of each cork. At the bottom center wedge in a phonograph needle or carefully wedge in a sewing neeedle. This will make the dart stick when you throw it. There are six darts to this game, but you could make more if you like. The idea is to throw the darts at the circled cardboard and see how many times you can hit the center ring. Keep score. Have a prize for the one who has the highest score.

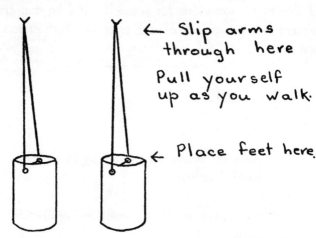

← Slip arms through here

Pull yourself up as you walk.

← Place feet here

Remove tops of cans — leave bottoms.

181. STILT CAN WALKERS

You will need:

> 2 empty cans both the same size
> Heavy string
> A hammer
> A nail

IT TAKES ABOUT 10 minutes to make these and many hours of fun to play with. See that the tops of the cans are off, but the bottoms should be attached. Punch a hole at each top side of the can about ½ inch from the top edge with the nail and hammer. See that the holes are directly opposite each other. Do this to both cans. Pass pieces of heavy string through the holes and bring the ends up long enough to reach from your feet to your elbows. Join the 2 ends of each string, each can separately. Slip your elbows under the string, and put your feet on the cans, and pull yourself up as you walk. Isn't that lots of fun?

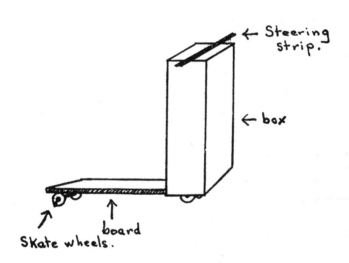

182. SCOOTER

You will need:

>A wooden pear box
>A board 3 feet long and 5 inches wide and 1 inch thick
>A small narrow stick
>An old skate
>Nails and a hammer
>Paint

SANDPAPER THE BOARD and the box. Nail the board to the inside of the box as it is shown in the picture. Separate the skate into 2 sets of 2 wheels a set. Nail these to the underside of the board. The scooter will move on these skate wheels. Nail the thin piece of wood to the top of the box for a steering handle. Paint the whole scooter. Oil the wheels to make your scooter go smoothly.

---

183. HOOP GAME

You will need:

> 3 pairs of embroidery hoops
> Paint
> 3 sticks of wood about 12 inches by 2 inches and about ½ inch thick

ASK MOTHER if she has any embroidery hoops or frames that she doesn't need. If not, you can get them at the dime store. Separate the pairs of hoops so that 3 pairs will give you 6 hoops. Paint the hoops any color you like. Paint the sticks of wood any color you like. At the top of each stick paint a number, as 5 on the first, 10 on the second, and 15 on the third. This game is best played in the garden or any place where you can stick the pieces of wood into the ground. Place the sticks firmly into the ground so that the first is 10 feet from you, the second is a little bit behind the first and the last stick is the farthest. Try to throw the hoops so that they will land on the sticks. Keep score when you play with your friends. Add up the number of rings you have on each stick, and that will be your score. For example, if you have 2 hoops on the 5 stick that's a score of 10. If you have 2 hoops on the 10 stick that's

20. And if you have 2 hoops on the 15 stick that's 30. Add these all up together, 10, 20, 30, and your score is 60. The idea or trick is to get all the hoops on the last stick.

Place this end of can to ear or mouth.

Wrapping paper tied around bottom of can.

Wire tied to button inside can.

Remove top and bottom of can.

Attach other end of wire to another can.

184. TELEPHONES

You will need:

> 2 empty tin cans
> A piece of wrapping paper
> String
> A pair of scissors
> A small roll of very fine wire, about 15 to 20 feet long
> 2 buttons

REMOVE THE TOPS and the bottoms of both cans. Tie a piece of wrapping paper over the bottoms of both cans, with a piece of string. See that the paper is very tightly fitted around the bottoms of the cans and that there are no wrinkles. Pass one end of the wire through the center of the wrapping paper, and fasten it securely by tying the wire to a button or a small toothpick or matchstick. This will prevent the wire from slipping out of the wrapping paper. The button, matchstick or toothpick, of course, will be inside the can. Pass the other end of the wire through the bottom or wrapping paper of the other can and fasten it the same way. The wire will transmit or carry the sound of the voices. The cans are the phones. When one person speaks he puts the can close to his mouth and talks quietly into the can. His voice will go over the wire, and to the person holding the other can close to his ear. Hold the cans so that the wire is stretched straight out as tightly as possible without tearing the wrapping paper. When the person who is listening wants to talk, he just has to remove the can from his ear and put it to his mouth. This is a swell gadget to have when playing games.

------

185. SPINNER

You will need:

> A small empty pill box with the cover on it
> A lollypop stick
> Pasting paper or adhesive tape

SHARPEN BOTH ENDS of the lollypop stick. Paste the cover of the box to the box with pasting paper. Push the lollypop stick through the center of the box until the box is half way down the stick. Twirl the top of the stick on the ground and watch the box spin. Make a few of these and try to keep them all spinning.

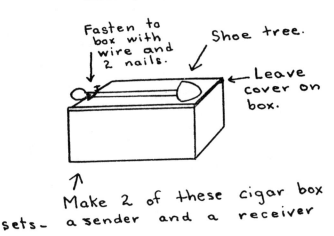

Fasten to box with wire and 2 nails.

Shoe tree.

Leave cover on box.

Make 2 of these cigar box sets— a sender and a receiver

186. TELEGRAPH SET

You will need:

2 cigar boxes
A pair of shoe trees
4 small nails and a hammer
A piece of wire

SEE THAT the cigar boxes have covers, and that the boxes are made of wood. At the top of the box along one of the smaller sides, in the center, nail 2 small nails an inch apart. Leave the heads sticking out a little. Do this to both boxes. Place a shoe tree, one with a metal rod in it, so that the back knob of the shoe tree hangs over the outside of the box, and the rod is between the 2 nails. Fasten the shoe tree down to the box by winding wire over the nails and over the rod of the shoe tree. Do this very tightly. The toe end of the shoe tree will thus be slightly raised above the box. In order to tap out signals to your friends all you have to do is to tap the toe end of the shoe tree lightly on the box into any scheme of signals you have made up. Two boxes like this will make a set for you and a friend.

Fill dish
with water.

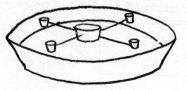

Fasten
small corks
to large
cork with
needles.

Attach camphor to
tops of small corks.

187. CAMPHOR SPINNER

You will need:

1 large flat cork
4 small corks
4 needles
4 small pieces of camphor
Nail polish or glue
Large shallow dish of water
Any small picture cut out of a magazine

WITH THE NAIL POLISH or glue attach the pieces of camphor to the tops of the 4 small corks. Stick a needle into the bottom of each cork. Stick the other end of the needle into the large flat cork. Do this to the 4 corks until they are evenly stuck around the flat large cork like 4 arms. Paste the little picture you have cut out to the large flat cork. Try to get one of a little boy or girl, and make it stand up on the cork. Place this whole cork combination carefully into a flat dish of water. Watch it spin, as the camphor acts up in the water.

188. TOP

You will need:

> A lollypop stick
> A circle of cardboard about 3 inches across
> Crayons

DECORATE BOTH SIDES of the cardboard circle with the crayons. Make colored circles if you can as they will look nice when the top spins. Punch a hole through the center of the cardboard circle. Sharpen one end of the lollypop stick into a point. Stick this pointed end through the hole in the cardboard. Spin it on the ground. It spins very fast.

---

189. BATTLE SHIELDS AND SWORDS

You will need:

> A sheet of newspaper for the pattern
> A pair of scissors
> A large piece of cardboard
> Crayons
> 2 paper fasteners
> 2 pieces of wood
> Paint
> A few nails

CUT A PATTERN for your shield out of the newspaper, as it is in the picture. Trace this on the cardboard, and cut out the shape of your shield on the cardboard. Draw a coat of arms or a design on the face of the shield and color it. Make a handle on the back to hold it by cutting a strip of cardboard,

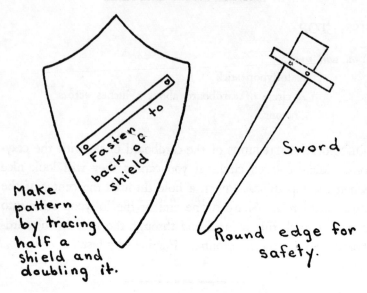

Make
pattern
by tracing
half a
shield and
doubling it.

Fasten to
back of
shield

Sword

Round edge for
safety.

189. BATTLE SHIELDS AND SWORDS

4 inches wide and as long as the width of the shield. Fasten it across the back of the shield with the paper fasteners. To make a sword to match, sharpen the end of a stick 20 inches long and 2 inches wide. Don't sharpen it too much or you may stick yourself. Two inches from one end of the stick nail a smaller piece of wood across as a handle for your sword. Paint the sword a bright color.

---

190. WHIRLER

You will need:

> A milk bottle top
> A piece of string
> 2 clothespins

MAKE 2 SMALL HOLES in the center of the milk bottle top.

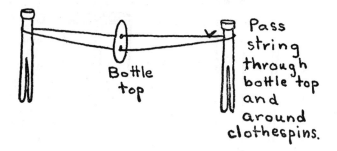

190. WHIRLER

Pass the string through the two holes. Tie the ends of the string around the clothespins. Hold the clothespins in your hands, let the string be slack a little, then pull on the clothespins. Do this several times and the bottle top will begin to wind and unwind very rapidly. Paint the clothespins if you like and color the bottle top with crayons.

---

191. CAT'S EARS

You will need:

> A man's handkerchief
> A piece of string

THIS IS NICE to make when playing outdoor games or when going to a club meeting. The whole trick in making this is in the folding. The string is used to tie the ears to your head so that they will stay on.

Fold the top part of the handkerchief to the center of the handkerchief. Bring the bottom edge up to meet the top edge, in the center. Fold this in half so that the two edges are on the outside. Hold it now so that the folded edge is at the bottom. Do the next step slowly. With your right hand grasp

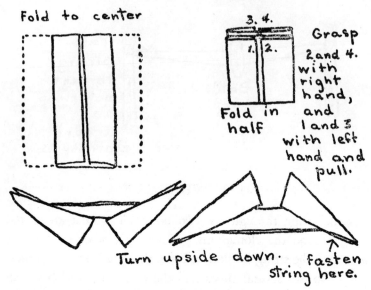

Fold to center

Fold in half

3. 4.
1. 2.

Grasp 2 and 4. with right hand, and 1 and 3 with left hand and pull.

Turn upside down. fasten string here.

191. CAT'S EARS

the point of the handkerchief which is at your right hand together with the point of the handkerchief which matches this on the other side of the handkerchief. Grasp the front point of the left hand side of the handkerchief and the back point in your left hand. You will have 2 points in your right hand and 2 points in your left hand. Pull both hands. The handkerchief will spread leaving 2 folded points sticking out like cat's ears. Turn this upside down so that the ears are sticking up, tie a piece of string to the ends which you were holding, and tie it around your head. If you make these ears out of colored handkerchiefs they will look nicer.

---

192. BEANIE

You will need:

> **An old felt hat**

A pair of scissors
Needle and thread
Club pins, buttons, clips, small ornaments

CUT AWAY THE BRIM of an old felt hat. It could be a man's or lady's hat. Leave the crown. If you don't want a cuff turned up on your hat, cut away part of the crown until you have enough left to stay on top of your head. If you want a cuff at the bottom of your beanie, fold up a piece all around the crown about 2 inches. Whether you have a cuff or not, make a trimming all around the edges by cutting points with your scissors. The next step is where you use your imagination. Make cutouts all around and all over the beanie in different shapes, like little circles, triangles, and boxes. Your hair will show through these cutouts. In between the cutouts sew the pins, buttons, clips, and any little "dojiggers" that you may have that you would like to have on your beanie. If you belong to a club, let each member make a beanie for himself and wear it to club meetings.

Why not get some boys together, and make a club, just to make all these things to play with, out of scrap material found around the house. You could easily add many other interesting things that you yourselves will invent as you go along. It would cost very little to do this and would certainly be a worthwhile thing to do. Anyone's brother would be very happy to join such a club. Make up your own name, slogan, and meet in each other's house whenever you have the time.

TOYS FOR THE YOUNGEST

EVERYONE likes to please a baby. The toys in this chapter are for babies of any age so that you certainly have a wide choice. I'm sure you will enjoy making some of these for any youngster you know. And I suspect you'll enjoy playing with them yourself.

---

193. TOY BASKET

You will need:

> An empty bushel basket from the vegetable store
> Paint
> Decals or small pictures
> Paste
> Sandpaper

WASH THE BASKET thoroughly. When it is dry sandpaper all the rough edges so that the youngsters won't scratch themselves. Paint the basket a bright color. When it is dry paste pictures all around the outside of the basket or paste decals from the dime store all around the basket. Put it in the children's playroom or let the children use it as an outdoor toy chest.

---

194. SANDBOX
You will need:

> 4 boards measuring 4 feet by 1 foot, and about 1 inch thick
> 4 triangle shaped pieces of wood measuring 12 inches on each side

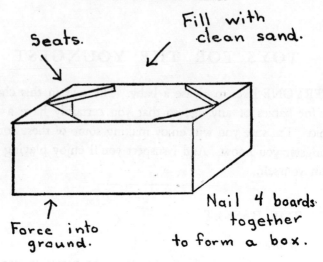

Seats.

Fill with clean sand.

Force into ground.

Nail 4 boards together to form a box.

194. SANDBOX

Paint
Hammer and nails
Sandpaper
Clean sand

MAKE A BOX of the 4 boards by nailing them together. This box won't have a bottom. Place the box in the garden where there is no grass. Force the boards into the ground a little so that the box won't move. Nail the triangle shaped pieces of wood across each corner of the box. These are seats for the children to sit on when they are playing in the sandbox. Sandpaper all rough edges. Paint the box a bright color and paint the seats a different color. Fill the box with nice clean sand that you can bring from the beach, when the box is finished. The children will love it and it will keep them out of mischief for many hours.

If you'd like to add more fun to this outdoor play yard have an outdoor pool. A big washtub filled with water and some paint brushes are all you will need. Children get a "kick" out of "painting" with plain water, on the sidewalk or cellar door. It dries up leaving no marks.

---

195. BEAN BAG

You will need:

> Heavy material or felt
> Small beans or rice or corn
> A needle and thread

CUT THE MATERIAL into 2 squares or 2 circles. Sew them together leaving a one inch opening. Through this opening fill the bag with the beans or corn or rice. Then sew over this opening. This is easy to make and nice to throw. Make a game with the bean bag by drawing several circles. Try to throw the bag into the circles.

---

196. QUICKIE APRON

You will need:

> 6 sheets of newspaper
> A needle and thread
> 4 strips of cloth or tape or ribbon
> Crayons

HOLD THE NEWSPAPERS the long way. See that all the edges are even. If they are too long, cut off a piece from the bottom. Sew 2 pieces of ribbon at the top 3 inches from the center. Sew 2 strips or pieces of ribbon at each side edge half way

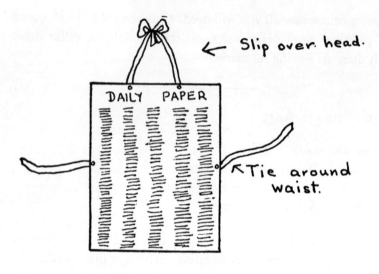

Slip over head.

DAILY PAPER

Tie around waist.

196. QUICKIE APRON

down. Decorate the front of the apron with the crayons or write the child's name for whom you are making the apron. Tie a bow at the top for a child to slip his head through, and the side ribbons can be tied around his waist. Then you won't worry if he dirties himself or the apron because you can always throw the apron away and make another one in a jiffy.

---

197. PICTURE DICTIONARY

You will need:

> A package of colored paper from the dime store
> Paste
> A pair of scissors
> Pictures from magazines
> A piece of ribbon
> A crayon

CUT PICTURES from the magazine that represent a different thing, like a picture of a boy, a girl, a house, a dog, an apple, a doll, and any other objects that you can find. Paste a different picture on each one of the sheets of colored paper. Paste a picture on the other side too so that you will have a bigger dictionary. Punch 2 holes at the top center and slip a ribbon through them and tie a bow so that the pages will be attached to each other. With the crayon print the name of each object at the bottom of each page. This will help the children identify the pictures and won't they be pleased when they can read the words themselves.

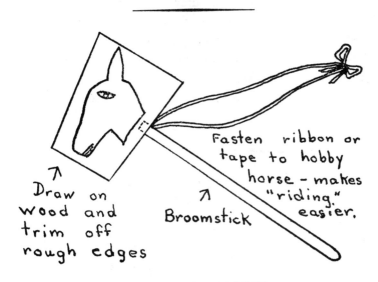

Draw on wood and trim off rough edges

Broomstick

Fasten ribbon or tape to hobby horse - makes "riding." easier.

198. HOBBY HORSE

You will need:

A broomstick
A thin piece of wood
A picture of a horse's head from a magazine
Paste

Sandpaper
Paint
A piece of ribbon or tape
Some small nails
A hammer

CUT THE BROOMSTICK down until it is about 3 feet long or less. Smooth the rough edges with sandpaper. Cut the thin piece of wood into a triangle roughly, or an oblong which has one side narrower. Nail this to one end of the broomstick. Paste a picture of a horse's head on both sides of this piece of wood. If you can't find one draw one yourself with crayons. Where the head is attached to the broomstick nail a piece of ribbon about a foot long, through the center, and tie a bow. The youngster who rides this hobby horse can hold on with this ribbon or tape. Make 2 or 3 so that when company comes all the children will have one with which to play.

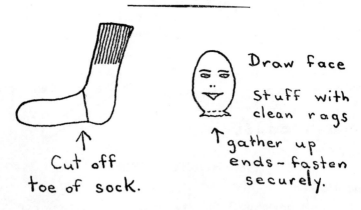

Cut off
toe of sock.

Draw face

Stuff with
clean rags

gather up
ends – fasten
securely.

199. SOFT BALL

You will need:

A clean white sock

[204]

Crayons
Clean rags or cotton
A needle and thread

CUT OFF THE TOE of the sock. Draw a face on the sock with the crayons. Stuff the sock with clean rags cut into little pieces, or with cotton. Draw up the ends of the sock and sew the edges together with the needle and thread. This is a safe, light ball for children to throw.

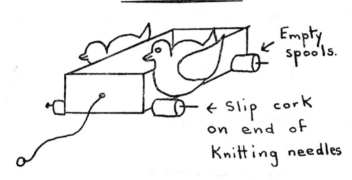

200. ANIMAL WAGON

You will need:

      Any cardboard box, as a square cereal box or candy box
      2 animal pictures or duck pictures
      Cardboard
      Paste
      2 knitting needles
      2 small corks
      A pair of scissors
      A piece of string and a bead or a button
      Crayons or paint
      4 empty spools of thread

CUT OFF THE SIDE of a cereal box or remove the cover of a candy box. Paint the box. Cut out the animals and paste them on cardboard. Then paste them at the sides of the box. Put an empty spool on each knitting needle, and pass the needle through the front bottom and back bottom of the box. When the point of the needle comes out through the other side of the box, slip another spool over the point and then stick a cork over the point of the knitting needle so that the spools won't slip off. Make a small hole in the front of the box, tie the string through the hole, and tie a button or bead at the other end of the string. Any child would be delighted to pull such a wagon.

---

201. STANDING ANIMALS

You will need:

> Pictures of animals from the magazines
> Cardboard
> Paste
> A pair of scissors
> Thumbtacks
> Empty thread spools

CUT OUT THE PICTURES and paste them on cardboard. Cut out the cardboard too. This will make the animals stronger. Cut the bottom of the animals ½ inch longer and fold up this tab. Fasten the animal to an empty spool with a thumbtack by means of the tab at the bottom of the animal. Make a set of these.

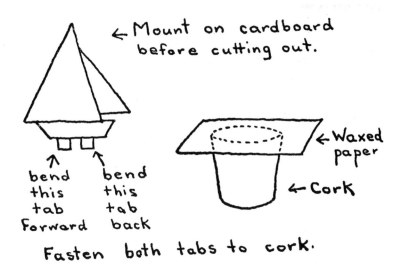

← Mount on cardboard before cutting out.

↑ bend this tab Forward
↑ bend this tab back

← Waxed paper

← Cork

Fasten both tabs to cork.

202. BATH TUB FLOATS

You will need:

      Small pictures of ducks, or birds or boats
      Cardboard
      Corks
      Waxpaper
      Thumbtacks

CUT OUT PICTURES of ducks, birds or boats from a magazine. They should be small ones. Paste them on cardboard. Cut them out but leave a piece of cardboard at the bottom of the picture, and cut out 2 tabs next to each other. Fold one tab toward you and one away from you. Cover the top of a large flat cork with waxed paper. Fasten the birds to the cork by pushing a thumbtack through each tab into the cork. They'll float in any bath tub, or in a fish tank.

[207]

203. BLOCKS

You will need:

>Lumber ends and empty spools
>Sandpaper
>Paint

ASK THE MAN in the lumber yard for scrap ends of lumber. They don't have to be square. They could be of different sizes, shapes or thicknesses. Ask Dad for scraps of lumber. When you have quite a few collected, sandpaper these blocks on all sides. Paint them different colors. Use vegetable dyed paint to protect the youngsters. You could decorate them with pictures or paint letters on some of them. Any child will be delighted to build with a set of these blocks. Put them in a small wooden box that you have sandpapered and painted. Add empty spools of various sizes. Sandpaper and paint them. Tie some spools on a string before adding them to the box.

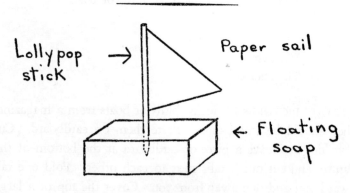

Lolly pop stick → Paper sail

← Floating soap

204. SAILBOAT

You will need:

>A bar of floating soap

A lollypop stick
A small triangle of colored paper
Paste

SHARPEN ONE END of the lollypop stick. Paste the triangle of paper around the stick to look like the sail of a boat. Stick the pointed end of the lollypop stick into the center of the bar of soap, but not all the way through. This will make taking a bath lots of fun.

---

205. A BEACH PAIL

You will need:

An empty coffee can
Paint
A piece of heavy string
A spoon

PAINT THE CAN a bright color. You could paste pictures around the can if you like. Punch a hole on each side of the can at the top edges. Tie the string through these holes for a handle. For a shovel put a large spoon in the can. You could paint the spoon to match the pail.

---

206. DOLL'S BED

You will need:

A cigar box or a shoe box
4 empty spools of thread or checkers
Glue
4 clothespins

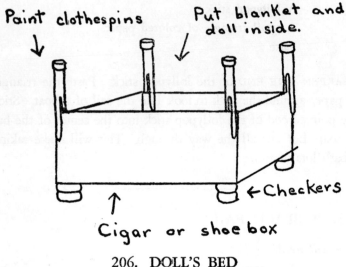

Paint clothespins ↓

Put blanket and doll inside. ↙

←Checkers

↑ Cigar or shoe box

206. DOLL'S BED

PASTE OR GLUE the spools or checkers to the bottom corners of the box. Stick a clothespin at each top corner of the box for bed posts. Paint the whole bed. Put a piece of blanket in it for a mattress and let any little girl enjoy making this bed comfortable for her doll.

---

207. WINDOW SHADE FUN

You will need:

      An old discarded window shade
      Black paint

PIN UP an old window shade. Paint it black. You can write on it with any colored chalk, and wash it off when you are finished. This is an excellent blackboard. Or paint the window shade another color. Give the children a jar of paste, a pair of blunt edged scissors, and an old magazine. Let them cut out the pictures and paste them all over the window shade. This is guaranteed to keep the walls clean as the children would rather cover the window shade than scribble up the walls.

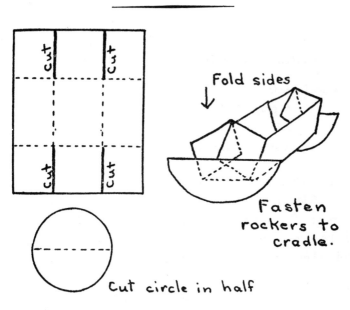

Fold sides

Fasten rockers to cradle.

Cut circle in half

208. DOLL'S CRADLE

You will need:

> A large sheet of cardboard
> Wallpaper and paste or paint
> A pair of scissors

THE LARGER THE PIECE of cardboard the larger the cradle will be. With a pencil measure the cardboard and divide it into thirds, in the width and the length. Draw lines like the picture. Make a cut with your scissors where the heavy lines are. Fold and paste up the ends of the cardboard into points, to form the head and the foot of the cradle. Cut out a large circle wider than the width of the cradle. Cut this circle in half. These are the rockers. Paste or fasten these to the front and the back of the cradle, curved or round side down. This cradle will really rock.

---

209. CARRYING DOLL BED

You will need:

>A grape basket
>Paint
>A piece of ribbon

GET A VEGETABLE BASKET with handles from the vegetable store. Clean it thoroughly. Paint it a soft shade of blue or white or pink. Tie a bow on the handles with the ribbon. Put soft cloths at the bottom for a mattress. Little sister can carry her doll wherever she likes in this basket bed.

---

210. SHAKER

You will need:

>A round stick about 2½ feet long, as from a child's broom
>Crepe paper
>A thumbtack

CUT STRIPS of crepe paper, about 1 inch wide and all different lengths. Cut about 20 strips. Hold them together, and fasten them to the top of the stick with the thumbtack, through the

Fasten strips
of crepe
paper to
top of stick

Broomstick from
a toy broom.

210. SHAKER

center of the strips of crepe paper. The children will like to carry one of these, and shake the stick and watch the strips of crepe paper fly around. Use different colors for the crepe paper. You could paint the stick to match the crepe paper.

---

211. BABY'S RATTLE

You will need:

> A baking powder can with its cover
> Paint or colored paper and paste
> Some small buttons

COVER THE CAN with the colored paper, or paint it. Put the buttons in the can and cover the can. This takes a few minutes to make and will make the baby very happy.

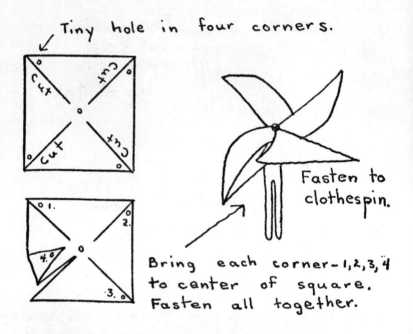

Tiny hole in four corners.

Cut

Fasten to clothespin.

Bring each corner—1,2,3,4 to center of square. Fasten all together.

212. PINWHEELS

You will need:

> A clothespin
> A pin or thumbtack
> A pair of scissors
> A piece of colored paper or any kind of paper

CUT A 5 INCH SQUARE of the paper. From each corner cut toward the center but stop when you get to an inch from the center. Make a hole at each alternate corner as it is in the picture, with the pin. Bring the ends with the holes in them to the center and fasten them through the holes and the center to the top of the clothespin, with the thumbtack. Turn the pinwheel paper over when you fasten it so that the curved edges

[214]

are underneath. Don't push the thumbtack in too far or the wheel won't turn. You might paint the clothespin. If you are in a hurry you could make these of newspaper.

---

213. ROLL UP GIFT

You will need:

> A roll of crepe paper 6 inches wide
> Small toys
> A large safety pin

LOOK THROUGH this book and find some easy to make small toys. Make about a dozen of them. Add some dime store novelties. Wind up the toys in the crepe paper into a large ball. Start with one,toy, wind the paper over it a few times, add another toy and keep this up until all the toys are wrapped up. When you have wound up all the toys and you have a large ball of crepe paper, fasten down the end with the large safety pin. Give this gift to a little boy or girl and just see how pleased they will be when they start to unwrap the gift. It will be worth the effort.

Did you have a good time making these for the youngsters? Good—I'm glad you did. Get your friends to make them too and give them to the Red Cross for distribution to other children who aren't lucky enough to have someone like you to make toys for them.

JUST PAPER

THESE THINGS made of paper are just for fun. Some of them can be made in a few minutes. All of them are very easy to make and the whole family will get a real treat in watching you.

214. DECORATED PAPER

You will need:

> A sheet of wrapping paper
> Different colored paints—water colors preferred
> Water

CRUSH THE WRAPPING PAPER in your hands. Open it up. Drop blobs of paint all over the paper. When it is dry run it quickly under the faucet. Let it dry. Fold it and press it between the covers of a large book. This is very attractive to use when wrapping gifts.

215. PAINTING ON CELLOPHANE

You will need:

> Clear or white cellophane
> Paint
> Colored paper

CUT A SQUARE of cellophane as large as you want your picture to be. Paint a picture or design on the cellophane. Bind the edges like a picture frame, with the colored paper. They'll decorate any wall.

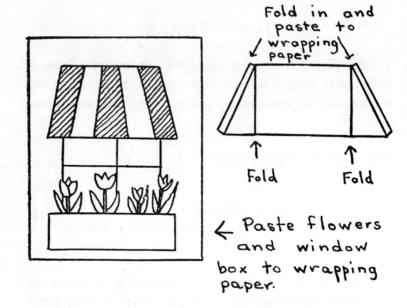

Fold in and paste to wrapping paper

Fold

Fold

← Paste flowers and window box to wrapping paper.

216. AWNINGS AND WINDOW BOXES

You will need:

A large sheet of wrapping paper
Paste
A large sheet of heavy paper or thin cardboard
Colored paper
A pair of scissors

PRACTICE this first on a small paper. Then you can make it large and pin it up on the wall and fool your friends into thinking that you have an extra window in the house.

Pin the wrapping paper up on the wall. Cut the heavy paper or thin cardboard into a square with triangle wings attached, and enough left at the outer edge of the triangle to fold a ½ inch flap down. This is the awning with its sides. Paste this

[218]

high up on the wrapping paper. Paste colored paper flowers and leaves near the bottom of the wrapping paper. Cover the bottom of the wrapping paper and also cover the stem ends of the flowers, with a sheet of colored paper to look like a window box. Draw lines on the wrapping paper between the awning and the flowers to look like window panes. This is very easily made.

217. MATS

You will need:

> Several sheets of different colored paper
> A pair of scissors
> Paste
> Cardboard

PASTE THE COLORED PAPER on the cardboard. Cut out different shapes as ovals, circles, and triangles. Make one larger than the other. Paste one on top of the other so that the largest is at the bottom and the smallest is at the top. Paste each one in the center of the other. Use your own ideas in making the shapes. Make them all ovals, one larger than the other, or all squares. Make up several combinations.

----

218. TENTS

You will need:

> A sheet of paper
> A pair of scissors
> Paste or paper fasteners

THE LARGER THE PIECE of paper you will use the larger your

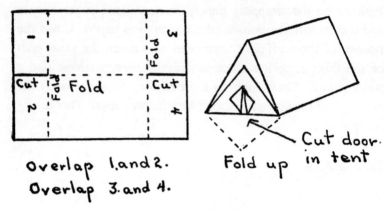

Overlap 1. and 2.
Overlap 3. and 4.
Fold up
Cut door in tent

218. TENTS

tent will be. Fold the paper in half. Open it. Fold each side down a little way. If you are using a sheet of paper 9 inches by 12 inches then fold the sides in 2½ inches. Open up the paper. Make a slit at the center crease where it is in the picture. Fold the tent until the back pieces overlap. Fold up the bottom pieces. Fasten with paste or a paper fastener. Do the same to the other side, but cut a slit for flaps for your tent. Use brown paper if you can.

---

219. SILHOUETTES

You will need:

> A sheet of colored paper, but not too dark
> Any picture
> Sunlight

GET A PICTURE that has a definite shape to it, like the picture of a person in profile, or of an animal or tree. Place it in the center of the colored paper. Place this in the sun for a few hours. When you remove the picture from the paper, the part of the paper not covered by the picture will have faded in the sun and will be a lighter color than the part of the paper covered by the picture. Experiment with different colored paper.

Paste windows and chimneys on outside of house.

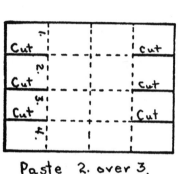

Cut

Cut

Cut

Cut

Cut

Cut

Paste 2. over 3.
Paste 4. over 2.
Paste 1. over 4.

220. A HOUSE

You will need:

>A square piece of paper
>A pair of scissors
>Paste
>Scraps of paper

FOLD THE PAPER in half, and in half again. Open it up. Turn it the other way and fold it in half and in half again. Open up the paper. You will have 16 boxes. Cut along 2 opposite sides, one box up. Fold in the pieces overlapping until you have shaped the paper into a house with a roof. Paste these flaps down. With scraps of paper make a chimney and paste it to the roof. Paste windows all around the house and don't forget the door. It would be nice to make a fence out of cardboard around your house.

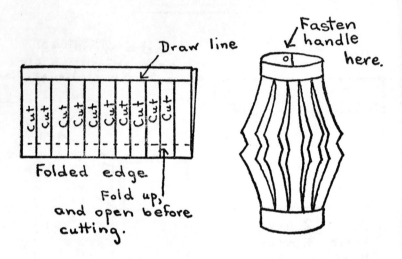

221. PAPER LANTERN

You will need:

> A sheet of paper longer than it is wide
> A pair of scissors
> Paste or a few paper fasteners

FOLD THE PAPER in half the long way. Draw a line across the top opposite the folded edge, ¾ of an inch down. Cut from the folded edge to the line you have drawn at the top, making each cut about ½ inch apart. Open up the paper, and fasten the top and the middle and the bottom of the lantern with the paper fasteners, after you have rolled the 2 side edges together. Fasten a strip to both sides for a handle. To make the lanterns a little fancier, before you start cutting the strips, fold up **the** bottom or folded edge up about an inch, open up the fold **and** then cut. This will make a ridge around the middle of **your** lantern. These are lovely when made of colored paper.

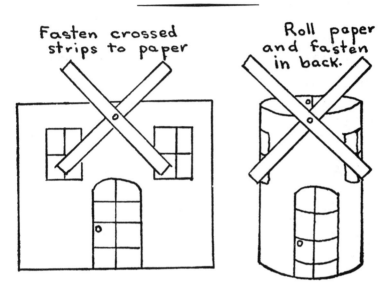

Fasten crossed
strips to paper

Roll paper
and fasten
in back.

222. WINDMILL

You will need:

> A sheet of drawing paper
> A smaller piece of paper
> Paper fasteners
> A pair of scissors
> Crayons
> Paste

WITH THE CRAYONS draw 2 windows high up on the paper, and a door at the bottom. Cut 2 strips of the smaller paper, cross them in the center and fasten them in the middle of **the** paper. Roll the drawing paper around until the side edges touch. Overlap them and fasten them with paper fasteners or with paste.

———————

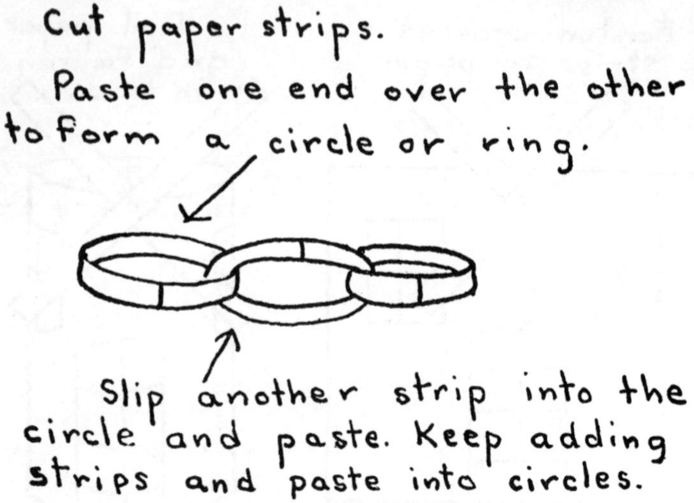

Cut paper strips.
Paste one end over the other to form a circle or ring.

Slip another strip into the circle and paste. Keep adding strips and paste into circles.

223. PAPER CHAINS

You will need:

> Colored paper
> Paste
> A pair of scissors

CUT THE COLORED PAPER into strips 4 inches long and ½ inch wide. Make one circle by pasting the ends of one strip together. Slip a strip through the circle and paste the ends of the second strip together, into a circle. Keep on doing this until you have as long a string of circles as you want.

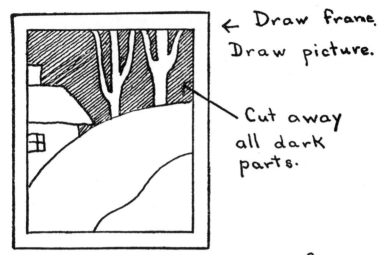

← Draw frame.

Draw picture.

Cut away all dark parts.

Paste tissue paper in back of picture — then paste on window.

224. TRANSPARENCIES

You will need:

A large sheet of colored paper

A pair of scissors

A sheet of tissue paper

Paste

DRAW A FRAME around the paper about 1½ inches wide. Inside the frame draw any picture you like, as a bird or an animal. You might like to trace a picture. Be sure that the picture is attached to the frame in several places. Cut out the background of the picture. This will leave the picture attached to the frame. Paste the tissue paper on the back of the colored paper. The tissue paper will show through the spaces you have cut out around the picture. Paste it to the window and the light will shine through the tissue paper making your picture stand out. These are nice to make on holidays.

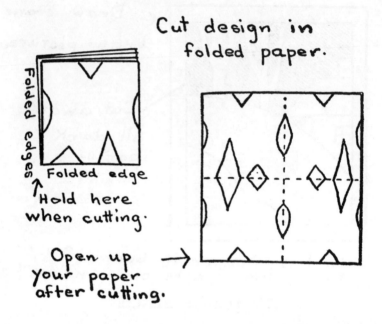

Cut design in folded paper.

Folded edges

Folded edge

↑ Hold here when cutting.

Open up your paper after cutting. →

225. PAPER CUTOUT DESIGNS

You will need:

> A piece of colored paper
> A piece of white paper
> A pair of scissors
> Paste

FOLD THE COLORED PAPER in four. Hold it with the folded corner in your left hand, and with the pair of scissors in your other hand cut any design through the four pieces of paper. Open up the paper. You will have the same design on all four sides. Paste the white sheet of paper on it. This is nice pasted on book covers or booklets, or used to make a border around a child's room.

226. PAPER STRAW FUN

You will need:

   Paper straws
   Colored paper
   A pair of scissors
   A piece of string

CUT THE STRAWS into 2 inch pieces. Cut squares of the colored paper about 2 inches. String the pieces of straw and the colored squares alternately on the string. Make other shapes with the paper instead of squares. Make circles or triangles. Use any combination you like.

———————

Save all the greeting cards and envelopes you get. You could use them for bookmarks, or as picture decorations, calendars, for scrapbooks, or to decorate stationery. Save the linings from envelopes. They can be used to decorate book covers or scrapbooks. These are just a hint and I know you can add others to this list.

MORE PAPER POINTERS

BY NOW you should have a grand collection of lots of scrap paper, such as blotters, book jackets, calendars, labels from canned foods, posters, used stamps and a host of other similar things. When you have such a collection you can make a world of interesting things. Here are some more paper pointers.

---

227. DECORATED WRITING PAPER

You will need:

> A package of writing paper
> A pair of scissors
> Paste
> Used greeting cards

SAVE THE GREETING CARDS that you get from friends and relatives at holidays and at birthdays. Cut out the pictures from the front of the greeting cards. Paste a different picture in the upper left hand corner of each sheet of writing paper. Wrap the package in fancy wrapping paper and there you have a novel and useful gift at no extra cost to you.

---

228. PLACE MATS

You will need:

> A sheet of cardboard
> Colored paper
> Shellac
> A pair of scissors

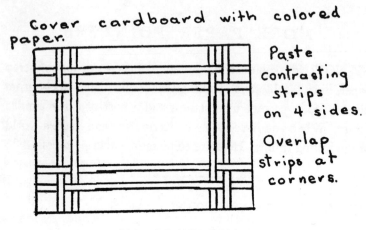

Cover cardboard with colored paper.

Paste contrasting strips on 4 sides.

Overlap strips at corners.

228. PLACE MATS

SAVE A HALF dozen cardboards from the next laundry that mother gets. Cut them into pieces 10 inches by 16 inches or larger if you like. Cover them with sheets of different colored paper. Cut strips of contrasting paper ½ inch wide. Paste 2 strips ½ inch apart and one inch from each edge. You will then have 2 colored strips on each side. Overlap them where they cross each other at the corners. Paste them down carefully so that you don't smear them at the edges. When the paste is dry shellac them well on both sides. Since these may get wet when being used, another coat or even 2 more of shellac will make the mats sturdier.

---

229. BATIK PAPER

You will need:

> 2 sheets of wrapping paper
> Crayons
> A dull knife

SPREAD ONE SHEET of wrapping paper on a table. With the dull knife shave different colored crayons all over the wrapping paper until it is fairly well covered. Mix the colors so that not one color stands out more than the other. Cover it with the other sheet of wrapping paper. If you are afraid to move the paper for fear the crayons will move around too much, then do the next step on the same table on which you started. Slip a blanket or doubled towel under the 2 sheets of wrapping paper. Slip a newspaper over this blanket or towel. Iron over the top sheet of wrapping paper with a hot iron, quickly. If you are bold enough then move the wrapping paper carefully to the ironing board which you will have covered with a sheet of newspaper. The trick is to iron over the 2 sheets of wrapping paper with the hot iron so that the crayons melt into each other and blend into lovely patterns. This is nice to use when you wrap gifts, or cover books or lamp shades.

---

230. SUN HAT

You will need:

> A large sheet of thin cardboard
> Crayons
> A pair of scissors
> Heavy string or ribbon

TRY TO GET a piece of cardboard that is already colored, as the top or bottom of a box from the dress store. Cut a circle by using a pot cover as a pattern. The larger your circle the larger your hat will be. Get the largest cover you can. Make a slit from the outer edge to the center of the circle. If your cardboard is colored you don't need to do the next step. If it is

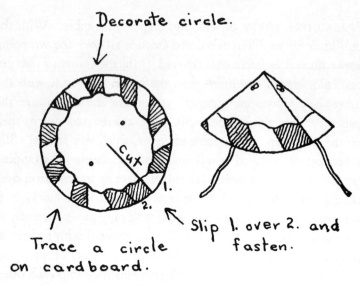

Decorate circle.

Trace a circle on cardboard.

Cut

1.
2.

Slip 1. over 2. and fasten.

230. SUN HAT

not colored then decorate the circle on the side you want to use as the outside of your hat. Slip one side of the cardboard where you made the slit, under the other edge of the slit, a little way, and paste it down. This will give shape to your hat. Make a small hole about 3 inches from the center on 2 equal sides, slip a piece of ribbon through the holes, put a knot in the ribbon at the top of the hat so that the ribbon won't slip out, and tie this "easy to make hat" under your chin the next time you go for a walk in the sun.

---

231. PLEATED PAPER FANS

You will need:

    A sheet of drawing paper for each type of fan
    Crayons
    A piece of string or ribbon
    A pair of scissors

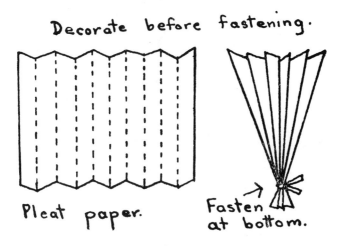

Decorate before fastening.

Pleat paper.   Fasten at bottom.

231. PLEATED PAPER FANS

PLEAT ONE SHEET of drawing paper by folding it about an inch, and then folding that back on itself for an inch, and continue folding that way, first forward, and then back until you have reached the end of the paper. You will have a stick of paper all folded together. Tie this by winding a piece of string or ribbon at one end an inch from the bottom, and tie a bow. Hold it at the tied end and the top will open into a fan. For another folded fan fold it the same way but make the folds about 1½ to 2 inches wide, and when it is folded and tied, with a pair of scissors cut triangle shaped wedges out from the top edges, or scallops to trim the fan. If you want to decorate your fan color it with crayons into a picture or design before you start folding, or fold it, open it up, decorate it between the folds, refold the fan and tie it. You can make one of these in a few minutes for yourself, the family and for your friends.

[233]

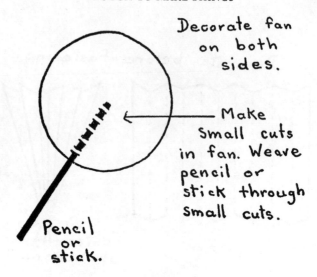

Decorate fan on both sides.

Make small cuts in fan. Weave pencil or stick through small cuts.

Pencil or stick.

232. CARDBOARD FAN

You will need:

> A piece of cardboard
> A pencil
> A pot cover
> A pair of scissors
> Crayons

TRACE A CIRCLE on the cardboard with the pot cover. Cut it out. Decorate it with the crayons, on both sides. Make small cuts about an inch apart from one edge of the circle to the center. Weave a pencil in and out of the cuts until you have reached the center. The pencil will be your handle.

---

233. CANDY PAPER CUP TRIMMING

You will need:

> Candy paper cups

Wool yarn

A needle

SAVE THE SMALL PAPER cups from the candy boxes that you get. When you have enough saved arrange them into nice color patterns and string them on colored wool yarn. Be sure to make a knot in the wool an inch or 2 between each cup or they will slide into each other. These look nice as wall trimmings or as ornaments on the Christmas tree. For the latter, make them in sets of 6 and tie them with a bow to the tree.

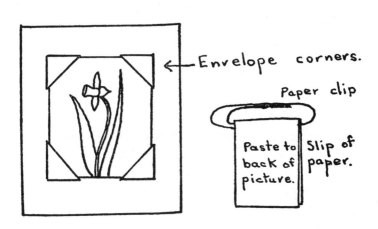

234. MOUNTED PICTURES

You will need:

> A piece of cardboard about 9 inches by 7 inches
> Colored paper
> Paste
> A pair of scissors
> An envelope

Cover the cardboard with colored paper. Cut off the four corners of the envelope and slip them over each corner of your favorite picture. Place paste on the back of each corner of the envelope and paste this in the center of the covered cardboard. These corners will hold the picture firmly to the cardboard, in such a fashion that you can easily slip the picture out of the frame whenever you like. To hang this picture up paste a slip of paper through a paper clip, fold the paper in half, and paste it to the back of the picture.

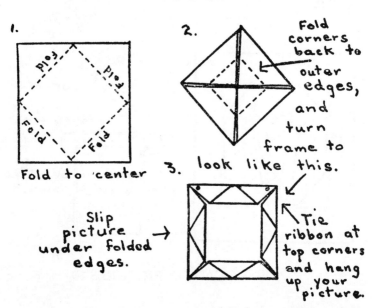

1. Fold to center

2. Fold corners back to outer edges, and turn frame to look like this.

3. Slip picture under folded edges. → Tie ribbon at top corners and hang up your picture.

235. FOLDED PICTURE FRAME

You will need:

A sheet of heavy paper about 12 inches square or larger
Paste
A pair of scissors

FOLD EACH CORNER of the paper toward the center until they meet evenly. Hold the creases down, and fold back each point towards the fold. This will make a square in the center. Slip your picture into this square and paste it down. You can decorate the four folded back corners or cut them off. Tie a string through a hole at each corner and hang up your picture.

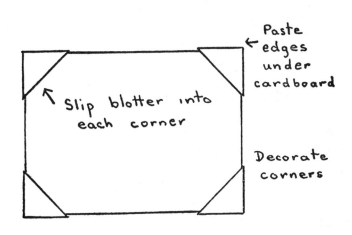

Paste edges under cardboard

Slip blotter into each corner

Decorate corners

236. CORNERED DESK BLOTTER

You will need:

    A piece of cardboard
    Some oilcloth or heavy paper
    Paste
    A pair of scissors

CUT THE CARDBOARD as large as the desk blotter. In each corner of the cardboard paste a triangle of heavy paper, or oilcloth or even heavy material. Paste the edges under the cardboard, to form a triangle shaped pocket in each corner. Dec-

orate the corners with crayons if you like. Slip **your** clean
blotter into the corners and the blotter will be held firmly. This
is a "quickie" blotter and very easy to make.

Paste one piece of cardboard over
another to form ridges

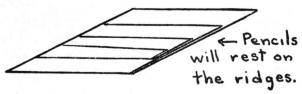

← Pencils
will rest on
the ridges.

Decorate the pieces
before you paste them.

237. PENCIL TRAY

You will need:

> Several pieces of cardboard
> Paste
> A pair of scissors
> Crayons
> Shellac

COLOR THE SHEETS of cardboard before you start cutting them.
Cut one piece 9 inches square. Cut a second piece 9 inches by 8
inches, another piece 9 inches by 7, another 9 by 6, another 9 by
5. You might make more smaller pieces if you like. Paste each
piece of cardboard on top of the other piece, keeping the largest
piece on the bottom, the next larger on top of that and so on

until all the pieces are pasted. But keep the sides which measure 9 inches, together, until you have built up the ridges. Pencils won't slip off this tray. Shellac the whole thing when the tray is dry.

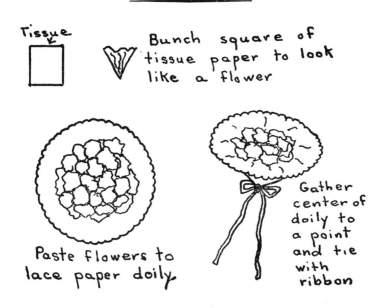

Tissue

Bunch square of tissue paper to look like a flower

Paste flowers to lace paper doily

Gather center of doily to a point and tie with ribbon

238. PAPER BOUQUET

You will need:

>A lace paper **doily**
>A piece of ribbon
>Paste
>A pair of scissors
>Tissue paper

CUT 4 INCH SQUARES of many colors of tissue paper. Bunch them into flowers and paste them all over a lace paper doily. When the doily is all covered (and don't paste any flowers further than an inch from the edge all around the doily), bunch up the center of the doily on the underside, and tie this with a piece of ribbon, letting several inches of the ribbon hang down as streamers.

---

239. TISSUE FLOWERS

You will need:

> Small thin sticks about 8 inches long, or paper straws
> A sheet of colored tissue paper
> A pair of scissors
> Paste
> A cheese box
> Paint
> Clean sand

PAINT THE CHEESE BOX. Fill it with clean sand. Cut tissue paper squares about 4 inches square. If you are using 2 colored sheets of tissue paper, place one square catticorner over the other square, bunch it in the center and paste this flower to the thin stick or paper straw. Place a half dozen of these, or more, in the sand in the cheesebox and dress up your window sill.

---

240. CIRCLE FLOWERS

You will need:

> 12 inch squares of wrapping paper
> A sheet of drawing paper
> A pair of scissors
> Crayons
> Paste

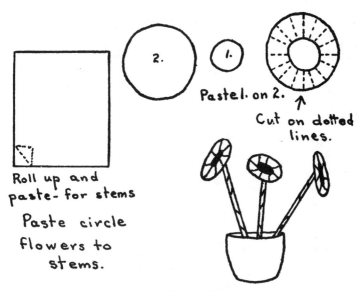

Pastel on 2.

Cut on dotted lines.

Roll up and paste- for stems

Paste circle flowers to stems.

240. CIRCLE FLOWERS

BEGINNING AT ONE corner of the wrapping paper, roll it up into a thin stick and paste down the edges. This is the stem of your flower. Trace a circle on the drawing paper with a small glass. Cut this out. Trace a smaller circle with a smaller glass. Cut this out. Color one circle one color and the other circle a contrasting color. Paste the smaller circle in the center of the larger circle. Fringe the edges of the larger circle with the scissors, and cut to the edge of the smaller circle. Paste this to the paper stick that you have made. Fill a glass vase with a dozen of these flowers. They are very colorful.

241. ART PORTFOLIO

You will need:

> 2 pieces of cardboard 8 inches by 10 inches
> Crayons

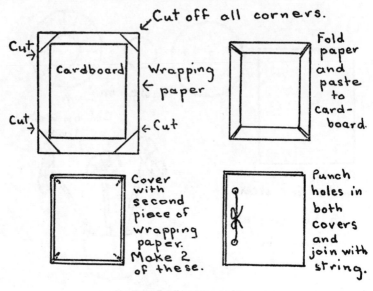

Cut off all corners.

Cut → Cardboard Wrapping ← paper ← Cut

Cut →

Fold paper and paste to cardboard.

Cover with second piece of wrapping paper. Make 2 of these.

Punch holes in both covers and join with string.

241. ART PORTFOLIO

Wrapping paper
A pair of scissors
Paste

COLOR AND DECORATE a large sheet of wrapping paper. Cut 2 pieces out of the wrapping paper an inch larger than the 2 pieces of cardboard, all around. Place the cardboard in the center of a piece of cut wrapping paper. Cut off the points of the paper near the corners of the cardboard. Paste all edges of the wrapping paper and fold them down on the cardboard. Cut another piece of wrapping paper the exact size of the cardboard. Cover it with paste and cover the cardboard over the folded edges of the wrapping paper. With a hole puncher make a hole near one side on each piece of cardboard about 2 inches apart at the center and tie the 2 pieces of cardboard (the second piece covered like the first piece) with a piece of ribbon or string. This is a nice folder to hold papers or clippings.

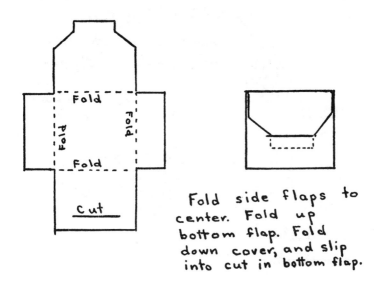

Fold side flaps to center. Fold up bottom flap. Fold down cover, and slip into cut in bottom flap.

242. PAPER PORTFOLIO

You will need:

A piece of heavy paper 12 inches by 8 inches
A pair of scissors
A ruler

DRAW A LINE 1½ inches from each edge of the 12 inch sides. Draw the pattern on the paper as it is in the picture. Cut around the edges leaving the 2 flaps on each side made by the 1½ inch line you have drawn. Fold in the flaps, and the top and bottom to make a pocket. In order to slip the top flap into the bottom flap make a slit in the center of the bottom flap as wide as the top flap. If you make this smaller it will make a nice folder to hold important papers in your inner coat pocket. Decorate it if you like.

Wind tightly.
Add 4 or 5 rolls
of party streamers

Push down
at center

Paste all ends down
carefully.

243. PARTY STREAMER TRAYS

You will need:

       Colored party streamers
       Paste
       Shellac

GET SOME ROLLS of party streamers from your next party or at the dime store. You could use all one color, or just 2 colors, or as many colors as you like. Start by folding the end of one of the party streamers back on itself about 2 times, and then very tightly wind it around and around, but not too tightly so that it will break. When you have finished with one roll of paper, paste the end of another roll at the end of the first roll, hold it a minute or 2 until it dries (but don't let the roll out of your hand, or it will start to unwind), and continue to wind the second roll. Keep on adding as many rolls as you like until you think that your tray is large enough. Four or five rolls is a good size to start with. When you have carefully finished winding the last roll, paste the end down smoothly. When the paste is dry, hold the tray in both hands and slowly and carefully shape your tray or bowl by pushing down the center. Shape the bowl as you push. The trick is not to push too far or the streamers will pop out of their moorings, and you'll have to start winding all over again. When it is shaped the way you want it to be, shellac it on both sides. Use it for an extra pin tray on your dresser. If you want to use it as an ashtray, better put a small glass dish inside this paper tray or you'll spoil its appearance.

---

244. LACE PAPER DOILY PLACE MATS

You will need:

> A package of round or square lace paper doilies
> Colored paper
> A pair of scissors
> Paste

THESE ARE NICE to use when company comes for dinner. They may be placed right on the tablecloth and under the serving plate. Get the largest doilies that you can. Place a doily on a sheet of colored paper. Paste it to the colored paper in several places around the edges. Trim the colored paper so that it is even with the doily. That's all there is to it. You could use one as a centerpiece under a vase with flowers.

If you would like to make a permanent one, use a square doily, line it with colored paper, place it between 2 pieces of glass the same size or a little larger than the doily, and bind all edges together with black pasting paper. This is very effective.

———————————

Keep a large envelope in the kitchen drawer so that the family will know that's the spot for collecting the paper scraps that you will need to make many things in this book. Then when you are in the mood to make something it will be lots of fun to go to this envelope and take out some of these scraps and go to work with the feeling that you're ready to make the nicest thing you can in the quickest way you can and at the least cost possible.

LET'S MAKE MUSIC

ONE OF THE MOST exciting things you and your friends could do would be to start a rhythm band. It is a very easy thing to do. Decide what instruments you want and make them yourselves. Here are almost a dozen and a half of splendid things to make for a rhythm band. Some only take a few minutes to put together. All of them will make some kind of a sound. A group of them together will make you the envy of the whole neighborhood. Get busy right now and organize your band immediately.

---

245. RHYTHM BLOCKS

You will need:

> 2 blocks of wood
> 2 clothespins

GO TO THE LUMBER YARD and get 2 small blocks of wood from the scrap heap. They could be any size, 6 inches by 6 inches or larger. If you want to, you could sandpaper the blocks and shellac or paint them but it isn't really necessary. Use 2 clothespins to tap out rhythms, by lightly tapping the clothespins on the blocks of wood. Easy, isn't it?

---

246. SAND BLOCKS

You will need:

> 2 square pieces of wood about 4 inches by 4 inches and
> 1 inch thick

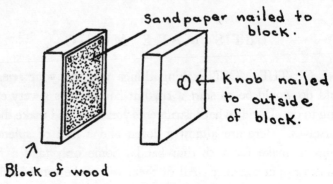

Sandpaper nailed to block.

Knob nailed to outside of block.

Block of wood

246. SAND BLOCKS

Sandpaper
Small nails
A hammer
2 dresser drawer knobs or small spools

CUT THE SANDPAPER to fit the outside of the blocks. Nail a piece of sandpaper to the outside of both blocks, or to one side only. On the other side in the center, nail the knobs or spools so that you can have something to grip when you hold the sand blocks. To make sounds rub the blocks together, slowly ot fast, hard or lightly, to get various sounds. This is another "quickie."

----

247. BOTTLE XYLOPHONE

You will need:

6 to 8 milk bottles
Water
Blue or red ink
2 small spoons

PLACE THE MILK BOTTLES in a row. Fill each bottle with water at a different level. Have the bottle with the most water first and the bottle with the least water last. To color the water drop a few drops of blue or red ink into each bottle. Test the sound of each bottle by tapping the sides lightly with a spoon. Compare it with the notes on the piano and add or take away water from each bottle until you get the sounds or notes that you like. If you think that you could handle it add more than 6 or eight bottles, thus giving you more notes to your xylophone. In case you want to save these bottles and you have to throw the water away to store the bottles, paste a small piece of paper on the outside of each bottle at the level of the water. Then all you will have to do the next time you use them is to set the bottles up, add water to the height of the paper pasters, and tap out your tunes. Always tap lightly on the bottles to get the best sounds. You could use small knives or forks instead of spoons. This is lots of fun to play.

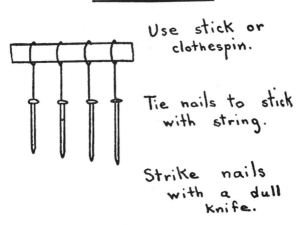

Use stick or clothespin.

Tie nails to stick with string.

Strike nails with a dull knife.

248. BELLS

You will need:

    String

    A large clothespin or a small stick

> 4 large heavy nails
> A dull knife

TIE STRING around the heads of the 4 heavy nails. Tie the other ends of the string around the stick or clothespin about 1 inch apart. Have the string no longer than 6 inches. Hold the stick in one hand, the nails dangling, and strike the nails lightly with a dull knife. They will give a bell like sound.

------

249. TRIANGLE

You will need:
> A horseshoe
> A fork or a spoon
> Heavy string

TIE A LOOP of heavy string at the curve end of the horseshoe. Hold the string in your hand, the horseshoe hanging, and lightly strike it with a fork or a spoon. It will produce a single clear sound.

------

250. COFFEE CAN DRUM

You will need:
> A coffee can with its cover
> String
> 2 pencils
> 2 spools

PUT THE COVER on the empty coffee can. Punch a hole in the center bottom of the can and in the center of the cover. Pass

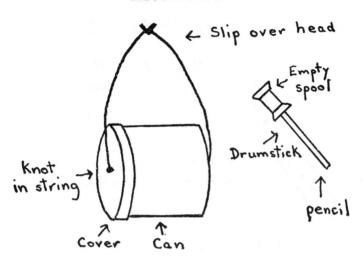

250. COFFEE CAN DRUM

a heavy string through the holes and make a knot close to the bottom of the can, and close to the cover so that the cover won't slip off. Tie a double knot to join the string so that you can slip it over or around your neck and have both hands free to play the drum. Stick a pencil through one end of an empty spool, do it to the other pencil and spool, and there you have 2 drumsticks in a jiffy.

251. BENT TRIANGLE

You will need:

>A metal rod or a curtain rod
>A small rod
>Some strength

BEND THE ROD until you have shaped a triangle. Tie a small piece of string at the top corner to hold the triangle, and hit it with a smaller rod or a fork. It works.

[251]

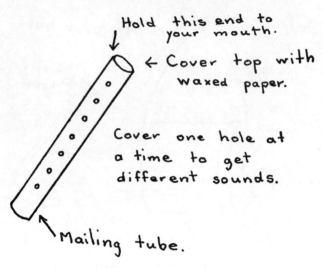

Hold this end to your mouth.

← Cover top with waxed paper.

Cover one hole at a time to get different sounds.

Mailing tube.

252. FLUTE

You will need:

A mailing tube or any roll of cardboard
Wax paper
Paste
A pair of scissors
Crayons

COVER THE TOP of the mailing tube with a piece of waxpaper glued over or pasted over the opening. Decorate the tube with crayons. With a pencil or any other pointed article punch holes down one side of the tube from the top to the bottom, making the holes less than an inch apart. Sing or hum into the tube at the waxpaper end. Experiment by covering one hole at a time or 2 or more holes to get different sounds. Try singing into the opposite end of the tube too, to see what sounds you get. Make more than one flute by using different lengths of mailing tubes. These will add dash to your orchestra.

253. COCOANUT DRUM

You will need:

>A cocoanut shell
>A piece of inner tubing
>Small nails
>A hammer
>A pair of scissors

CUT A PIECE of inner tubing a little larger than the open side of the cocoanut shell. Nail it tightly around the shell with the small nails.. To get rhythm out of it, beat on the inner tubing which you have stretched across the shell, with your knuckles. If you can't get a cocoanut shell, use a small wooden box or a tin can.

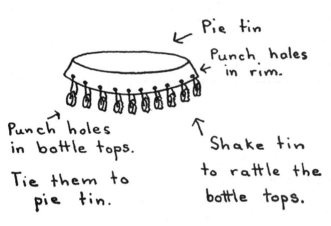

Pie tin

Punch holes in rim.

Punch holes in bottle tops.

Tie them to pie tin.

Shake tin to rattle the bottle tops.

254. TAMBOURINES

You will need:

>A pie tin or a round cereal box cover
>Bottle tops
>String

[253]

MAKE HOLES all around the edges of the cereal box cover. If you are using a pie tin, punch holes in the outer rim of the tin with a nail and a hammer. Punch holes through the center of a bunch of metal cork lined bottle tops. You could remove the cork if you like. Tie the bottle tops to the pie tin or the other cover, with small pieces of string. Don't let the tops hang too far down. Have them close to the pie tin. Shake the tin when the tops are all tied and you'll get a real treat when you hear your tambourine play.

---

255. HUMMER

You will need:

> A clean comb
> A piece of tissue paper

COVER A CLEAN COMB with a piece of tissue paper. Hold it close to your mouth and sing through it. You'll get a funny tickling sensation while you do it but you'll be pleasantly surprised at the humming sounds which result.

---

256. BANDSTAND

You will need:

> 2 orange boxes or egg boxes
> Nails
> A hammer
> Paint
> A small cheese box

THE LEADER of your orchestra should have a table or stand on

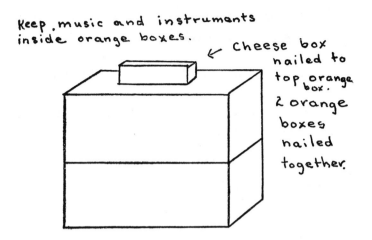

Keep music and instruments inside orange boxes.

← Cheese box nailed to top orange box.

2 orange boxes nailed together.

256. BANDSTAND

which to hold his music and extra instruments. Place one orange box over the other so that the bottoms of the boxes are in a line with each other and are facing out. Nail the boxes together. Nail a small cheese box to the top of this, in the middle. Paint all the boxes. That takes only a short time to make. You could keep your instruments in the inside of this music stand as there will be four compartments made by the two orange boxes being nailed together.

---

257. QUICKIE DRUM

You will need:

> A child's washboard
> 2 thimbles or clothespins

ALL YOU HAVE TO DO to get rhythm out of this is tap on the washboard with the clothespins, or put the thimbles on one finger of each hand and tap out any rhythm you want. If you have some more time, paint and decorate the wooden part of the washboard, and the clothespins. If you want to hang this around your neck, if it is a small washboard, thumbtack a string to each side long enough to go around your neck and shoulders. If you want to get lots of sound out of this, put three thimbles on each hand, and won't you be pleased when you start to tap on the board.

---

258. STURDY DRUM

You will need:

> A small nail keg
> A piece of unbleached muslin
> Some small nails
> A pair of scissors
> Shellac
> 2 small sticks and 2 empty spools

CUT A PIECE OF MUSLIN a little larger than the open top of a small nail keg. Draw it very tightly as you nail the muslin. Shellac the muslin. To make it stronger shellac it twice, letting it dry between each coat of shellac. Force a small stick into an empty spool, do this to two of them and there are your drumsticks. It could be painted or left alone. This makes a dandy drum.

---

259. FANCY DRUM STICKS

You will need:

> A pair of shoe trees
> Ribbon the color of your club colors
> Glue or a needle and thread

WIND RIBBON around the metal part of the shoe trees. Fasten the ends down with glue or by making a small stitch with a needle and thread. Use the tops or backs of the shoe trees to tap out sounds on your drums, or use both ends at different times. Make a set or two as spare drumsticks.

---

260. MUSICAL RATTLER

You will need:

> A baking powder can with its cover
> A few pebbles or buttons or lima beans
> Paint

FILL THE CAN with the buttons or the pebbles or lima beans. Put the cover on tightly and just shake it to make it rattle. If you haven't a can with a cover, then cover the open end of the can by covering it with a piece of cloth held over the can with a rubber band. Paint the can the color you like best. Make two or three as extras to add a little musical flavor to the band.

---

261. MUSIC BOX TO HOLD MUSIC

You will need:

> A hat box
> Brown wrapping paper
> Paste
> Paint—2 or more colors
> Old comb

FIRST WE'LL DECORATE the wrapping paper. Cover a large

sheet of wrapping paper with paste. Cover every bit of it. Drop small blobs of paint all over the wrapping paper. With an old comb, comb the paint into the paste. Make swirling designs. When you have gone over the whole sheet of wrapping paper let it dry. When it is thoroughly dry, paste it over and around the outside of the hatbox. Trim off any rough edges sticking up. Isn't that an attractive music rack? You could use this same paper for book covers too.

You could easily add your own ideas in increasing your rhythm band. Real bells could be used. Pot covers held by the handles make perfect cymbals, when you slap them together. Oil cans make good drums if you have them around. Mother's chopping bowl, turned upside down and tapped on with clothespins is a good drum substitute. Gourds make good rattles to beat rhythms. If you'll look back to the chapter on Indian Craft, you'll find instructions for making a Tom Tom drum. This drum uses wrapping paper for the top. If you oil this paper it will make a better sound. I suspect you probably will have a super rhythm band when you use these ideas.

HELPFUL HOLIDAY HINTS

HOLIDAY TIME is always a happy time. It means time for fun, visiting your friends and neighbors, sharing ideas and generally enjoying yourself. The holidays that most of us celebrate are New Year's Day, which comes January 1, Valentine's Day, February 14, Lincoln's Birthday, February 12, Washington's Birthday, February 22, Easter in March and sometimes April, St. Patrick's Day on March 17 (when we use the color green, high hats, clay pipes and the shamrock), April Fool's Day on April the first, Mother's Day in May, May Day on the first of May, and its gay Maypole, Memorial Day on May 30, Father's Day in June, Flag Day on June 14, Independence Day on July 4, Arbor Day in September, Columbus Day, October 12, Hallowe'en at the end of October, November brings Armistice Day on the 11th, and the welcome of Thanksgiving on the last Thursday in November, and best of all, Christmas on the 25th of December. All these holidays mean a good time. Here are some suggestions that will make you enjoy every holiday as it comes during the year.

---

262. WASHINGTON HATS

You will need:

> A large piece of cardboard
> Blue paint or crayon
> Paper clips, fasteners or a stapler
> Red, white, and blue ribbon

MAKE A PATTERN on newspaper first, like the pattern in the

Make 3 of these

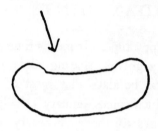

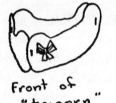

Fasten the 3 pieces together

Front of "tricorn"

262. WASHINGTON HATS

picture. It should be 10 inches long and 4 inches wide. Trace this pattern on the cardboard 3 times. Cut out the 3 pieces. Color them blue. With the stapler or fasteners or clips, fasten each piece at the corners until you have a tri-cornered hat. The top will be open but don't worry about that as your head won't show through. Make a bow of the red, white, and blue ribbon, and fasten it on one side of the hat near the point, and let that be the front point of the hat.

263. LINCOLN'S LOG CABIN

You will need:

> 2 sheets of drawing paper
> Brown crayon
> A pair of scissors
> Paste

TURN BACK TO chapter 15 and you will find directions for making a house. Follow these directions, making a house out of one sheet of drawing paper. Before you paste it together, color the paper lightly on the outside with brown crayon. Make

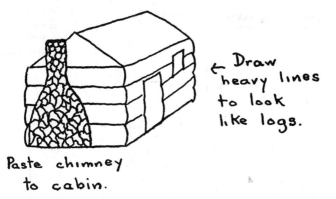

← Draw heavy lines to look like logs.

Paste chimney to cabin.

263. LINCOLN'S LOG CABIN

lines across each side of the house in heavy brown to look like logs. Draw a chimney on the second sheet of drawing paper, and make lines on the chimney to look like stone. Paste the chimney to one side of the house. Be sure to put a door and a window in the log cabin.

---

264. FLUTTERING VALENTINE

You will need:

A sheet of heavy white paper
A piece of red paper
A pair of scissors
Black crayon or red crayon

MAKE 4 CUTS in the white paper as they are shown in the picture. Make the center cuts near each other, and make all the cuts about 1½ inches long. The paper could be about 5 inches square. On the red paper draw a heart not quite 5 inches high and about 4 inches wide or less. Cut this heart down the center. Paste a tab near the center of each half of a heart at the cut edge, making the tab ½ inch wide and 3 inches long.

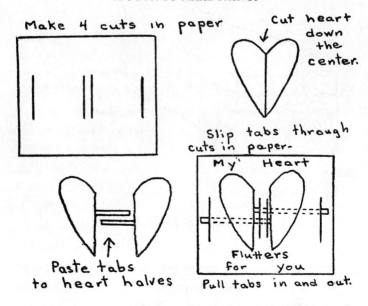

264. FLUTTERING VALENTINE

When the tabs are dry, slip them through the cuts so that a tab is extended from each side of the paper. If you pull these tabs slowly in and out the heart will flutter. At the top or bottom of the white paper or on the heart itself print, "My heart flutters for you." This is lots of fun if you mail this to your favorite Valentine on Valentine's Day.

---

265. VALENTINE

You will need:

        A sheet of drawing paper
        A sheet of red paper
        A valentine verse from a magazine or newspaper
        Paste and a pair of scissors

CUT A LARGE white heart out of the drawing paper. Cut a

red heart a little smaller than the white heart. Paste this red heart in the center of the white heart. Cut another white heart smaller than the red heart. Paste this smaller white heart in the center of the red heart. On this white heart paste the verse that you have cut from a magazine or a newspaper, or if you can, put in one that you have made up yourself. Try to fit it in so that no edges stick out. Cut a red heart still smaller than all the others. This will be a cover for your poem. Paste this over the poem but only at the top so that you can lift it up to read the poem underneath. On the top heart print "Open my heart and read my thoughts." This certainly ought to get you many valentines.

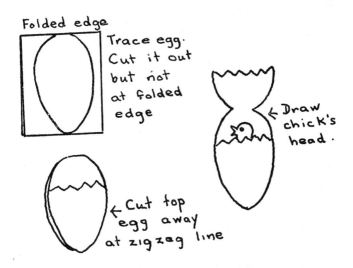

266. EASTER EGG

You will need:

    A sheet of drawing paper

    A pair of scissors

    Crayons

FOLD THE DRAWING PAPER in half. Draw a large Easter egg, the top being right on the fold. Cut out the egg but be careful to leave it attached at the fold so that when you open it you will have 2 eggs attached to each other. Cut off one egg above the center with zigzag lines to look as though the egg is cracked. Trace this cut edge on the egg underneath. Lift up the top piece and draw a chicken's head. Color the egg any color, the top half egg and the whole bottom egg, color the chicken yellow, with a tiny black eye, and fold down the top piece. When you look at this Easter egg with the top piece down it is a plain egg, but when you lift up the top, presto! There's the baby chick coming out ready to celebrate a happy Easter.

---

267. FLAG

You will need:

> 2 sheets of drawing paper
> Paste
> Red and blue crayons
> White chalk

BEGINNING AT ONE corner of one sheet of drawing paper, roll a very tight roll for the stick of your flag. Paste down the last corner. On the other sheet of drawing paper, make a flag of thirteen stripes, seven red, six white, alternating, and a field of blue in the upper left hand corner. Make forty-eight stars with the white chalk on the blue field. Paste the left edge of the flag to the stick that you have made. Make enough for all your friends.

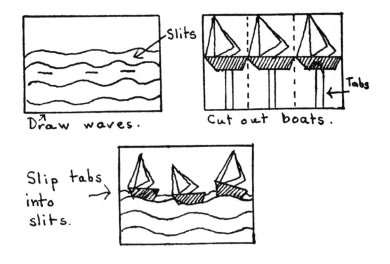

Draw waves.

Cut out boats.

Slip tabs into slits.

268. COLUMBUS' SHIPS

You will need:

A sheet of drawing paper

A pair of scissors

Crayons

CUT THE PAPER IN HALF. Fold one of the pieces of paper into thirds. Draw a boat on each third, and draw a long tab at the bottom of each boat. Cut these out. Draw waves on the other half of the paper. Color the sky blue. Color the boats. Make 3 slits across the waves. Slip the tabs attached to the boats, into these slits. It will look as though the ships are sailing across the ocean. Print the names of the ships across them, the Nina, the Pinta, and the Santa Maria. If you want to have more fun try making this on large sheets of paper.

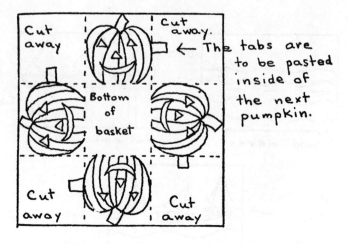

Cut away

Cut away.

← The tabs are to be pasted inside of the next pumpkin.

Bottom of basket

Cut away

Cut away

269. HALOWE'EN PUMPKIN BASKET

You will need:

> A sheet of drawing paper 9 inches square
> A pair of scissors
> Paste
> Crayons

FOLD THE DRAWING PAPER into thirds. Open it up. Turn it to the second or opposite side and fold it again in thirds. Open it up. You will now have nine boxes. The center box is the bottom of the basket. The middle boxes are the ones on which you will draw a pumpkin. Draw a nice smiling pumpkin in these boxes. Color the eyes and nose and mouth red. Color the stem green. Make black ridges down the pumpkin and around the outside and the stem of the pumpkin. Draw a tab about an inch long in the center of the right side of each pumpkin, and ½ inch wide. Cut out the pumpkins carefully, without cutting them away from the center box, and without cutting off the tabs. Fold up the pumpkins, and paste the tabs on the inside to hold the box together. This is very attractive to use at a Hallowe'en party. You could make them larger or smaller if you like.

---

270. HALLOWE'EN LANTERNS

You will need:

> A piece of cardboard 9 inches square, for each lantern
> A large sheet of tissue paper, red or yellow
> Orange, black and green crayons
> A pair of scissors
> A long string
> Paste

IF YOU THINK you won't be able to make a large round pumpkin on each piece of cardboard, then trace a circle on the cardboard with a large plate or pot cover. Put a stem at the top of your pumpkin. Make 2 triangle eyes, a triangle nose, and a large grinning mouth. Cut these out carefully. Color the pumpkin orange. Paste yellow or red tissue paper in the back of each pumpkin. It will show through on the other side. Make another pumpkin just like the first one and paste this on top of the first pumpkin, over the tissue paper, back to back so that you will see a pumpkin face on both sides, and the eyes, nose and mouth will show on both sides. Make a hole in the stem end with a pencil, and string the lanterns up on a long string. Make a knot between the pumpkins at regular intervals so that they won't slide into each other. String them across the room at your next Hallowe'en Party.

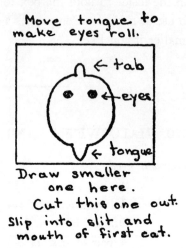

271. HALLOWE'EN CAT

You will need:

> 2 sheets of drawing paper
> Black and yellow crayon
> A pair of scissors

DRAW A FACE of a cat on one sheet of drawing paper. Cut out the eyes and mouth. Draw a shape of the cat, but smaller, containing the eyes, and having a long tongue. See if yours looks like the picture. Make a slit at the top of the cat. Slip the tongue through the cat's mouth and the top part through the slit in the cat's head. When you are sure it will fit, remove it. Color the cat black. Color the second part so that the eyes are yellow, outlined in black, and the tongue yellow, or red if you like. Slip it back again. To make the cat's eyes roll, move his tongue or the little tab at the top.

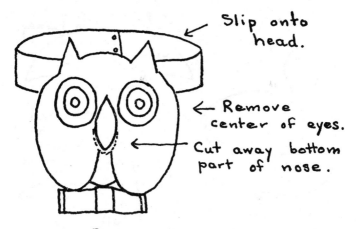

Slip onto head.

Remove center of eyes.

Cut away bottom part of nose.

Paste owl to headband.

272. HALLOWE'EN MASK

You will need:

Crayons
A pair of scissors
2 sheets of drawing paper

DRAW AN owl's face on one sheet of drawing paper. Cut out the eyes. Cut the nose in such a way that it is still attached to the mask at the top of the nose. Color the mask black and orange. Cut the other sheet of paper down the center. Join the two pieces to form a headband to fit around your head. Fasten the owl's face to the headband. Slip it on your head and have some fun with it on Hallowe'en.

273. PAPER TURKEY

You will need:

A sheet of drawing paper

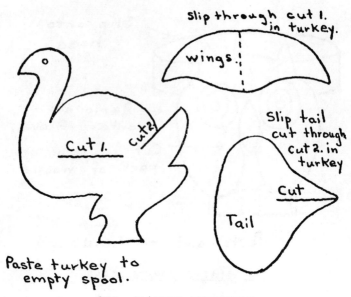

Slip through cut 1.
in turkey.

wings!

Cut 1.

cut2!

Slip tail
cut through
cut 2. in
turkey

Cut

Tail

Paste turkey to
empty spool.

273. PAPER TURKEY

Crayons

A pair of scissors

Empty spools

IF THIS TURKEY comes out good, then make a larger one out
of cardboard. Draw a turkey on the drawing paper as large as
you can. Make a cut in the center of the turkey as it is in the
picture. Draw and cut out the wings, and fold them in half.
It would be easier to fold a piece of the drawing paper in half,
cut it out, but not on the fold, and open it up. Make the tail
as it is in the picture and cut it from the point to the center.
Slip the wings into the cut in the turkey. Make a cut at the
edge of the turkey. Slip the tail onto the turkey, cut end over
the cut in the turkey. When you are sure the pieces fit, take
them apart, and color them with crayons, then put them together again. Paste the turkey to an empty spool. Make a
few of these to march across the table at Thanksgiving.

Roll together and fasten.

Slip cardboard ring over top of hat.

274. PILGRIM HAT

You will need:

A piece of cardboard from a suit or dress box
Paste or fasteners
A pair of scissors
Silver paper

MAKE A PATTERN out of newspaper like the one in the picture. Make it large enough to go around your head. Trace this on the cardboard, and cut it out. Roll it together and paste or fasten the edges with fasteners. Cut a large circle of cardboard, cut a hole in the center as large as your head. Slip this circle over the top of the roll or top of the hat until it goes to the bottom. It won't slip off. Trim off the under edge if it is too long. If you have gray cardboard or black cardboard your hat will look real. Make a cardboard buckle, cover it with silver paper and fasten it to the front of your hat.

275. CHRISTMAS TREE POSTER

You will need:

 A large red blotter
 A large green blotter
 A pair of scissors
 Paste
 Colored paper
 Cellophane tape

CUT OUT A GREEN TREE from the green blotter. Paste this on the red blotter. If you haven't any blotters, get large red and green mounting paper. Cut out ornaments from the colored paper. Paste this all over the tree. Paste colored streamers across it too, and paper candles. Put a large bright star at the top. Fasten it to the wall with cellophane tape so that you won't injure the wall when you take it down after Christmas.

---

276. CHRISTMAS DECORATIONS

You will need:

 Popcorn
 Cranberries
 Peanuts
 Thick cotton string
 A needle

STRING THE POPCORN and the cranberries and the peanuts on long string to hang on the Christmas tree or around the room. String them separately or together making different combinations. Paint the tips of the peanuts with nail polish if you like. Try to get colored popcorn as it is so attractive. This is a novel decoration.

277. TREE ORNAMENTS

You will need:

>A cardboard roll or mailing tube
>Christmas wrapping paper
>Paste
>A knife

PASTE THE DECORATED PAPER around the mailing tube. When it is dry let Dad or older brother do the next step, as you may cut yourself. Have them cut pieces off the tube about an inch apart. These rings when tied with a bright ribbon can be tied all around the tree or can even be used as souvenir napkin rings at the dinner table.

278. CHRISTMAS BELLS

You will need:

>Cardboard
>A pair of scissors
>Paste
>Christmas wrapping paper or silver, red, and green paper

CUT OUT bells from the cardboard 5 inches high and 4 inches wide. Paste the colored paper or wrapping paper on both sides, and trim off the edges. Put a small hole at the top of each bell. String them on ribbon, making a knot after each bell so that they won't slide into each other. At the top tie a large red or silver or blue ribbon bow. Hang them in the doorway.

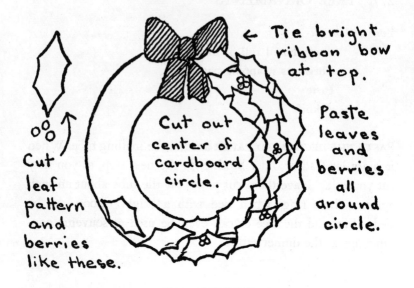

← Tie bright ribbon bow at top.

Cut out center of cardboard circle.

Paste leaves and berries all around circle.

Cut leaf pattern and berries like these.

279. CHRISTMAS WREATH

You will need:

> A large piece of cardboard
> A pair of scissors
> A sheet each of red, dark green, and light green paper
> Paste
> A piece of silver or red ribbon

CUT A LARGE circle of the cardboard. Cut out the center so that the frame of your wreath is 2½ to 3 inches wide. Cut out leaves from both sheets of green paper. Make them large. Cut out small red circles. Paste these leaves and the red berries all over the cardboard so that no cardboard shows. Tie a large ribbon bow around one side, and hang it up in the window at Christmas time.

Fasten 4 trees to outside of box. Join tops of trees with ribbon. Decorate trees.

280. A STANDING CHRISTMAS TREE

You will need:

A large square piece of cardboard
A pair of scissors
Colored paper
A cheese box or a wooden chalk box
Small nails
A hammer
Crayons or paint

CUT OUT four triangles all the same size, out of the cardboard. Cut out different shaped ornaments to paste on the tree. Color the four pieces of cardboard on both sides in bright green. Paste on the ornaments. Paint the small wooden box (a cigar box will do), a bright red. Put a weight in the box. Nail the four trees to each side of the box. Put a small hole at the top point of the trees, and join them by tying a bright gold or silver ribbon through the holes and making a bow. The trees will bend toward each other at the top and make it look more realistic. Put it on the Christmas dinner table.

Paste 2 colored circles together.

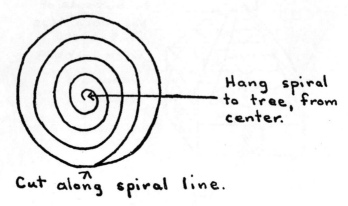

Hang spiral to tree, from center.

Cut along spiral line.

281. SPIRALS

You will need:

> 2 pieces of paper, red and green
> String
> A pair of scissors
> A cup

PASTE THE RED PAPER to the green, and you will have one piece, red on one side and green on the other. Trace a circle with the cup and cut this circle out. Cut a spiral toward the center and stop when you reach the center. Tie a piece of string through the center, making a knot on the under side and tie these spirals to the tree. The two colors can be changed to others if you are going to make several of these.

---

282. CORNUCOPIAS

You will need:

> A heavy piece of paper
> A pair of scissors

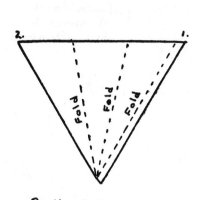

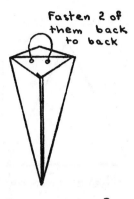

Fasten 2 of them back to back

Paste 1. to 2. to form cornucopia.

Decorate before pasting.

282. CORNUCOPIAS

Paste
Colored ribbon

CUT THE PAPER as it is in the picture. Paste it together to form a cone. Make two of these. Paste or clip them back to back and trim off the top edges if they are not straight. Make two small holes near each other at the top edge where the two cornucopias are pasted to each other. Slip a piece of ribbon through the holes and hang them up. The larger the paper the larger your cone.

---

283. ANGELS

You will need:

A sheet of drawing paper
A pair of scissors
Paste

CUT OUT a triangle on the drawing paper. Paste it together to

[277]

Paste face of angel to top of triangle.

Paste paper wings to back of triangle.

Paste circles for hands; and music between them.

Paste triangle into a cone.

283. ANGELS

form a roll that will stand up. Draw an angel's head from the scrap pieces of the drawing paper, and paste this at the top of the cone. Cut out two wings and paste these at the back of the cone so that they will stick out at the sides. Paste two circles at the front center for hands, and carefully paste a piece of paper between them with notes written across it for music. When you make the angel's face make the eyes downcast. This is nice as a window decoration or as a shelf decoration.

---

284. BELL CHAIN

You will need:

> Colored paper
> A pair of scissors
> Paper drinking straws
> String
> Paste

WITH A SMALL GLASS trace circles on the colored paper. Cut

them out. Cut out a small wedge from each circle toward the center. Paste the circle together at the edge where you have removed the wedge. It will look like a small bell. Cut 2 inch lengths of straw or longer, and string the bells and the straw alternately on the string (going through the center of the bells) until your chain is as long as you want it to be.

Most of this chapter seems to be devoted to Christmas. But that shouldn't stop you from planning many more things for all the other holidays. Have a good time making all these things no matter what holiday you are helping to make a gay one.

BACK TO NATURE

HERE ARE some ideas borrowed from nature. Some will need seeds to make them a success, but most of them need only a few spare minutes to make and enjoy.

---

285. EGGSHELL FLOWER POTS

You will need:

      Empty egg shells
      Some earth
      A flower seed or a bean

THE NEXT TIME mother is making a cake ask her for the empty egg shells. Rinse them out and fill them with earth. Put a flower seed or a bean in each egg shell. Water them in a dish and set them on the window sill. Watch your garden grow.

---

286. GUM DROP TREE

You will need:

      A short branch from a tree
      A package of gumdrops
      A pair of scissors
      A flat deep jar filled with clean sand, or a flowerpot

TAKE A BRANCH from a dead limb of a tree so as not to injure the tree. Make a cut in several gumdrops of different colors and stick them on the branches so that it looks as though

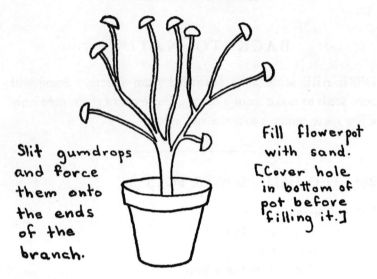

Slit gumdrops and force them onto the ends of the branch.

Fill flowerpot with sand. [Cover hole in bottom of pot before filling it.]

286. GUM DROP TREE

flowers are growing on the tree. Stick the covered branch into the sandfilled jar. If you are using a flowerpot, cover the hole in the bottom of the pot with a piece of cardboard so that the earth or sand won't run out. This is a very fine table decoration.

---

287. WINDOW GARDEN

You will need:

> A muffin tin
> Paint
> Earth
> Tiny flower pots

PAINT THE muffin tin. Paint the tiny flower pots. Fill them with earth and plant a seed in each pot. Put the tiny pots in the muffin cups, one pot in a cup. If you like you could fill the muffin tin directly with earth instead of using the tiny flower pots. Plant a seed in each one. Put it on the window sill, water it a little each day, and soon you'll have a lovely window garden.

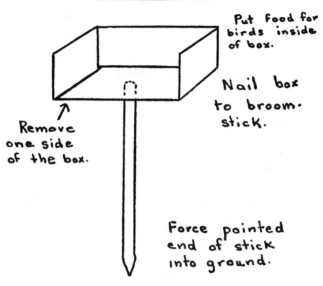

Put food for birds inside of box.

Nail box to broom-stick.

Remove one side of the box.

Force pointed end of stick into ground.

288. BIRD FEEDING TRAY

You will need:

    An old broomstick
    A cigar box
    A few nails
    A hammer

MAKE A POINT at one end of the broomstick. Remove the cover and one side of a cigar box which you have cleaned carefully so that there is no cigar odor to frighten the birds away. Nail the box at the center to the top of the broomstick, but not to the pointed end. Stick the pointed end in the ground, in the garden. Put bread crumbs and suet in it every day. You'll enjoy watching the birds dine in your garden daily.

289. WINDOW BOX DRAINAGE

You will need:

      6 small flowerpots with plants in them
      Yellow paint
      A baking tin
      Adhesive tape
      A package of colored pebbles
      Clean sand

PAINT THE FLOWERPOTS on the outside with the yellow paint. Cover the inside bottom edges of the baking tin with strips of adhesive tape to prevent leakage. Fill the bottom of the tin with a layer of clean sand. Cover the sand with a layer of colored pebbles. Set the six flowerpots in the pan three in a row, in two rows. Set the pan on the window sill. The water will drain into the sand, and the whole arrangement will look pleasing on the window sill.

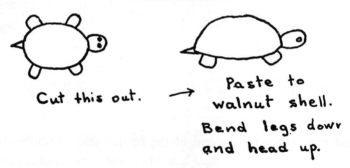

Cut this out.   →   Paste to walnut shell.
Bend legs down and head up.

290. TURTLE

You will need:

      A walnut shell
      A small card
      Paste and a pair of scissors

PLACE A WALNUT shell half on a card. Trace around the shell. Draw four legs and a head and a tail on this tracing on the card. Cut this out. Paste it to the open side of the shell. Bend the legs down, and the head and tail up. It will look like a real turtle. Fool your friends. Paint the shell halves different colors for fun.

---

291. BERRY BASKET GARDEN MARKERS

You will need:

> An empty berry basket
> Seed envelopes
> Sticks
> Paste
> Shellac
> Small nails
> A hammer

BREAK OUT the sides of the berry baskets. Paste the envelopes containing the seeds (after you have used the seeds) to each side of one of the sides of the basket. Shellac both sides. When the shellac is dry, nail them to a stick, and put them in the garden. You could shellac them after they are nailed to the sticks.

---

292. SEED PICTURES

You will need:

> Small cards
> Paste
> Seeds of different flowers or trees
> A crayon

GET SEEDS, like the "pollynoses" from maple trees. Paste them in any design on the card. Fill in faces or shapes or outlines or designs around the seeds with the crayons. You can make up many of these with different seeds.

---

293. HANGING BASKET

You will need:

>   A coffee can
>   Paint
>   3 pieces of wire 9 inches long
>   A ring

PAINT THE CAN a bright color. With a nail punch out three holes evenly spaced around the top rim of the can. Tie a piece of wire in each hole. Bring the three ends together at the top and wind them over two or three times around a small metal ring. Punch a small hole in the bottom center for drainage. Put a flower pot in it that has a plant with hanging leaves, as an ivy plant, and hang it up.

---

294. CEREAL BOX HANGING BASKET

You will need:

>   A round cereal box
>   A pair of scissors
>   Paint
>   Heavy string

CUT OUT A PIECE of the side of a cereal box, leaving the cover

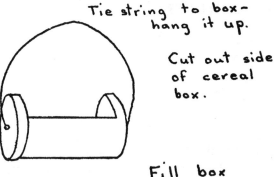

Tie string to box—
hang it up.

Cut out side
of cereal
box.

Fill box
with wild
berries.

294. CEREAL BOX HANGING BASKET

on, and leaving a one-inch margin at the top and bottom. Cut a piece out about 4 inches wide. Paint the box on the outside. Make a hole in the cover and the bottom of the box at the center. Tie a piece of heavy string through these holes, about 12 inches long, making a knot on the ends so that it won't slip out. Hang this up and fill it with winter berries or straw flowers.

---

295. GOURD FLOWER POTS

You will need:

      A large gourd
      A spoon
      Paint

ASK DAD TO CUT the top off the gourd. Scoop out the inside of the gourd with the spoon. When it is thoroughly scraped make a small hole in the bottom of the gourd. This will be for drainage when you have filled it with earth and a plant. Paint the gourd on the outside. Fill it with earth and a plant. Set it on a plate on the window sill.

296. LEAF PICTURES

You will need:

> Cards
> Paste
> Leaves
> A black crayon or other colors

PASTE A LEAF in the center of the card. Use this as the body. Draw people by drawing heads, feet, arms and trousers or skirts around the leaf. Color them if you like. Make a few of these for your friends.

---

297. PINE CONE BIRD

You will need:

> A pine cone
> A small block of wood
> Thumbtacks
> Pipe cleaners

MAKE A FACE and legs from the pipe cleaners. Fasten them to the pine cone with thumbtacks the same color as the pine cone. Fasten the bird to the small block of wood. Make several birds, each having a different head.

---

298. MOUNTING YOUR ROCK COLLECTION

You will need:

> Plaster of Paris
> A discarded ashtray

The rock or any other specimen you want to mount

MIX SOME PLASTER of Paris with some water until it is as thick as cream. Turn an old ashtray over on its back. Make a lump of the plaster of Paris, after it has set for a few minutes, and put this lump on the back of the ashtray. Set your specimen into this lump of plaster and let it harden. Then you can keep your collection on display. Be sure to rinse the pan in which you mixed the plaster of Paris or you'll have to discard it. You can paint the ashtray and the plaster lump a light color when it is set.

---

299. MOUNTING LEAVES

You will need:

> Small squares of cardboard
> Cellophane tape
> Cellophane paper
> White paper
> Colored paper
> Paste

COVER THE CARDBOARD with the white paper. Place a leaf in the center and fasten it down with cellophane tape. Label the leaf. Cover the leaf with a piece of cellophane the same size as the cardboard. Fasten all the edges together by pasting narrow colored strips of paper all around the edges.

---

300. LEAF CHAINS

You will need:

> Leaves with fairly long stems
> Patience

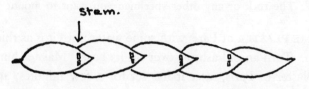

Break off stems. Use them as pins.

300. LEAF CHAINS

ELM LEAVES are nice to use for this but you can use other leaves too. Break off the stems carefully. These are your pins. Place the leaves one on the other, and pin them with the stem ends that you have broken off. Make your chain as long as you like.

---

301. NATURE SCRAP BOOK

You will need:

>   Seed catalogues
>   A pair of scissors
>   Paste
>   An old notebook

REMOVE THE USED PAGES in an old notebook. Cover the outside of the notebook with an attractive cover from a seed catalogue. Cut out flower, fruit and vegetable pictures from the catalogues. Paste them in the notebook and write a little story under each picture. This is nice to make on a rainy day.

That's a good start. Now add some more of your own thoughts to make this a really delightful nature chapter.

USE PAPER PLATES

MANY TIMES when you go to a picnic or a party there are some paper plates left over. Here are some ideas as to what to do with those left over plates.

---

302. FRUIT PLATES

You will need:

> A paper plate
> Paste
> A small picture
> Shellac

PASTE A SMALL PICTURE in the center of a paper plate. If you are very careful you could paste small pictures all around the inside and the outside rim of the plate. When the paste is dry shellac the plate on both sides. Give it two coats letting each coat dry before you apply the other coat. That's all there is to it. If you feel very ambitious paint the plates before you paste the pictures on the plate.

---

303. PAPER PLATE COASTERS

You will need:

> A small paper plate
> A decal or small picture
> Shellac and varnish

PASTE A SMALL PICTURE in the center of the plate. When it

is dry, give the plate two coats of shellac, letting each coat dry before applying the next one. When both coats of shellac are dry apply a coat of clear varnish. This will make it washable and it could also be used as an ashtray.

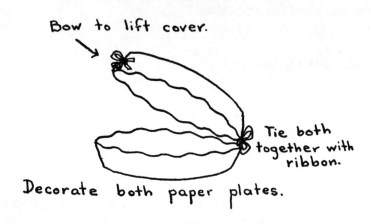

Bow to lift cover.

Tie both together with ribbon.

Decorate both paper plates.

304. JEWELRY BOX

You will need:

    2 paper plates of the same size
    Paint
    A picture
    Paste
    A piece of ribbon

PASTE A PICTURE on the outside center of one paper plate. This will be the cover of your box. Paint both plates on both sides before pasting the picture on the cover. When they are dry, place one plate inverted (the cover), over the other plate. To keep the cover attached to the bottom plate, make a small hole in the rim of the bottom plate and a small hole in the rim of the cover. Slip a piece of ribbon through the two holes and tie a small bow. This will hinge the two plates together. In the front of the cover make a small hole in the rim. Slip a piece of ribbon through, make a small bow, and you will then have a tab with which to lift the cover when you want to put in or take out your trinkets.

---

305. PAPER PLATE MASK

You will need:

> A paper plate
> Crayons or paint
> A pair of scissors
> 2 pieces of string or ribbon

DRAW EYES and a nose and a mouth on the inside of a paper plate. Cut these out. Try to make the eyes come where your own eyes come. Turn the plate to the outside, and decorate the face, filling in eyebrows, and even hair around the upper edges of the plate. Make two small holes on each side of the rim, tie a piece of string or ribbon through these holes, and tie the mask around your head.

---

306. POT HOLDER CONTAINER OR NOTE HOLDER

You will need:

> 2 paper plates
> Wool yarn
> A needle
> A hole puncher

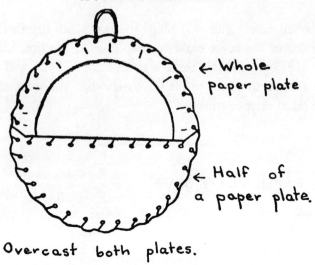

← Whole
paper plate

← Half of
a paper plate.

Overcast both plates.

306. POT HOLDER CONTAINER OR NOTE HOLDER

CUT ONE of the paper plates in half. Punch holes all around the rim of the whole paper plate and the half paper plate, making the holes ½ inch apart. Place the half plate inverted over the whole plate, keeping the edges or rims together, forming a pocket. Join the two plates together by sewing an overcasting stitch all around the half plate and the rest of the whole plate, with the wool. Make a loop to hang up the container, by braiding a piece of the yarn, tying it at the top of the plate and hanging it up. You could paint the plates before you start to sew them together or decorate them in any fashion you like. This is a fine simple container for pot holders, or for kitchen notes.

307. PICNIC PAPER PLATES
You will need:

> As many plates as there are people
> Nail polish

THE NEXT TIME you have a party, or go to a picnic, take a bottle of colored nail polish with you. When you open the lunch, write the name of each person on the outside rim of a paper plate. This will save plates, as a person won't need a second one if he puts his plate down. His name will tell the others whose plate it is, and spare the other plates. You could do this to paper cups too. Another good idea is to put the initials on regular glasses on the outside, with the nail polish, so that you won't get the glasses mixed when serving drinks. A little nail polish remover will take off the polish from the glasses when the party is over. The paper plates and cups, of course, can be discarded.

Cover handle with wool yarn.

Attach handle to plate.

Cover rim of plate with wool, yarn.

308. COOKIE TRAY

You will need:

    A paper plate
    A piece of cardboard
    Shellac
    Paint
    A needle
    Wool yarn

PAINT A LARGE paper plate a nice color. When it is dry give it two coats of shellac. With the wool and the needle, sew around and around the rim, covering the whole rim from the bottom of the plate to the top of the rim, keeping the stitches as close together as possible, until the rim is all covered with the wool. Cut the cardboard into an inch strip about 12 inches long. Wind wool around this cardboard until it is all covered. Fasten this to the rim of the plate with a few stitches, to form a handle. Line the plate with a lace paper doily when you fill it with cookies.

---

309. SCRAPER SET

You will need:

> A large paper plate
> A pair of scissors
> A piece of ribbon
> A hole puncher

TRY TO GET a paper plate that is already decorated, otherwise decorate it yourself. Cut the plate into two pieces, not through the center but about one third up the plate. Use the smaller piece for the scraper and the larger piece for the crumb catcher. Make a hole in the rim in the center, slip a piece of ribbon through it and tie it into a loop so that you can hang it up. Do this to both pieces. This will make scraping crumbs from the tablecloth a very simple matter.

---

310. PAPER PLATE LANTERNS

You will need:

> 2 paper plates

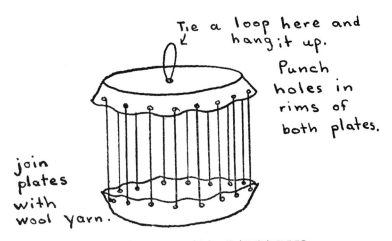

Tie a loop here and hang it up.

Punch holes in rims of both plates.

join plates with wool yarn.

310. PAPER PLATE LANTERNS

A hole puncher
Wool yarn

PUNCH HOLES around the rims of small paper plates about ½ to 1 inch apart. Cut pieces of yarn 10 inches long. Tie these pieces of yarn around one paper plate, all around the rim. Then attach the other ends of the yarn to the holes in the rim of the other paper plate, which you will invert. Make a hole in the center of one paper plate. Tie a piece of yarn into a loop through this hole so that you can hang up the lantern. The two plates will be connected all around by the 10 inch pieces of yarn between them.

311. CLOCK

You will need:

A large paper plate
A black crayon or paint
A piece of cardboard
A paper fastener

[297]

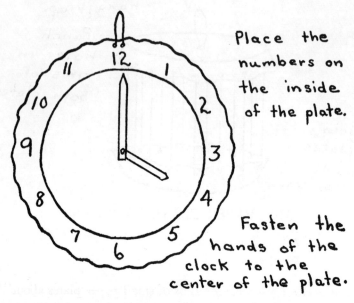

Place the numbers on the inside of the plate.

Fasten the hands of the clock to the center of the plate.

311. CLOCK

AROUND THE RIM of the plate on the inside of the plate write or paint the numbers, as on a clock face. If you like, put the numbers on the plate close to the rim. Be sure the twelve is on the top and the six is directly opposite it. Cut out two clock hands from the piece of cardboard, one smaller than the other. The larger hand should be as long as from the center of the plate to the rim of the plate. Color the hands. Fasten them to the center of the plate with the paper fastener. If you want to make your clock fancy, paste a small picture under each number. Tie a piece of string or ribbon to the top of the plate and hang it up. Although this clock won't keep time, it is good as a reminder by setting the hands at the time you want to remind you to do something.

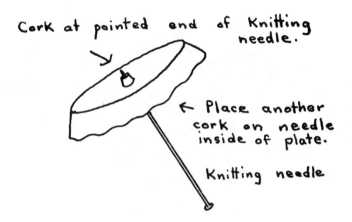

Cork at pointed end of Knitting needle.

← Place another cork on needle inside of plate.

Knitting needle

312. TOY UMBRELLA

You will need:

> A large paper plate
> A knitting needle
> 2 corks
> Crayons

DECORATE THE PAPER plate with the crayons, on both sides. Invert the plate. Stick a knitting needle point up through the plate in the center. Place a cork about an inch and a half past the point of the needle before you put it through the plate. When the plate is on the needle, and resting on this cork, slip another cork on the pointed end of the needle. Any little girl will be proud to have one of these.

---

313. PAPER PLATE HAT

You will need:

> A paper plate
> Glue

Paste paper cup to paper plate.

Cover cup and plate with crepe paper.

Ribbon.

313. PAPER PLATE HAT

A paper cup
Crepe paper
A pair of scissors
2 pieces of ribbon

COVER THE PAPER cup with a piece of crepe paper, any color. Cover the paper plate on one side with crepe paper, pasting or gluing down the crepe paper. Turn the plate upside down so that the rim goes downward. Leave the crepe paper around the paper cup a half inch longer so that you can paste the cup to the center of the plate by means of this half inch of paper. When the cup is pasted to the plate, and it is dry, make a small hole on each side of the plate near the cup, slip a piece of ribbon through the holes, make a knot at the top so that the ribbon won't slip through, and presto, the hat is finished and ready to tie with a nice bow under your chin. It's quite tricky, isn't it?

314. PAPER PLATE TOY TABLE

You will need:

> A large paper plate
> A round cereal box
> Crayons, paint, or colored paper
> Paste

COVER THE CEREAL BOX with the colored paper or the paint. Decorate the outside of a paper plate. Place this inverted plate on the cereal box, in the center, and fasten it down as a table top with glue, paste or a paper fastener.

It's nice making things out of paper plates because they are so easy to handle, and they give such quick results.

TIN CANS, MILK CONTAINERS, AND BOTTLE TOPS

IF YOU WILL look through the pages of this book you will find many suggestions for making things out of tin cans. Here are some extras for good measure, and also some ideas on using milk containers and bottle tops. They're all easy to make.

---

315. SOAP FLAKER

You will need:

> A baking powder can and the cover
> Paint
> A nail

PAINT THE CAN and the cover. When they are dry, put the cover on the can and with a nail punch holes in the cover. Fill the can with dish powder or soap flakes. They'll shake out of the can quickly. Paste a picture on the outside of the can, if you like.

---

316. CANDY TRAY

You will need:

> 2 cream container covers
> 3 thin strips of wood about 12 inches long
> Paper fasteners
> Paint
> Shellac
> Sandpaper

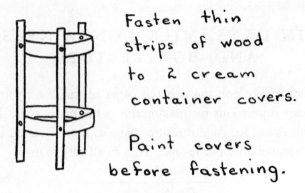

Fasten thin
strips of wood
to 2 cream
container covers.

Paint covers
before fastening.

316. CANDY TRAY

PAINT THE COVERS on both sides. When they are dry, shellac them. Smooth the edges of the wood with sandpaper and give them two coats of shellac. Fasten the strips of wood around the covers as shown in the picture. Punch a hole in the wood first, and use the paper fastener to hold the strips to the covers. This is very attractive when it is finished.

---

317. TOOTH BRUSH HOLDER

You will need:

A quart sized milk container or a smaller size
Paint or colored paper
Paper fastener
Shellac

USE THE LARGER CONTAINER if you have a lot of brushes, but cut it in half, only using the bottom half. If you only have a few brushes then cut off the top of a half pint-sized milk container. Paint it or cover it with colored paper. Since the container is already waxed on the outside hold the colored paper to it with the paper fastener. Shellac it on the outside. Keep it in the bathroom for the toothbrushes. A nice idea would be to make a small one for each one in the family, putting the name on the outside of each with initials cut out of contrasting paper.

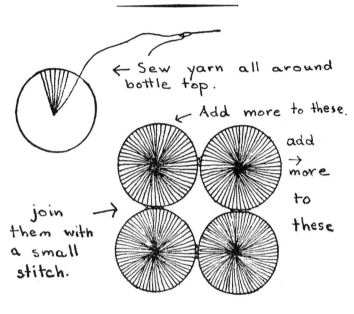

← Sew yarn all around bottle top.

← Add more to these.

add → more to these

join them with a small stitch. →

318. PLACE MATS

You will need:

> About 42 milk bottle tops
> Wool yarn or raffia
> A needle

THIS IS INTERESTING to make because you can make a little of it at a time without spoiling your work. Make each bottle top the same way. Cover it with raffia or wool yarn by sewing around and around from the center out until the top is covered on both sides. Arrange them in rows of six, and make about eight to ten rows. The more tops you have the larger your mat will be. Attach the tops to each other by sewing them with a small stitch at the edges where they touch, and making a double knot. If you are using raffia, then shellac the mat when all the tops are sewed together.

---

319. HANDY ASH TRAY

You will need:

> An empty shoe polish can
> A nail and a hammer

WHEN YOU HAVE finished using the shoe polish, wash the can thoroughly. Keep the cover on it. With a large nail hammer a hole in the cover large enough for a cigarette to pass through. The thing that makes this ash tray so handy is that it can be carried around by the smoker without spreading ashes on the floor. It is also fireproof, as a lighted cigarette can be slipped into the can and it will be put out immediately. You can paint the can if you want to.

---

320. BELT

You will need:

> Milk bottle tops
> Hole puncher
> Ribbon or wool yarn
> Crayons or paint

PAINT OR CRAYON both sides of the milk bottle tops. Punch two holes $\frac{1}{2}$ inch apart at one edge of the top, and do the same

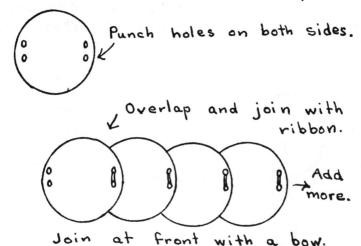

Color both sides of bottle tops.

Punch holes on both sides.

Overlap and join with ribbon.

Add more.

Join at front with a bow.

320. BELT

to the other edge directly opposite. Place the tops together until the holes match, and tie them with a piece of ribbon or yarn. Keep adding milk bottle tops to your belt until it is as long as you want it to be. Tie a bow in the front to join the ends of the belt. You could paint a design in the center of each top with nail polish.

321. CREAM CONTAINER FLOWER POTS

You will need:

> A cream container and the cover
> Paint and shellac

PUT THE COVER on the bottom of the cream container so that the bottom will be that much sturdier. Paint the container on the outside. When it is dry paste pictures on the outside, if you like, give it two coats of shellac, and you're finished. Put a small plant in the center of it after you have filled it with good earth. A few of these on the kitchen window sill will please mother.

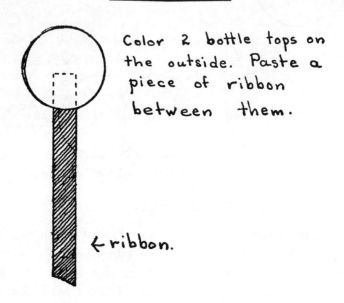

Color 2 bottle tops on the outside. Paste a piece of ribbon between them.

← ribbon.

322. BOOK MARKS

You will need:

> 2 milk bottle tops
> Crayons
> Paste
> Ribbon

COLOR THE BOTTLE tops on one side only. Put paste on the other side, and slip a piece of ribbon about 10 inches long between the two tops as you paste them together. This will hold your place when you are reading a book.

323. IDENTIFICATION TAG

You will need:

> A milk bottle top
> A piece of paper
> **Paste**
> A pair of scissors
> Indelible ink

PASTE THE PAPER on both sides of the bottle top. Trim off the edges. Write your name and address on both sides with indelible ink. Punch a small hole at the top and wear it under your blouse on a thin ribbon, or put it on your key chain.

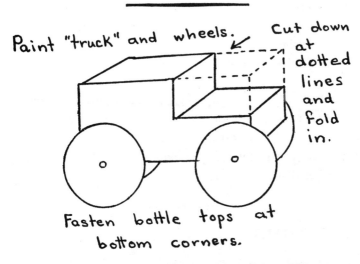

Paint "truck" and wheels. Cut down at dotted lines and fold in.

Fasten bottle tops at bottom corners.

324. MILK CONTAINER TRUCK

You will need:

> A quart sized milk container
> 4 milk bottle tops

> 4 paper fasteners
> A pair of scissors
> Paint

PUT THE CONTAINER down on its side. Cut down from the top at the center half way. Fold down the top pieces to form the engine of the truck. You could paste a picture of a driver here to make it look real. Attach the bottle tops at the bottom for wheels. Paint the whole truck and the wheels. Make a set of these.

___

325. TIN CAN WASTEPAPER BASKET

You will need:

> An oil can
> Paint
> Adhesive tape

ASK DAD TO CUT off the top of an oil can. Clean it thoroughly. Bind the cut edges with adhesive tape so that you won't cut your hands. Paint the can on the inside and the outside. Decorate the outside with pictures, if you like. This is a handy and quick wastepaper basket to make.

___

326. COASTERS

You will need:

> Tops of cream bottles
> Small pictures
> Paste
> Shellac

THE TOPS of wide mouthed cream bottles are larger than bottle tops, and have a high rim usually colored red. Paste a small picture in the center of the cover and shellac it with two coats. Wasn't that a quickie?

---

327. TIN CAN BANK

You will need:

>A baking powder can and cover
>Paint
>A nail

PAINT THE CAN and the cover. When the cover is on make a slit in the top by punching it with a nail. You can take off the cover when you want to take out money from your bank. The wiser thing to do is not to take the money out but to try to fill up the bank to the very top.

---

328. CRAYON BOX

You will need:

>A flat can of fifty cigarettes
>Alphabet soup initials
>Glue
>Paint

PAINT THE OUTSIDE of a flat can of cigarettes. When it is dry carefully glue the initials from a package of alphabets used for soup, across the top to form your name. It will hold many crayons and look nice at the same time.

329. COOKIE CUTTER

You will need:

> A tin can
> A mechanical can opener
> A knob from a drawer
> Glue

USE A FLAT round can for this. Ask mother to use the mechanical can opener to cut off the top so that it will be smooth. Boil the can in hot water to sterilize it. Fasten the drawer knob with glue to the bottom of the can, then when mother cuts out cookies she will have a handle to hold the cutter.

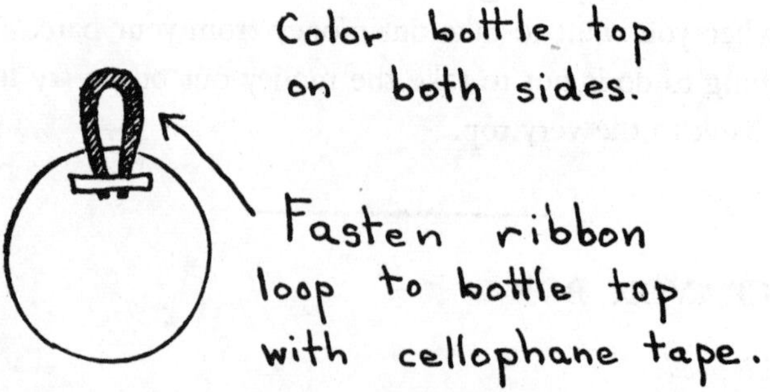

Color bottle top on both sides.

Fasten ribbon loop to bottle top with cellophane tape.

330. TRIMMINGS

You will need:

> Bottle tops
> Colored ribbon
> Crayons
> Cellophane tape

THESE COULD be used at Christmas or at any other festive occasion. Color the tops on both sides. Make a loop of the ribbon and fasten it to the milk bottle top with cellophane tape. Make the loop as long as the bottle top. Use different colors for the tops and for the ribbon.

---

331. SOAP DISH

You will need:

>A sardine can
>Adhesive tape
>Paint

IF YOU HAVE a mechanical opener then cut around the edges of the can so that the edges won't cut you. To be sure that they won't, cover the edges of the can with adhesive tape after you have thoroughly cleaned the can. Paint the sardine can on the outside and the inside, and if you want to, glue a washer underneath so that it won't slip on the sink. Make one for the bathroom and one for the kitchen.

---

332. QUICKIE CHRISTMAS TREES

You will need:

>Coffee can
>Red paint
>Clean sand
>Sprigs of spruce trees

PAINT THE CANS red on the outside. Fill them with clean sand. Stick a sprig of spruce in each can. Put them on the window sill at Christmas time. If you want to use these at other times, then paint the cans to match your room, and fill them with straw flowers.

———————————

Always be careful when you handle the tin cans that you don't cut yourself. If you are doubtful about using them, ask Dad or big brother to help. They'll be only too glad to help you and will probably want to finish the whole thing themselves. The best trick then would be to get doubles and let them make one for themselves while they are helping you, then you'll all have a good time.

SOMETHING FOR THE HOUSE

HERE ARE MORE than two dozen suggestions to make your home a very interesting one. It is a real thrill to make something for the house and to have someone who is visiting you exclaim over something that you have made. It will make people remember your home as being a "lived in" one because of the personal touches that you were so thoughtful in adding.

---

333. FUN WITH OLD RECORDS

You will need:

> An old phonograph record
> Hot water
> Paint

SOAK AN OLD PHONOGRAPH record in hot water until it becomes soft enough to shape. Shape it into anything you like, a dish, a flowerpot, a fruit bowl or anything else. Let it harden and dry. Paint it after it is dry. This will surprise many people when they see the results.

---

334. COVERED PICTURE FRAME

You will need:

> A cardboard circle
> Raffia or wool yarn

CUT A CIRCLE OF CARDBOARD large enough to frame your

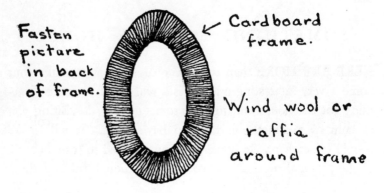

Fasten picture in back of frame.

← Cardboard frame.

Wind wool or raffia around frame

334. COVERED PICTURE FRAME

favorite picture. Have the circle at least 1½ inches wide. Wind wool or raffia around and around the circle until it is completely covered. Join the ends with a knot. if you are using raffia you could shellac it to preserve it. Paste or fasten your picture to one side of the frame. If you prefer an oval shaped frame then cut your cardboard that shape and cover it the same way.

← Paint rim of jar.

← Paste colored pieces of paper all over the jar.

Give it 2 coats of shellac.

335. PAPER COVERED JARS

You will need:

    A jelly jar

Magazines
A pair of scissors
Paste
Shellac
Paint

WASH THE JAR carefully. Cut out small pieces from colored pages of the magazine into triangles, circles, and squares. Paste these all over the jar until it is all covered. Overlap the pieces if necessary. Cover the jar almost up to the rim. Paint the rim a bright color. Shellac the jar with two coats of shellac. This is nice for fresh cut flowers.

set clip in back of picture.

The shape of your pan will determine the shape of your picture.

Be sure to let plaster set for a few hours before removing from pan.

336. PLASTER PICTURES

You will need:

Plaster of Paris

Cold cream or vaseline
A picture
Shellac
A paper clip
A shallow pan

THE SHAPE OF YOUR PICTURE will be determined by the shape of the pan.   If you use a square pan it will be nicer.   Cover the inside of the pan with a coating of cold cream, or vaseline if you have no cold cream.   Smooth it out so that it doesn't show too many finger marks.   Cut out the picture that you want to frame.   It could be a magazine picture, or your own photo, cut out so that you are alone without a background. Very carefully place this picture face down in the pan and on top of the cold cream.   Be sure it is in the center before you place it as you'll smudge it if you have to shift it too much. Make a mixture of plaster of Paris and water until it is as thick as cream.   If you want to color the plaster then put a few drops of blue ink or red ink or coffee or tea into the water as you mix it with the plaster.   When the mixture is as thick as you want it to be, pour this into the pan slowly, while lightly holding the picture.   Pour it for a little more than an inch. Then take away your hand.   Let the plaster set.   After about a half hour or longer put a paper clip slantwise into the plaster, in the middle, to hang up your picture.   If you are making a round picture make a mark on the pan so that you know which will be the top of your picture.   Let the plaster harden thoroughly for a few hours.   Then all you have to do is turn the pan over, tap it on the sides, and the plaster picture will slide right out.   Wipe off the grease with a clean cloth and hang up your picture.

337. BATHROOM SET

You will need:

    3 mayonnaise jars of different sizes, with screw tops
    Paint
    Fancy labels and paste

WASH THE JARS and the covers that you have collected. Try to get three jars of various sizes to make the set or use the ½ pint jar size. Paint the outside of the covers. Paste a fancy label that you can make yourself, one for cotton, one for band-aids, and one for cotton swabs. The jars will keep these things handy and clean and you'll be able to see them when you need them. You could use them for many other things besides.

―――――――――

338. FAMILY BULLETIN BOARD

You will need:

    A large cork place mat
    A piece of wood larger than the place mat
    2 screw eyes
    6 screw hooks, the kind to hang up cups
    Thumbtacks and note paper
    Paint

PAINT THE WOOD the color of the kitchen or hall wall. Place the place mat cork side out in the center and thumbtack it to the board. Put the screw eyes in the upper corner of the wood and hang it up on the wall. Put the six hook screws across the top of the board one inch below the edge of the cork mat. These are handy for hanging keys, and kitchen gadgets. Put a few thumb-

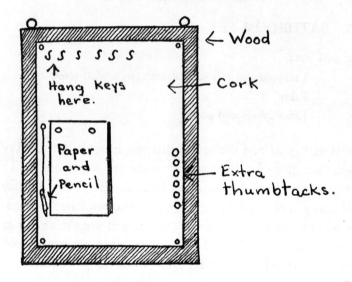

338. FAMILY BULLETIN BOARD

tacks on the side, and tack up a few sheets of note paper to write notes. The extra thumbtacks are to tack up reminders or newspaper or magazine articles that you want the family to see.

If you can get a large piece of beaver board nail it to the wall in the children's room. Thumbtack large sheets of newspaper on this or wrapping paper, tie a thick crayon to a string and thumbtack this to the beaver board and let the youngsters color this up. It will keep your walls clean and give them hours of pleasure.

---

339. ICE CREAM CARTON WASTEPAPER BASKET

You will need:

        An ice cream carton

        Paint

Shellac

Large pictures

ASK THE ICE CREAM store man to save a carton when he has finished with it. It is a large round one. Wash it thoroughly. When it is dry, paint it a bright color. A good idea would be to paint the upper half tan and the bottom half blue or brown. Paint the inside one color. Paste some pictures around the outside. Shellac it on the inside and the outside with two coats of shellac.

Pleat paper. Punch holes in top. Join to frame, with string.

← Join paper at side.

340. PLEATED LAMPSHADE

You will need:

    2 sheets of drawing paper

    Paste

    Crayons

    Hole puncher

    Colored string

PASTE THE TWO sheets of drawing paper at the edges to make it one long piece of paper. Draw a design on the paper and color it. Pleat it by making one-inch folds back and forth like an accordion. Paste the two ends together to join the shade. With a hole puncher punch holes in every pleat. Slip this over the lamp shade frame and wind colored yarn or string or ribbon through the holes in the paper and over the frame of the lamp shade until you come back to where you started to wind. Have a long enough piece so that you can end it with a bow. If you like you can do this at the bottom of the shade too.

---

341. BREAD BOARD

You will need:

> A piece of wood 12 inches by 9 inches and 1 inch thick
> Sandpaper
> A small picture
> A nail
> Shellac or varnish
> Paste

YOU COULD USE the top of an orange or fruit box to get the wood. Sandpaper all around it to make it smooth. Paste a small picture at one end on both sides. Shellac it or varnish it with two coats. Heat a nail in a pair of pliers and burn a hole in it at one end so that you can hang up the bread board when you are not using it.

---

342. BOOKCASE

You will need:

> 3 boards—each as wide as a brick and lengths 4 feet,
> 3 feet and 2 feet

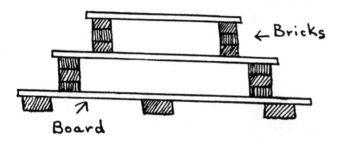

Paint boards. Place on bricks. This is a movable bookcase.

← Bricks

Board

342. BOOKCASE

Paint
15 bricks

PAINT ALL THREE BOARDS on both sides. For a smoother finish you could sandpaper the boards first. When they are dry, place the 4 foot board so that it is resting on a brick at the end and in the center. On top of the board place three bricks at each end. Place the 3 foot board on top of these bricks. Place three bricks at the end of the 3 foot board and place the 2 foot board on top of these bricks. Your bookcase is finished and can be moved quickly from room to room.

---

343. JUNIOR CLOSET

You will need:

An old towel rack
6 large hooks

DO YOU HAVE trouble putting away your clothes because you can't reach into the closet? Ask mother if she'll allow you to do this. Place the six hooks on the back of your bedroom door. Place them low enough for you to reach. A little to one side of these hooks fasten the towel rack. Now you can put your clothes away yourself. When the door is flat against the wall the clothes won't show and will be neatly put away.

———

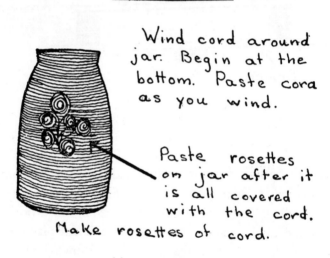

Wind cord around jar. Begin at the bottom. Paste cord as you wind.

Paste rosettes on jar after it is all covered with the cord.

Make rosettes of cord.

344. CORDED JARS

You will need:

> A glass jar
> Colored heavy cord
> Paste
> Shellac

START AT THE bottom on the underside of the jar. Put a little paste on the jar and wind colored cord on it. Keep winding the cord close together, adding a little paste, then winding the cord. The cord will paste to the jar. Wind it closely so that no spaces show through. When you have to add more cord just paste it close to the end of the previous cord. When the whole jar is covered use other colored cord and make rosettes and paste these around the jar. Shellac it when the paste is dry. You could also use crepe paper cord instead of real cord. Make crepe paper cord by cutting strips of crepe paper about ¾ inch wide, and passing it through a hole in a large button, twisting as you pull it through. This will twist the crepe paper into cord. It is just as effective as real cord.

---

345. FOOTSTOOL

You will need:

> 3 cheese boxes
> Nails and a hammer
> 4 chair slides
> A piece of blanket
> Oilcloth
> Thumbtacks
> A pair of scissors

NAIL THE CHEESE BOXES together. Fold the blanket in two and in two again and nail it to the top of the boxes. Trim off the edges. Cover the whole thing with oilcloth, fastening it down on the underside with thumbtacks. Nail 4 chair slides to the bottom and there you have a comfortable and washable footstool.

---

346. KITCHEN RACK

You will need:

> A cheese box
> Paint

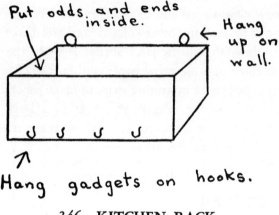

Put odds and ends inside.

← Hang up on wall.

↗ Hang gadgets on hooks.

346. KITCHEN RACK

Several screw hooks as used for cups
2 screw eyes

PAINT THE BOX inside and outside. Put the screw eyes in the back corners to hang up the box. On the outside in the front of the box put a few screw hooks to hang up things in the kitchen. The inside of the box could be used for bills and odds and ends needed in the kitchen.

----

347. TEAKETTLE WATERING CAN

You will need:

        An old teakettle
        Paint
        Decals

LOOK AROUND your cellar for an old teakettle that mother no longer needs. Clean it thoroughly inside and outside. Paint it a bright color. Yellow would be nice. Around the center of it paste some pretty flower decals. That's all there is to it.

It will be handy to water the flower pots with this as the kettle spout can reach into the pots without disturbing the plants. It will also look nice on the porch or in the garden.

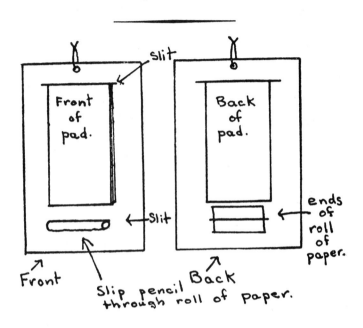

348. KITCHEN REMINDER

You will need:

> A piece of cardboard
> A piece of colored paper
> Paste
> A pair of scissors
> A small piece of wrapping paper
> A pad and a pencil

PASTE THE COLORED PAPER on the cardboard. Cut it around until it measures 9 inches by 6 inches. One and a half inches from the top make a slit an inch from each side. Do the same one and a half inches from the bottom. Slip the back of a pad in the top slit so that the pages are in front of the reminder. Cut a piece of wrapping paper three inches long and as wide as the bottom slit. Hold the two edges together but don't crease the paper, slip the two edges into the slit in the front, slip a pencil through the loop of paper, and paste the two ends down flat on the left side. There is your pad and pencil ready to use. Make a small hole in the top, tie a piece of string through it so that you can hang it up.

---

349. LETTER BOX FILE

You will need:

> An old letter box
> Paint
> Screws or nails

Do you have an old letter box that has become rusty? Don't throw it away. Remove it from the outside of your house. Clean it and paint it. Then screw it to the inside of the kitchen closet. This is very handy for holding bills and little reminders that you want to keep on hand. Mother would like one for herself. You could get one in the dime store brand new and put it inside your own closet door for the same purpose.

---

350. PAINTED JARS

You will need:

> An empty jar
> Paint—2 colors

A PICKLE JAR is a good one to use. Wash it thoroughly. Paint it carefully on the outside. When it is dry, turn it upside down and paint the bottom and a little bit of the sides of the jar with the other colored paint. Let it drip down a little until it dries. When it is dry and you turn it up, it will have made a nice design on the jar.

351. NOTICES

You will need:

> A pad
> Thumbtacks
> A pencil
> A piece of string

VERY OFTEN when you or mother are away and you expect a package to be delivered, you'd like to leave a note. Sometimes you have to leave a note for the milkman. To do this conveniently, fasten a pad next to your door with the thumbtacks. Tie a piece of cord around a pencil and fasten this next to the pad. You could write the note on the pad, and if there will be an answer, you'll find it when you come back.

352. CANDY TRAY

You will need:

> 4 shallow box tops of cardboard, all the same size
> A pair of scissors
> Paint
> Shellac

CUT OFF ONE RIM or side of a cardboard cover. Make a small

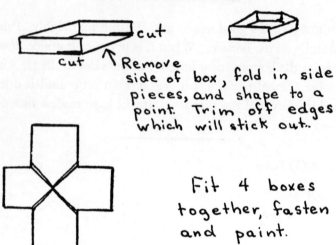

cut

cut

↑ Remove side of box, fold in side pieces, and shape to a point. Trim off edges which will stick out.

Fit 4 boxes together, fasten and paint.

352. CANDY TRAY

cut as shown in the picture into the two side rims. Bring them together and paste into a point. Trim off the edges. This will give your box a point. Do this to the other three covers. Put the four covers together, points fitting together and glue them securely. When the glue is dry, paint the boxes, and give them two coats of shellac. This dish will hold four kinds of candy.

---

353. SHADE OR LAMP PULLS

You will need:

> Empty thread spools
> Colored cord
> A bead and a tassel

YOU COULD PAINT the spools or leave them their natural color. Tie a tassel to a large bead, and this to a heavy cord, and pass it through a spool. Tie the other end of the cord to a window shade or to a light pull on the lamp.

[330]

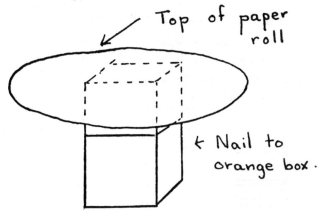

Top of paper roll

← Nail to orange box.

Paint the whole table.

354. MODERN OUTDOOR TABLE

You will need:

> An orange box or egg box
> The circular top of a large paper roll
> Small nails and a hammer
> Paint

IF THERE IS a newspaper plant in your neighborhood ask them if you may have the large roll around which paper is bound. Remove the circular cardboard or sometimes wood at the end of the roll. Place this on an orange box which you have turned open side down. Nail the large circle to the orange box. Paint the whole table. This is very convenient to use outdoors.

---

355. NAPKIN RING

You will need:

> Spring clothespins
> Paint

PAINT THE CLOTHESPINS any color. Paint the names of the members of your family separately on each clothespin. Paste a tiny flower on it if you like. All you have to do is clip each napkin to each colored clothespin.

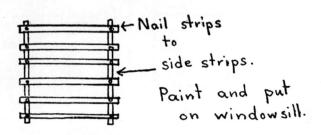

← Nail strips to side strips.

Paint and put on windowsill.

356. PLANT STAND

You will need:

    Strips of wood

    Nails and a hammer

    Paint

MAKE A LATTICE of the strips of wood as it is in the picture. Use two pieces as side frames and on these pieces nail other strips across. The size of the strips will depend upon how large a flower pot you are going to put on it. The average size would be 7 inches long for each strip, nailing them so that there is a little space between each piece. Paint the frame the same color as the window sill. When you put a flower pot on this it won't soil the window sill.

---

357. CARDBOARD NAPKIN RINGS

You will need:

    A paper towel roll

Wool or raffia

A pair of scissors

CUT 2 INCH RINGS from a cardboard. Wind colored wool or raffia around and around it until no cardboard shows. Join the ends with a small double knot on the inside. You're all finished. If you are using raffia you could shellac the rings.

---

358. FLOWER POT FRAMES

You will need:

> Clothespins
> Heavy twine
> Paint

PAINT AS MANY clothespins as you think you will need, depending upon the size of your flower pot. Twenty to thirty clothespins may be sufficient. Tie heavy twine around the flower pot at the bottom of the rim or around the middle. Slip the clothespins over the twine and all around the pot. To make it firmer twist colored cord around the clothespin heads, over and under. You could also make a cover by reversing the clothespins so that the points are sticking up instead of the heads.

---

359. SHADE PULLS

You will need:

> Toy clothespins
> Paint
> Colored cord

PAINT TOY CLOTHESPINS a bright color and the heads another color. Tie colored string around the heads and attach them to the window shades.

Beach roll rolled up.

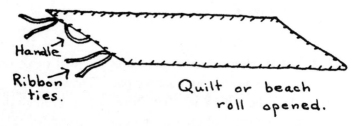

Handle →

Ribbon ties. →

Quilt or beach roll opened.

360. BEACH ROLL

You will need:

> An old quilt
> A heavy needle
> Wool to match or contrast with the quilt
> Four and a half feet of one-inch ribbon to match

SEE THAT THE QUILT is clean. Cut a strip 6 feet long, or as long as the quilt is, and 2½ feet wide. Sew an overcasting stitch all around the quilt with the wool. At one end of the strip, the narrow end, sew two pieces of ribbon, 6 inches from the end. Cut the ribbon into three pieces before you sew them on. Two pieces should be 2 feet each, and 6 inches should be left over. Sew the 2 feet pieces in the center to the edge of the quilt. This will tie around the quilt when you roll it up. The remaining 6 inches will make a handle to hold it or when you are pulling it around on the sand. Sew the handle in the center of the same edge that you sew the ribbon ties. You will enjoy using this on the beach, or in the garden.

---

361. STAMP TRAY

You will need:

      An old serving tray
      Used stamps
      Glue
      Shellac
      Paint

LOOK AROUND the house until you find an old serving tray that has seen better days. Paint the underside and the edges of the upperside. On the tray part which you did not paint, glue used postage stamps in any pattern until it is all covered. When it is dry give it two coats of shellac. This is an unusual tray and will be enjoyed by the family as well as by company.

You'll be spending many a happy hour making these things for your home and I am sure you'll get a big kick out of making them.

TRY INK AND PAINT

YOU CAN HAVE lots of fun with ink and paint. When you are making spatter prints do it outdoors so that you won't scatter paint in the house. Did you know that you could touch up the knicked edges of heels and toes of scuffed shoes with ink the same color as the shoes? Here are a dozen ideas for fun with ink and paint.

---

362. INK SPOTS

You will need:

> A sheet of paper
> Ink

FOLD THE PAPER in half. Open it up. On one half drop a few blots of ink. Fold the paper in half. Press it down with your fingers. Open it up and you will see some fancy designs. Experiment a few times and each time you will get a different pattern. Sometimes they look like butterflies.

---

363. INITIALED STATIONERY

You will need:

> A small piece of cardboard
> A package of writing paper
> Ink

DRAW YOUR INITIAL on the cardboard. Cut out the initial without breaking the edges of the cardboard. Place the initial on the corner of each sheet of writing paper, and carefully ink over the cardboard. Slowly lift the cardboard up without smearing the edges. Let it dry. Use colored ink for a change.

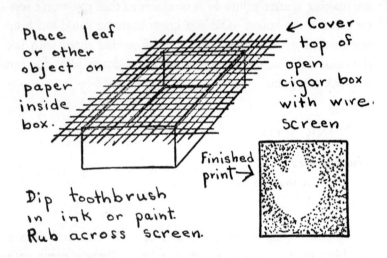

Place leaf or other object on paper inside box.

← Cover top of open cigar box with wire screen

Finished print →

Dip toothbrush in ink or paint. Rub across screen.

364. SPATTER PRINTS

You will need:

A cigar box with the cover off
A piece of wire screening
A toothbrush
Paint or ink

THESE COULD BE MADE into greeting cards or pictures. Pin a leaf or a picture to a sheet of paper. Put it in the cigar box. Cover the cigar box with the screen. Dip the toothbrush in ink or paint and lightly rub it across the screen. It will spatter on the paper. When you think that the paper is sufficiently spattered, let it dry and remove the leaf or the picture and you will be pleased with the results. If you haven't got a piece of wire screen then pass the toothbrush over an old comb.

365. CORK TRIMMED CURTAINS

You will need:

> Small corks
> Paint
> A nail
> String

MAKE A HOLE in each cork by heating a nail in a pair of pliers. Push the nail through the cork. Pull a piece of string through the cork, making a knot in the end so that it won't slip off. Dip the cork into paint. Hang the corks up to dry. Tie them around the bathroom curtains to give them that nautical air.

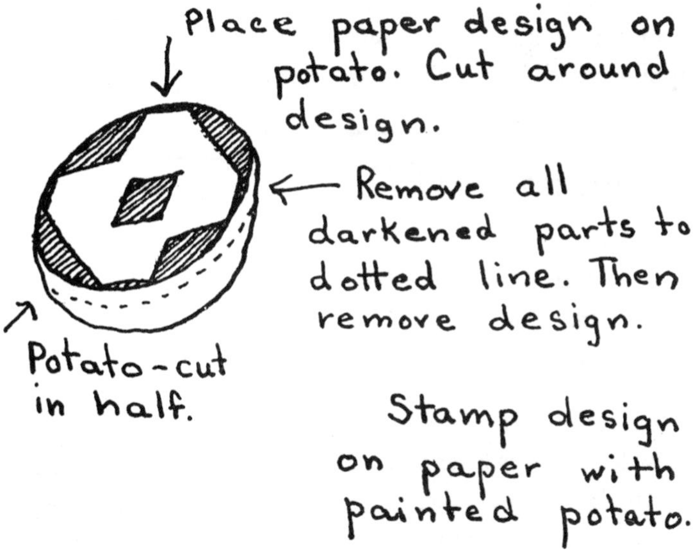

Place paper design on potato. Cut around design.

← Remove all darkened parts to dotted line. Then remove design.

Potato-cut in half.

Stamp design on paper with painted potato.

366. POTATO PRINTS

You will need:

> A potato

> A knife
> A pair of scissors
> A small piece of paper
> Paint or ink
> A large sheet of paper on which to print your design

CUT A FAIRLY large potato in half. Draw a design on the small piece of paper, cut it out and place it on the cut side of one half potato. With the knife cut around the design about one half inch down. Cut out the pieces inside the design too. When your design stands out from the potato, remove the piece of paper and you are ready to print. Brush the surface of the potato with paint or ink and press it evenly on the large paper. Each time you press the design, ink it first. Make rows across or alternate the design. Make another design with the other half of the potato. These will be useful for book covers or wrapping paper. The potato is good for a day.

---

367. DRESSER SCARF

You will need:

> A piece of unbleached muslin
> Indelible ink
> A pencil and a pin

FRINGE THE EDGES of the muslin with a pin, making it one inch wide. Do this after you have cut the muslin large enough to fit on the dresser. You make the fringes by pulling threads at the edges with the pin. When your friends come to the house ask them to write their names any place on the scarf in pencil. Then you go over it with indelible ink. You could dip the scarf in coffee to tint it before your friends put their names on it.

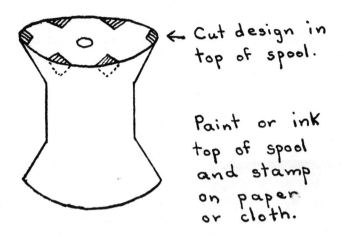

← Cut design in top of spool.

Paint or ink top of spool and stamp on paper or cloth.

368. SPOOL PRINTS

You will need:

    An empty spool
    A knife
    Ink or paint

THIS IS THE SAME idea as the stick print only you use the end of the spool instead of the end of a stick. Cut out your design. Make one at each end so that you will have two different designs. Ink it or paint the ends and press it on cloth. This can be used again and again.

---

369. STICK PRINTS

You will need:

    A wide stick
    A knife
    Ink or paint

CUT OUT a design at the end of a stick with a knife. Ink the end of it just as you inked the design on the potato and use this to print your design. This can be used longer than the potato, as it won't dry up.

Place blue print paper on cardboard. Place leaf on blue print paper. Place glass over all. Expose to light. Wash paper. When dry, place between glass and cardboard. ← Bind edges.

370. BLUE PRINTING

You will need:

>A piece of cardboard
>Blueprint paper
>A leaf or other specimen
>A piece of glass

CUT THE BLUEPRINT paper the size of the cardboard, which should be the size of the piece of glass that you are using. Lay the blueprint paper on the cardboard. Place the leaf in the center of the blueprint paper. Clamp the glass on top of this.

Try to do this in a darkened room so that the blueprint paper won't fade. Hold this in the sunlight about three or five minutes. Hold it at the very corners. If you want to do this by electric light then expose it for at least a half hour or longer. When it is exposed long enough, remove the glass and the flower or leaf, and wash the blueprint paper thoroughly in a pan of water. Dry between blotters or sheets of newspaper. Put books on it to press it flat. When it is dry, place the paper on the cardboard, the glass on the paper and bind all edges together with black pasting paper. If you want to label it before you put on the glass make a mixture of soda and water into a thin paste and with a toothpick write the name of the specimen. A row of these will look nice on the wall. Paste a slip of paper passed through a paper clip, to the back of the picture so that you can hang it up.

———————

371. LINOLEUM BLOCK PRINTING

You will need:

> A square of linoleum
> A knife
> Ink or paint

DECIDE WHAT DESIGN you are going to use. Draw this on the left side of the linoleum. Cut into the design with a knife, cutting away the parts that you don't want to show. Cut away at least one-eighth of an inch down. Paint with ink or paint. Stamp it on paper or cloth. After each print wipe it with a piece of cloth or paper, and re-ink it or repaint it. This will keep your design clear.

372. COMBED WALLS

You will need:
> Paint and a comb

ASK MOTHER OR DAD if you could paint a small wall in the playroom or the basement. When the wall is painted and still wet, take an old comb and run it over the wall, making designs with the comb as you run it on the wall.

---

373. NAME TAPE

You will need:
> A roll of tape ½ inch wide
> Indelible ink

PRINT YOUR NAME and address very small across the tape, several times. Cut off the pieces you have printed and sew them inside your coats, hats and jackets, even inside your school bag, so that you won't lose them.

The nicest thing to do in this chapter is the potato prints. But the trickiest is the blueprinting. Show your friends how to do this and see how grateful they will be. A bit of advice—go to the stationer's or ask at your local museum and they'll tell you where to get blueprint paper.

ODDS AND ENDS

HERE ARE some "extras" that will surely offer many hours of fun in the making.

---

374. SILHOUETTES

You will need:

      A sheet
      A bright light or a flashlight
      A sheet of wrapping paper
      Thumbtacks
      Safety pins
      A pencil or crayon
      A pair of scissors

THUMBTACK A SHEET on a wall that has no windows. On this sheet pin up the sheet of wrapping paper with the safety pins. The person whose silhouette you are going to make should sit in front of the sheet in such a way that while somebody holds the flashlight on him his shadow will fall on the wrapping paper. You may have to shift the person or the light until the shadow is cast just right. Trace around the shadow with a pencil or crayon. Cut out the picture you have traced and mount it on colored paper. Use a large colored paper instead of wrapping paper for variety.

375. GRAB BAG FOR A SICK CHILD

You will need:

> A large fancy bag or a small pillowcase
> Small toys or knickknacks wrapped up nicely

DO YOU KNOW some little boy or girl who is ill? Would you like to make him very happy? Here's a recipe for making any sick child your very best friend, and also make him get well quicker. Get a small fancy pillowcase or a fancy bag. Go through this book and pick out a few things that are easily made and are not too large. Make your own wrapping paper. Tie up each little gift with a fancy bow. Add a coloring book, a box of crayons, a doll or a small boat, and put them in the bag or pillowcase. Tie up the bag or the pillowcase with a ribbon and a bow, and pin a big label to the bag, on which you have printed, "For a very good boy (or girl) who is going to get well in a hurry." You'll be just as happy as he'll be when he opens the grab bag.

---

376. BUTTON PICTURES

You will need:

> Small cards
> Buttons
> A needle and thread
> Crayons

SEW BUTTONS on the cards with the needle and thread, forming pictures. Make a person by sewing a small button for a head, a large button for the body, and drawing in the rest of the figure. Sew three buttons in a row. Draw petals, stems, and

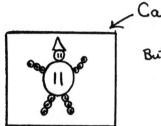

Card.

Button

Sew large
button in
center. Sew
smaller buttons
for arms and
legs.

Sew buttons
on card.
Draw petals
around
buttons.

376. BUTTON PICTURES

leaves around them and you have a garden of flowers. Use your imagination and make many others. Use them as party invitations or announcements.

377. SPONGE TREES

You will need:

> Sponges
> A pair of scissors
> Green paint
> Glue
> Empty pill boxes

CUT TREE SHAPES out of the sponges. Dip them in green

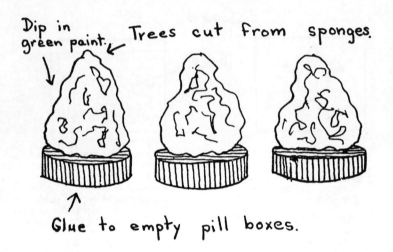

Dip in green paint. Trees cut from sponges.

Glue to empty pill boxes.

377. SPONGE TREES

paint. When they are dry glue them to empty pill boxes so that they will stand up.

---

378. CRACKER CONTAINER

You will need:

> A large napkin
> A minute's time

TRY TO GET a large, heavy, clean white napkin. Fold it in half. When you have folded it this way, fold it in thirds in the same direction as you have folded it in half. Overlap one third over the other third. Your napkin now looks like a narrow band. Hold an end in each hand, turn it under, and slip one end into the other. Put it on the table. Open it up at the top until an opening is made. Smooth this out and put your

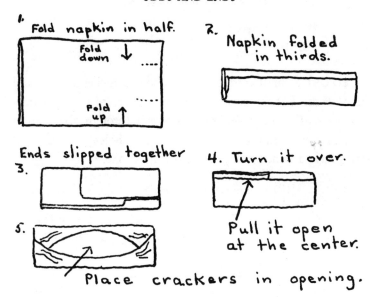

1. Fold napkin in half.

Fold down ↓ ....

Fold up ↑ ....

2. Napkin folded in thirds.

3. Ends slipped together

4. Turn it over.

Pull it open at the center.

5. Place crackers in opening.

crackers in this opening. If you are using toasted crackers this keeps them warm. Try it a few times and see how easy it is.

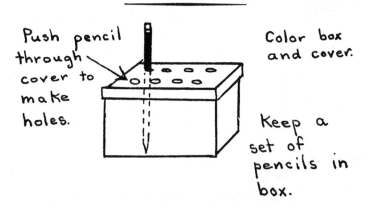

Push pencil through cover to make holes.

Color box and cover.

Keep a set of pencils in box.

379. PENCIL HOLDER

You will need:

A small cardboard box

Paint or crayons

Pencils

TRY TO GET a small cardboard box about 6 inches square, and with a cover. Put the cover on the box and color it with paints or crayons. On the cover, push a pencil through about eight times, in rows. Put your pencils in these holes and you will always have a pencil ready when you need one.

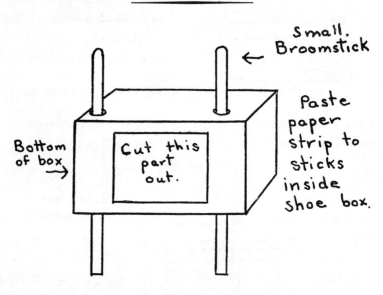

380. MOVIES

You will need:

A shoe box

2 sticks 8 inches longer than the width of the box

A pair of scissors

Several sheets of paper

Pictures

Paste

CUT OUT A PIECE from the bottom of the box large enough to leave a frame about two inches all around. Make a hole in the long sides of the box at the corners, thus making four holes. Turn the box on its side. Slip the sticks through these holes, leaving a piece of the stick sticking out at the top and the bottom. These will be the handles which turn your picture. Cut the paper into strips not quite as wide as the bottom of the box. Paste the strips to each other to make a long strip. Cut out pictures that tell a story and paste them all along the strip of paper. You can print in words between the pictures. Paste one end of the strip to one stick and roll the stick until almost all the paper is rolled around it. Paste the other end to the other stick. To show the movies rest the box on a table so that it is over the edge a little, so that you can turn the sticks. Now slowly turn the sticks so that the people sitting on the other side of you will see the movies as you turn the sticks, showing through the space that you have cut out of the bottom of the box. To make a larger movie use a cardboard carton for the movie and toy broomsticks for the sticks.

———————

381. EYE GLASS CASE

You will need:

> An old felt hat
> A pair of scissors
> A needle and wool yarn

BRUSH THE OLD FELT hat thoroughly until you are sure it is clean. Cut two pieces of felt 5½ inches long, 2½ inches wide. Place them together. Join them on three sides with an overcasting stitch with the wool. Slip a pair of glasses into it or slip an eyeglass case into it. Make one for every member of your family who wears glasses. They'll all appreciate having one of these.

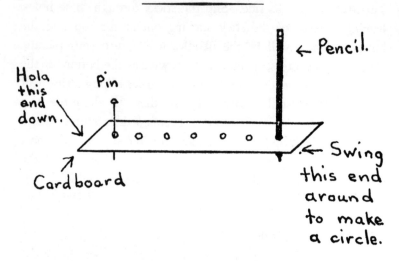

Hola this and down.

Pin

← Pencil.

Cardboard

← Swing this end around to make a circle.

382. COMPASS

You will need:

> A piece of cardboard
> A large needle
> A large pin
> A pencil

CUT THE CARDBOARD so that it measures 6 inches long and from ½ to 1 inch wide. With the large needle make holes ½ inch apart down the center of the cardboard. Put the pin at one end of the cardboard into the last hole. This is the pivot on which the cardboard will turn. The other holes will determine the size of your circle. If you want a large circle put the pencil in the last hole opposite the pin. Hold the pin firmly and swing the pencil and you will have a large circle. If you want a smaller circle then move the pin or the pencil toward the center of the cardboard into the other holes. This is a very easy and quick compass to use.

---

383. TRICK WALKER

You will need:

>An empty match cover
>A dull knife

CUT OFF THE ENDS of a paper match cover. Slip the folded piece of cardboard that you have left, over a knife, the dull edged silver kind. Hold the knife steady and carefully rest it on the table until the ends of the cardboard just barely touch the table. In a minute or so the vibration of your hand will make the match cover start to walk along the knife. Ask your friends to try it.

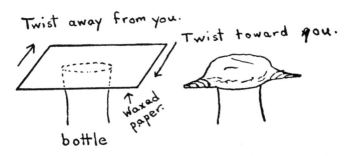

Twist away from you.

Twist toward you.

Waxed paper.

bottle

384. WAXED PAPER COVERS

You will need:

>Wax paper
>A pair of scissors

VERY OFTEN when you take a milk bottle or a jar out of the frigidaire or the ice box you lose the cover. Here's a cover that takes less than a minute to make. Cut out a square of wax-paper larger than the mouth of the bottle. Put it over the mouth of the bottle so that it is centered. Hold the edges or ends in your hands, and twist the left hand away from you and the right hand toward you until a little twist of paper is sticking out of each side. The bottle will be covered securely.

---

385. POP BOTTLE CANDLE HOLDERS

You will need:

> A pop bottle
> Colored candles
> A plate

PUT A POP BOTTLE, preferably a brown glass one, on a plate. Put a colored candle into it. Use it on the table. The wax will melt and drip down the sides. Let it drip until the candle is all finished. The next time you use it put another colored candle in the bottle and allow that to drip over the wax of the first candle. Each time use another color. Gradually all these colored wax drippings will cover the bottle and you will have a lovely, colored, wax-covered bottle.

---

386. NAPKIN RING

You will need:

> A piece of cardboard 6 inches by 2 inches
> Crayons
> A hole puncher
> A piece of ribbon

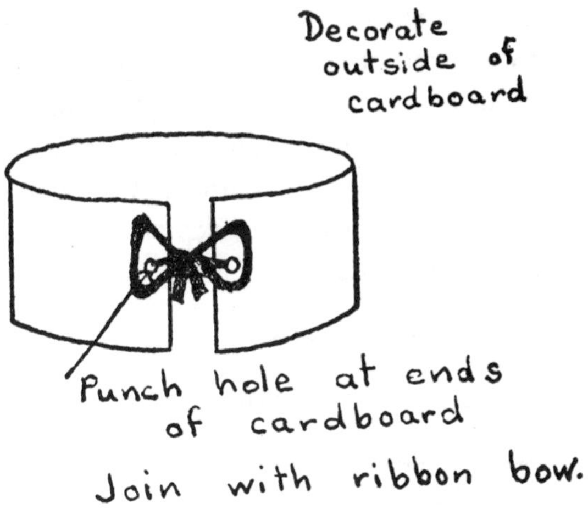

Decorate
outside of
cardboard

Punch hole at ends
of cardboard
Join with ribbon bow.

386. NAPKIN RING

DECORATE THE CARDBOARD on one side (the outside of the napkin ring) with the crayons. Punch a hole at the ends of the cardboard. Join the cardboard edges to make a ring by tying the ribbon through the holes and making a bow. You could make a half dozen of these in an hour.

---

387. SALT PICTURES

You will need:

       Salt
       Flour
       Water
       Small spoon
       Piece of cardboard or a table plate
       Paint
       Toothpick

MIX TWO PARTS of salt to one part of flour, add water slowly until you have made a paste. Use the cardboard or the paper plate as the background of your picture. Dip a toothpick into the mixture to make an outline of any picture that you want to make, as a face or a flag or an animal or a flower. With the spoon fill in the mixture into the outline. Use your hands to shape it as it will rise for about ½ inch above the cardboard or plate. When it dries paint it.

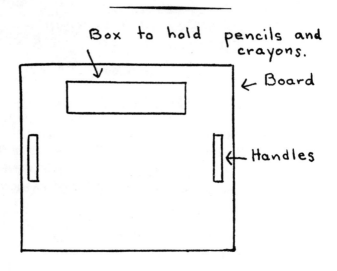

Box to hold pencils and crayons.

← Board

← Handles

388. GAME BOARD

You will need:

> A piece of thin wood 22 inches by 14 inches
> 2 drawer pulls or knobs and screws
> Small wooden or cardboard box
> A few small nails
> Paint

THIS IS A SPLENDID gift for a sick child. Sandpaper the board on both sides. Paint it carefully. On each side of the board screw the knobs or handles. This will make it easier to lift the board. At the top of the board nail the small box. This is handy for crayons, paste and a pair of scissors. Thumbtack a few sheets of drawing paper in the center of the board. This is easy to hold on your knees when you are in bed or sitting on the floor when you are playing.

---

389. SUGAR SCOOP

You will need:

> A large shell
> Paint and shellac

FIND A LARGE SHELL with smooth edges, when you go to the beach. Wash it clean when you are home. Paint it a color to match your kitchen. Give it two coats of shellac. Make another one for flour.

---

390. SPARE HOUR BLANKET

You will need:

> A basket
> Knitting needles
> A heavy sewing needle
> A crochet needle
> Wool yarn
> A piece of cardboard and a crayon

THIS IS FOR PEOPLE or boys and girls who can knit or crochet. With the crayon and cardboard make a sign which will say,

"Spare an hour and knit or crochet a 6 inch square. Help yourself to the materials." Place this sign in your clubroom or playroom or guest room. Under the sign put the basket filled with odds and ends of wool gathered from your home and the homes of your friends. Add knitting needles and crochet needles to the basket. You could also add this to the sign: "If you can't knit or crochet, then please sew some of these squares together." Have the heavy needle sticking into this part of the sign.

With all these materials on hand anyone who has an hour to spare could make a square. When all these squares are sewed together into a blanket then you could present it to the local chapter of the Red Cross which in turn would gladly contribute it to a hospital or other organization in need of such a gift. Many willing hands will be only too glad to "chip" in and make this wonderful blanket.

---

391. QUICKIE SHOPPING BAG

You will need:

> A small orange or onion sack
> Heavy cord
> Dye

WHEN MOTHER GOES shopping ask her to save the sack in which oranges are packed. It is usually about 18 inches long and 12 inches wide. Sometimes it is already colored orange. If it isn't then use any left over dye and color the sack any color. Make two handles of the heavy cord and fasten them to the top of the sack. This is easily carried when in use. When not in use it can be folded up and carried in a pocket or purse.

Felt

Scallop edges.

Loop to hang up.

Sew contrasting felt design on one side of potholder.

392. POT HOLDER

You will need:

> An old felt hat, any color
> A pair of scissors
> An old metal ring, or ribbon loop
> A needle and thread

BRUSH the hat so that you are sure it is clean. Cut out a six inch square. If you would like to make it round cut out a round piece, about six inches across. Cut out scallops or points all around the edges. At one corner sew the ring or ribbon loop so that you can hang it up. If you have another piece of felt of a different color, cut out a small figure and sew it in the center of the pot holder. A set of these would make a nice gift.

393. YARDSTICK

You will need:

> A tape measure

Thumbtacks
A pencil
A piece of string
Photographs of the members of your family
Paste

THIS IS TO BE MADE or fastened to the back of a door. Fasten a long tape measure from the bottom to the top of a door. Be sure that it touches the bottom of the door so that the measurements will be correct. Tie the string around the pencil and thumbtack the other end of the string next to the tape measure. Paste the pictures in a row across the door about 18 inches from the top of the door. Once a month measure each member of the family. Place a mark under the picture and watch the mark rise. This is very effective for little boys and girls, who will be delighted to watch how much they grow each month.

---

394. WASHCLOTHS

You will need:

> An old bath towel
> A pair of scissors
> A needle and thread

CUT OUT THE GOOD PARTS of an old towel, into 10 inch squares. Turn under all the edges on the same side and sew them down with a small stitch. If you want to make a loop in one corner to hang up the washcloth, then sew a small tape or ribbon loop in one corner. That's about ten minutes' work and will supply at least four washcloths from each worn out towel.

395. BABY HOLDER

You will need:

      Old stockings

      A needle and thread or safety pins

THE NEXT TIME you have to mind the baby or take the baby for a walk here's an easy baby holder to make. Take as many clean old stockings that you can get, of all colors. Braid them. Make a loop to fit around the baby's "tummy" and fasten it with a needle and thread or a large safety pin. Make two more braids and fasten them on each side of the loop. These are the handles that you will hold when baby is walking, so make them long enough for comfort.

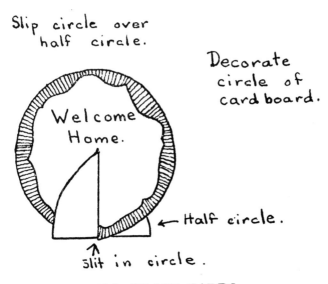

396. PLACE CARDS

You will need:

      2 small cardboard circles or large bottle tops

A pair of scissors
Crayons

CUT ONE CIRCLE of cardboard in half. Decorate the other circle. Make a slit in the decorated circle one-half way up. Stick the circle over the half circle by means of the slit, and the curved end of the half circle fitting into the slit. It will stand up by itself.

---

397. BED BOARD

You will need:

A thin board 24 inches by 24 inches
Sandpaper and paint
Material twice as large as the board
A needle and thread

SANDPAPER the board on both sides. Paint it a light color. Make a jacket for the board by folding the material in half so that the left side is on the outside. Sew the side edges. The folded edge and the two sides will thus be joined. The two open edges can be turned in a half inch and sewed down. This will make a large pocket. Slip the board into this pocket. Lean it against the headboard of your bed. Put your pillow against it. Isn't it more comfortable to lean against this when you are reading in bed?

---

398. DOORSTOP OR PAPER WEIGHT

You will need:

A bottle, any size
A sheet of paper

Colored sand, sugar or salt
Colored chalk

THE SIZE OF THE BOTTLE will decide whether or not it will be used as a paper weight or as a doorstop. The whole trick in making this is in how carefully you pour in the sand. Every time you go to the beach bring home some clean sand and save it. Try to get different colored sand. If you can't get sand then put some salt or sugar on a newspaper and color it by rubbing colored chalk over it. Make a funnel of the sheet of paper. Carefully pour some sand into a small bottle. Then pour another color over that. Keep on adding different colors until the bottle is filled. Try not to move the bottle while you are pouring in the sand. Try to pour it evenly so that the colored bands showing through the glass will also be even. This is very effective. When the bottle is filled to the top then cover it tightly.

---

399. HOT PLATE

You will need:

A large tile
4 rubber washers or a piece of felt
Glue
A pair of scissors

GLUE A PIECE of felt to the underside of a large tile. Trim off the edges. If you have no felt then glue a rubber washer to each corner on the underside of the tile. Make a set of these as a gift.

After you have had some experience making all the things in this book, here's a grand idea. Talk it over with your friends. Start a Hobby Club and call it the "Scrap Fun Club" or the "Be Scraptical Club," or give it any name you like. Collect materials to make things and get busy making them. Then when you have all cooperated in making as many as you can have a "Scrap Sale." Many people will be delighted to purchase your articles. You and your friends will be doing something worth while. Be sure to make enough to give away to some unfortunate children in your neighborhood, as well as enough to sell. The money that you earn could be shared and saved for the future or used to buy something for the club. Think it over, talk it over with Mother and Dad, and here's wishing you lots of luck in your venture.

WHAT TO MAKE

[369]

CATALOG OF DOVER BOOKS

Puzzles, Mathematical Recreations

SYMBOLIC LOGIC and THE GAME OF LOGIC, Lewis Carroll. "Symbolic Logic" is not concerned with modern symbolic logic, but is instead a collection of over 380 problems posed with charm and imagination, using the syllogism, and a fascinating diagrammatic method of drawing conclusions. In "The Game of Logic" Carroll's whimsical imagination devises a logical game played with 2 diagrams and counters (included) to manipulate hundreds of tricky syllogisms. The final section, "Hit or Miss" is a lagniappe of 101 additional puzzles in the delightful Carroll manner. Until this reprint edition, both of these books were rarities costing up to $15 each. Symbolic Logic: Index. xxxi + 199pp. The Game of Logic: 96pp. 2 vols. bound as one. 5⅜ x 8.
T492 Paperbound **$1.50**

PILLOW PROBLEMS and A TANGLED TALE, Lewis Carroll. One of the rarest of all Carroll's works, "Pillow Problems" contains 72 original math puzzles, all typically ingenious. Particularly fascinating are Carroll's answers which remain exactly as he thought them out, reflecting his actual mental process. The problems in "A Tangled Tale" are in story form, originally appearing as a monthly magazine serial. Carroll not only gives the solutions, but uses answers sent in by readers to discuss wrong approaches and misleading paths, and grades them for insight. Both of these books were rarities until this edition, "Pillow Problems" costing up to $25, and "A Tangled Tale" $15. Pillow Problems: Preface and Introduction by Lewis Carroll. xx + 109pp. A Tangled Tale: 6 illustrations. 152pp. Two vols. bound as one. 5⅜ x 8.
T493 Paperbound **$1.50**

AMUSEMENTS IN MATHEMATICS, Henry Ernest Dudeney. The foremost British originator of mathematical puzzles is always intriguing, witty, and paradoxical in this classic, one of the largest collections of mathematical amusements. More than 430 puzzles, problems, and paradoxes. Mazes and games, problems on number manipulation, unicursal and other route problems, puzzles on measuring, weighing, packing, age, kinship, chessboards, joiners', crossing river, plane figure dissection, and many others. Solutions. More than 450 illustrations. vii + 258pp. 5⅜ x 8.
T473 Paperbound **$1.25**

THE CANTERBURY PUZZLES, Henry Dudeney. Chaucer's pilgrims set one another problems in story form. Also Adventures of the Puzzle Club, the Strange Escape of the King's Jester, the Monks of Riddlewell, the Squire's Christmas Puzzle Party, and others. All puzzles are original, based on dissecting plane figures, arithmetic, algebra, elementary calculus and other branches of mathematics, and purely logical ingenuity. "The limit of ingenuity and intricacy," The Observer. Over 110 puzzles. Full Solutions. 150 illustrations. vii + 225pp. 5⅜ x 8.
T474 Paperbound **$1.25**

MATHEMATICAL EXCURSIONS, H. A. Merrill. Even if you hardly remember your high school math, you'll enjoy the 90 stimulating problems contained in this book and you will come to understand a great many mathematical principles with surprisingly little effort. Many useful shortcuts and diversions not generally known are included: division by inspection, Russian peasant multiplication, memory systems for pi, building odd and even magic squares, square roots by geometry, dyadic systems, and many more. Solutions to difficult problems. 50 illustrations. 145pp. 5⅜ x 8.
T350 Paperbound **$1.00**

MAGIC SQUARES AND CUBES, W. S. Andrews. Only book-length treatment in English, a thorough non-technical description and analysis. Here are nasik, overlapping, pandiagonal, serrated squares; magic circles, cubes, spheres, rhombuses. Try your hand at 4-dimensional magical figures! Much unusual folklore and tradition included. High school algebra is sufficient. 754 diagrams and illustrations. viii + 419pp. 5⅜ x 8.
T658 Paperbound **$1.85**

CALIBAN'S PROBLEM BOOK: MATHEMATICAL, INFERENTIAL AND CRYPTOGRAPHIC PUZZLES, H. Phillips (Caliban), S. T. Shovelton, G. S. Marshall. 105 ingenious problems by the greatest living creator of puzzles based on logic and inference. Rigorous, modern, piquant; reflecting their author's unusual personality, these intermediate and advanced puzzles all involve the ability to reason clearly through complex situations; some call for mathematical knowledge, ranging from algebra to number theory. Solutions. xi + 180pp. 5⅜ x 8.
T736 Paperbound **$1.25**

MATHEMATICAL PUZZLES FOR BEGINNERS AND ENTHUSIASTS, G. Mott-Smith. 188 mathematical puzzles based on algebra, dissection of plane figures, permutations, and probability, that will test and improve your powers of inference and interpretation. The Odic Force, The Spider's Cousin, Ellipse Drawing, theory and strategy of card and board games like tit-tat-toe, go moku, salvo, and many others. 100 pages of detailed mathematical explanations. Appendix of primes, square roots, etc. 135 illustrations. 2nd revised edition. 248pp. 5⅜ x 8.
T198 Paperbound **$1.00**

MATHEMAGIC, MAGIC PUZZLES, AND GAMES WITH NUMBERS, R. V. Heath. More than 60 new puzzles and stunts based on the properties of numbers. Easy techniques for multiplying large numbers mentally, revealing hidden numbers magically, finding the date of any day in any year, and dozens more. Over 30 pages devoted to magic squares, triangles, cubes, circles, etc. Edited by J. S. Meyer. 76 illustrations. 128pp. 5⅜ x 8.
T110 Paperbound **$1.00**

CATALOGUE OF DOVER BOOKS

MATHEMATICAL RECREATIONS, M. Kraitchik. One of the most thorough compilations of unusual mathematical problems for beginners and advanced mathematicians. Historical problems from Greek, Medieval, Arabic, Hindu sources. 50 pages devoted to pastimes derived from figurate numbers, Mersenne numbers, Fermat numbers, primes and probability. 40 pages of magic, Euler, Latin, panmagic squares. 25 new positional and permutational games of permanent value: fairy chess, latruncles, reversi, jinx, ruma, lasca, tricolor, tetrachrome, etc. Complete rigorous solutions. Revised second edition. 181 illustrations. 333pp. 5⅜ x 8.
T163 Paperbound **$1.75**

MATHEMATICAL PUZZLES OF SAM LOYD, selected and edited by M. Gardner. Choice puzzles by the greatest American puzzle creator and innovator. Selected from his famous collection, "Cyclopedia of Puzzles," they retain the unique style and historical flavor of the originals. There are posers based on arithmetic, algebra, probability, game theory, route tracing, topology, counter, sliding block, operations research, geometrical dissection. Includes the famous "14-15" puzzle which was a national craze, and his "Horse of a Different Color" which sold millions of copies. 117 of his most ingenious puzzles in all, 120 line drawings and diagrams. Solutions. Selected references. xx + 167pp. 5⅜ x 8.
T498 Paperbound **$1.00**

MATHEMATICAL PUZZLES OF SAM LOYD, Vol. II, selected and edited by Martin Gardner. The outstanding 2nd selection from the great American innovator's "Cyclopedia of Puzzles": speed and distance problems, clock problems, plane and solid geometry, calculus problems, etc. Analytical table of contents that groups the puzzles according to the type of mathematics necessary to solve them. 166 puzzles, 150 original line drawings and diagrams. Selected references. xiv + 177pp. 5⅜ x 8.
T709 Paperbound **$1.00**

ARITHMETICAL EXCURSIONS: AN ENRICHMENT OF ELEMENTARY MATHEMATICS, H. Bowers and J. Bowers. A lively and lighthearted collection of facts and entertainments for anyone who enjoys manipulating numbers or solving arithmetical puzzles: methods of arithmetic never taught in school, little-known facts about the most simple numbers, and clear explanations of more sophisticated topics; mysteries and folklore of numbers, the "Hin-dog-abic" number system, etc. First publication. Index. 529 numbered problems and diversions, all with answers. Bibliography. 60 figures. xiv + 320pp. 5⅜ x 8.
T770 Paperbound **$1.65**

CRYPTANALYSIS, H. F. Gaines. Formerly entitled ELEMENTARY CRYPTANALYSIS, this introductory-intermediate level text is the best book in print on cryptograms and their solution. It covers all major techniques of the past, and contains much that is not generally known except to experts. Full details about concealment, substitution, and transposition ciphers; periodic mixed alphabets, multafid, Kasiski and Vigenere methods, Ohaver patterns, Playfair, and scores of other topics. 6 language letter and word frequency appendix. 167 problems, now furnished with solutions. Index. 173 figures. vi + 230pp. 5⅜ x 8.
T97 Paperbound **$1.95**

CRYPTOGRAPHY, L. D. Smith. An excellent introductory work on ciphers and their solution, the history of secret writing, and actual methods and problems in such techniques as transposition and substitution. Appendices describe the enciphering of Japanese, the Baconian biliteral cipher, and contain frequency tables and a bibliography for further study. Over 150 problems with solutions. 160pp. 5⅜ x 8.
T247 Paperbound **$1.00**

PUZZLE QUIZ AND STUNT FUN, J. Meyer. The solution to party doldrums. 238 challenging puzzles, stunts and tricks. Mathematical puzzles like The Clever Carpenter, Atom Bomb; mysteries and deductions like The Bridge of Sighs, The Nine Pearls, Dog Logic; observation puzzles like Cigarette Smokers, Telephone Dial; over 200 others including magic squares, tongue twisters, puns, anagrams, and many others. All problems solved fully. 250pp. 5⅜ x 8.
T337 Paperbound **$1.00**

101 PUZZLES IN THOUGHT AND LOGIC, C. R. Wylie, Jr. Brand new problems you need no special knowledge to solve! Take the kinks out of your mental "muscles" and enjoy solving murder problems, the detection of lying fishermen, the logical identification of color by a blindman, and dozens more. Introduction with simplified explanation of general scientific method and puzzle solving. 128pp. 5⅜ x 8.
T367 Paperbound **$1.00**

MY BEST PROBLEMS IN MATHEMATICS, Hubert Phillips ("Caliban"). Only elementary mathematics needed to solve these 100 witty, catchy problems by a master problem creator. Problems on the odds in cards and dice, problems in geometry, algebra, permutations, even problems that require no math at all—just a logical mind, clear thinking. Solutions completely worked out. If you enjoy mysteries, alerting your perceptive powers and exercising your detective's eye, you'll find these cryptic puzzles a challenging delight. Original 1961 publication. 100 puzzles, solutions. x + 107pp. 5⅝ x 8.
T91 Paperbound **$1.00**

MY BEST PUZZLES IN LOGIC AND REASONING, Hubert Phillips ("Caliban"). A new collection of 100 inferential and logical puzzles chosen from the best that have appeared in England, available for first time in U.S. By the most endlessly resourceful puzzle creator now living. All data presented are both necessary and sufficient to allow a single unambiguous answer. No special knowledge is required for problems ranging from relatively simple to completely original one-of-a-kinds. Guaranteed to please beginners and experts of all ages. Original publication. 100 puzzles, full solutions. x + 107pp. 5⅜ x 8.
T119 Paperbound **$1.00**

CATALOGUE OF DOVER BOOKS

THE BOOK OF MODERN PUZZLES, G. L. Kaufman. A completely new series of puzzles as fascinating as crossword and deduction puzzles but based upon different principles and techniques. Simple 2-minute teasers, word labyrinths, design and pattern puzzles, logic and observation puzzles — over 150 braincrackers. Answers to all problems. 116 illustrations. 192pp. 5⅜ x 8.
T143 Paperbound **$1.00**

NEW WORD PUZZLES, G. L. Kaufman. 100 ENTIRELY NEW puzzles based on words and their combinations that will delight crossword puzzle, Scrabble and Jotto fans. Chess words, based on the moves of the chess king; design-onyms, symmetrical designs made of synonyms; rhymed double-crostics; syllable sentences; addle letter anagrams; alphagrams; linkograms; and many others all brand new. Full solutions. Space to work problems. 196 figures. vi + 122pp. 5⅜ x 8.
T344 Paperbound **$1.00**

MAZES AND LABYRINTHS: A BOOK OF PUZZLES, W. Shepherd. Mazes, formerly associated with mystery and ritual, are still among the most intriguing of intellectual puzzles. This is a novel and different collection of 50 amusements that embody the principle of the maze: mazes in the classical tradition; 3-dimensional, ribbon, and Möbius-strip mazes; hidden messages; spatial arrangements; etc.—almost all built on amusing story situations. 84 illustrations. Essay on maze psychology. Solutions. xv + 122pp. 5⅜ x 8.
T731 Paperbound **$1.00**

MAGIC TRICKS & CARD TRICKS, W. Jonson. Two books bound as one. 52 tricks with cards, 37 tricks with coins, bills, eggs, smoke, ribbons, slates, etc. Details on presentation, misdirection, and routining will help you master such famous tricks as the Changing Card, Card in the Pocket, Four Aces, Coin Through the Hand, Bill in the Egg, Afghan Bands, and over 75 others. If you follow the lucid exposition and key diagrams carefully, you will finish these two books with an astonishing mastery of magic. 106 figures. 224pp. 5⅜ x 8. T909 Paperbound **$1.00**

PANORAMA OF MAGIC, Milbourne Christopher. A profusely illustrated history of stage magic, a unique selection of prints and engravings from the author's private collection of magic memorabilia, the largest of its kind. Apparatus, stage settings and costumes; ingenious ads distributed by the performers and satiric broadsides passed around in the streets ridiculing pompous showmen; programs; decorative souvenirs. The lively text, by one of America's foremost professional magicians, is full of anecdotes about almost legendary wizards: Dede, the Egyptian; Philadelphia, the wonder-worker; Robert-Houdin, "the father of modern magic;" Harry Houdini; scores more. Altogether a pleasure package for anyone interested in magic, stage setting and design, ethnology, psychology, or simply in unusual people. A Dover original. 295 illustrations; 8 in full color. Index. viii + 216pp. 8⅜ x 11¼.
T774 Paperbound **$2.25**

HOUDINI ON MAGIC, Harry Houdini. One of the greatest magicians of modern times explains his most prized secrets. How locks are picked, with illustrated picks and skeleton keys; how a girl is sawed into twins; how to walk through a brick wall — Houdini's explanations of 44 stage tricks with many diagrams. Also included is a fascinating discussion of great magicians of the past and the story of his fight against fraudulent mediums and spiritualists. Edited by W.B. Gibson and M.N. Young. Bibliography. 155 figures, photos. xv + 280pp. 5⅜ x 8.
T384 Paperbound **$1.25**

MATHEMATICS, MAGIC AND MYSTERY, Martin Gardner. Why do card tricks work? How do magicians perform astonishing mathematical feats? How is stage mind-reading possible? This is the first book length study explaining the application of probability, set theory, theory of numbers, topology, etc., to achieve many startling tricks. Non-technical, accurate, detailed! 115 sections discuss tricks with cards, dice, coins, knots, geometrical vanishing illusions, how a Curry square "demonstrates" that the sum of the parts may be greater than the whole, and dozens of others. No sleight of hand necessary! 135 illustrations. xii + 174pp. 5⅜ x 8.
T335 Paperbound **$1.00**

EASY-TO-DO ENTERTAINMENTS AND DIVERSIONS WITH COINS, CARDS, STRING, PAPER AND MATCHES, R. M. Abraham. Over 300 tricks, games and puzzles will provide young readers with absorbing fun. Sections on card games; paper-folding; tricks with coins, matches and pieces of string; games for the agile; toy-making from common household objects; mathematical recreations; and 50 miscellaneous pastimes. Anyone in charge of groups of youngsters, including hard-pressed parents, and in need of suggestions on how to keep children sensibly amused and quietly content will find this book indispensable. Clear, simple text, copious number of delightful line drawings and illustrative diagrams. Originally titled "Winter Nights Entertainments." Introduction by Lord Baden Powell. 329 illustrations. v + 186pp. 5⅜ x 8½.
T921 Paperbound **$1.00**

STRING FIGURES AND HOW TO MAKE THEM, Caroline Furness Jayne. 107 string figures plus variations selected from the best primitive and modern examples developed by Navajo, Apache, pygmies of Africa, Eskimo, in Europe, Australia, China, etc. The most readily understandable, easy-to-follow book in English on perennially popular recreation. Crystal-clear exposition; step-by-step diagrams. Everyone from kindergarten children to adults looking for unusual diversion will be endlessly amused. Index. Bibliography. Introduction by A. C. Haddon. 17 full-page plates. 960 illustrations. xxiii + 401pp. 5⅜ x 8½.
T152 Paperbound **$2.00**

Entertainments, Humor

ODDITIES AND CURIOSITIES OF WORDS AND LITERATURE, C. Bombaugh, edited by M. Gardner. The largest collection of idiosyncratic prose and poetry techniques in English, a legendary work in the curious and amusing bypaths of literary recreations and the play technique in literature—so important in modern works. Contains alphabetic poetry, acrostics, palindromes, scissors verse, centos, emblematic poetry, famous literary puns, hoaxes, notorious slips of the press, hilarious mistranslations, and much more. Revised and enlarged with modern material by Martin Gardner. 368pp. 5⅜ x 8.　　　　　　　　T759 Paperbound **$1.50**

A NONSENSE ANTHOLOGY, collected by Carolyn Wells. 245 of the best nonsense verses ever written, including nonsense puns, absurd arguments, mock epics and sagas, nonsense ballads, odes, "sick" verses, dog-Latin verses, French nonsense verses, songs. By Edward Lear, Lewis Carroll, Gelett Burgess, W. S. Gilbert, Hilaire Belloc, Peter Newell, Oliver Herford, etc., 83 writers in all plus over four score anonymous nonsense verses. A special section of limericks, plus famous nonsense such as Carroll's "Jabberwocky" and Lear's "The Jumblies" and much excellent verse virtually impossible to locate elsewhere. For 50 years considered the best anthology available. Index of first lines specially prepared for this edition. Introduction by Carolyn Wells. 3 indexes: Title, Author, First lines. xxxiii + 279pp.
T499 Paperbound **$1.35**

THE BAD CHILD'S BOOK OF BEASTS, MORE BEASTS FOR WORSE CHILDREN, and A MORAL ALPHA-BET, H. Belloc. Hardly an anthology of humorous verse has appeared in the last 50 years without at least a couple of these famous nonsense verses. But one must see the entire volumes—with all the delightful original illustrations by Sir Basil Blackwood—to appreciate fully Belloc's charming and witty verses that play so subacidly on the platitudes of life and morals that beset his day—and ours. A great humor classic. Three books in one. Total of 157pp. 5⅜ x 8.　　　　　　　　　　　　　　　　　　　　T749 Paperbound **$1.00**

THE DEVIL'S DICTIONARY, Ambrose Bierce. Sardonic and irreverent barbs puncturing the pomposities and absurdities of American politics, business, religion, literature, and arts, by the country's greatest satirist in the classic tradition. Epigrammatic as Shaw, piercing as Swift, American as Mark Twain, Will Rogers, and Fred Allen, Bierce will always remain the favorite of a small coterie of enthusiasts, and of writers and speakers whom he supplies with "some of the most gorgeous witticisms of the English language" (H. L. Mencken). Over 1000 entries in alphabetical order. 144pp. 5⅜ x 8.　　　　T487 Paperbound **$1.00**

THE PURPLE COW AND OTHER NONSENSE, Gelett Burgess. The best of Burgess's early nonsense, selected from the first edition of the "Burgess Nonsense Book." Contains many of his most unusual and truly awe-inspiring pieces: 36 nonsense quatrains, the Poems of Patagonia, Alphabet of Famous Goops, and the other hilarious (and rare) adult nonsense that place him in the forefront of American humorists. All pieces are accompanied by the original Burgess illustrations. 123 illustrations. xiii + 113pp. 5⅜ x 8.　　　　　　　T772 Paperbound **$1.00**

MY PIOUS FRIENDS AND DRUNKEN COMPANIONS and MORE PIOUS FRIENDS AND DRUNKEN COMPANIONS, Frank Shay. Folksingers, amateur and professional, and everyone who loves singing: here, available for the first time in 30 years, is this valued collection of 132 ballads, blues, vaudeville numbers, drinking songs, sea chanties, comedy songs. Songs of pre-Beatnik Bohemia; songs from all over America, England, France, Australia; the great songs of the Naughty Nineties and early twentieth-century America. Over a third with music. Woodcuts by John Held, Jr. convey perfectly the brash insouciance of an era of rollicking unabashed song. 12 illustrations by John Held, Jr. Two indexes (Titles and First lines and Choruses). Introductions by the author. Two volumes bound as one. Total of xvi + 235pp. 5⅜ x 8½.
T946 Paperbound **$1.00**

HOW TO TELL THE BIRDS FROM THE FLOWERS, R. W. Wood. How not to confuse a carrot with a parrot, a grape with an ape, a puffin with nuffin. Delightful drawings, clever puns, absurd little poems point out far-fetched resemblances in nature. The author was a leading physicist. Introduction by Margaret Wood White. 106 illus. 60pp. 5⅜ x 8.
T523 Paperbound **75¢**

PECK'S BAD BOY AND HIS PA, George W. Peck. The complete edition, containing both volumes, of one of the most widely read American humor books. The endless ingenious pranks played by bad boy "Hennery" on his pa and the grocery man, the outraged pomposity of Pa, the perpetual ridiculing of middle class institutions, are as entertaining today as they were in 1883. No pale sophistications or subtleties, but rather humor vigorous, raw, earthy, imaginative, and, as folk humor often is, sadistic. This peculiarly fascinating book is also valuable to historians and students of American culture as a portrait of an age. 100 original illustrations by True Williams. Introduction by E. F. Bleiler. 347pp. 5⅜ x 8.
T497 Paperbound **$1.35**

CATALOGUE OF DOVER BOOKS

THE HUMOROUS VERSE OF LEWIS CARROLL. Almost every poem Carroll ever wrote, the largest collection ever published, including much never published elsewhere: 150 parodies, burlesques, riddles, ballads, acrostics, etc., with 130 original illustrations by Tenniel, Carroll, and others. "Addicts will be grateful . . . there is nothing for the faithful to do but sit down and fall to the banquet," N. Y. Times. Index to first lines. xiv + 446pp. 5⅜ x 8.

T654 Paperbound **$1.85**

DIVERSIONS AND DIGRESSIONS OF LEWIS CARROLL. A major new treasure for Carroll fans! Rare privately published humor, fantasy, puzzles, and games by Carroll at his whimsical best, with a new vein of frank satire. Includes many new mathematical amusements and recreations, among them the fragmentary Part III of "Curiosa Mathematica." Contains "The Rectory Umbrella," "The New Belfry," "The Vision of the Three T's," and much more. New 32-page supplement of rare photographs taken by Carroll. x + 375pp. 5⅜ x 8.

T732 Paperbound **$1.65**

THE COMPLETE NONSENSE OF EDWARD LEAR. This is the only complete edition of this master of gentle madness available at a popular price. A BOOK OF NONSENSE, NONSENSE SONGS, MORE NONSENSE SONGS AND STORIES in their entirety with all the old favorites that have delighted children and adults for years. The Dong With A Luminous Nose, The Jumblies, The Owl and the Pussycat, and hundreds of other bits of wonderful nonsense. 214 limericks, 3 sets of Nonsense Botany, 5 Nonsense Alphabets, 546 drawings by Lear himself, and much more. 320pp. 5⅜ x 8.

T167 Paperbound **$1.00**

THE MELANCHOLY LUTE, The Humorous Verse of Franklin P. Adams ("FPA"). The author's own selection of light verse, drawn from thirty years of FPA's column, "The Conning Tower," syndicated all over the English-speaking world. Witty, perceptive, literate, these ninety-six poems range from parodies of other poets, Millay, Longfellow, Edgar Guest, Kipling, Masefield, etc., and free and hilarious translations of Horace and other Latin poets, to satiric comments on fabled American institutions—the New York Subways, preposterous ads, suburbanites, sensational journalism, etc. They reveal with vigor and clarity the humor, integrity and restraint of a wise and gentle American satirist. Introduction by Robert Hutchinson. vi + 122pp. 5⅜ x 8½.

T108 Paperbound **$1.00**

SINGULAR TRAVELS, CAMPAIGNS, AND ADVENTURES OF BARON MUNCHAUSEN, R. E. Raspe, with 90 illustrations by Gustave Doré. The first edition in over 150 years to reestablish the deeds of the Prince of Liars exactly as Raspe first recorded them in 1785—the genuine Baron Munchausen, one of the most popular personalities in English literature. Included also are the best of the many sequels, written by other hands. Introduction on Raspe by J. Carswell. Bibliography of early editions. xliv + 192pp. 5⅜ x 8.

T698 Paperbound **$1.00**

THE WIT AND HUMOR OF OSCAR WILDE, ed. by Alvin Redman. Wilde at his most brilliant, in 1000 epigrams exposing weaknesses and hypocrisies of "civilized" society. Divided into 49 categories—sin, wealth, women, America, etc.—to aid writers, speakers. Includes excerpts from his trials, books, plays, criticism. Formerly "The Epigrams of Oscar Wilde." Introduction by Vyvyan Holland, Wilde's only living son. Introductory essay by editor. 260pp. 5⅜ x 8.

T602 Paperbound **$1.00**

MAX AND MORITZ, Wilhelm Busch. Busch is one of the great humorists of all time, as well as the father of the modern comic strip. This volume, translated by H. A. Klein and other hands, contains the perennial favorite "Max and Moritz" (translated by C. T. Brooks), Plisch and Plum, Das Rabennest, Eispeter, and seven other whimsical, sardonic, jovial, diabolical cartoon and verse stories. Lively English translations parallel the original German. This work has delighted millions, since it first appeared in the 19th century, and is guaranteed to please almost anyone. Edited by H. A. Klein, with an afterword. x + 205pp. 5⅝ x 8½.

T181 Paperbound **$1.00**

HYPOCRITICAL HELENA, Wilhelm Busch. A companion volume to "Max and Moritz," with the title piece (Die Fromme Helena) and 10 other highly amusing cartoon and verse stories, all newly translated by H. A. Klein and M. C. Klein: Adventure on New Year's Eve (Abenteuer in der Neujahrsnacht), Hangover on the Morning after New Year's Eve (Der Katzenjammer am Neujahrsmorgen), etc. English and German in parallel columns. Hours of pleasure, also a fine language aid. x + 205pp. 5⅝ x 8½.

T184 Paperbound **$1.00**

THE BEAR THAT WASN'T, Frank Tashlin. What does it mean? Is it simply delightful wry humor, or a charming story of a bear who wakes up in the midst of a factory, or a satire on Big Business, or an existential cartoon-story of the human condition, or a symbolization of the struggle between conformity and the individual? New York Herald Tribune said of the first edition: ". . . a fable for grownups that will be fun for children. Sit down with the book and get your own bearings." Long an underground favorite with readers of all ages and opinions. v + 51pp. Illustrated. 5⅜ x 8½.

T939 Paperbound **75¢**

RUTHLESS RHYMES FOR HEARTLESS HOMES and MORE RUTHLESS RHYMES FOR HEARTLESS HOMES, Harry Graham ("Col. D. Streamer"). Two volumes of Little Willy and 48 other poetic disasters, A bright, new reprint of oft-quoted, never forgotten, devastating humor by a precursor of today's "sick" joke school. For connoisseurs of wicked, wacky humor and all who delight in the comedy of manners. Original drawings are a perfect complement. 61 illustrations. Index. vi + 69pp. Two vols. bound as one. 5⅜ x 8½.

T930 Paperbound **75¢**

History, Political Science

THE POLITICAL THOUGHT OF PLATO AND ARISTOTLE, E. Barker. One of the clearest and most accurate expositions of the corpus of Greek political thought. This standard source contains exhaustive analyses of the "Republic" and other Platonic dialogues and Aristotle's "Politics" and "Ethics," and discusses the origin of these ideas in Greece, contributions of other Greek theorists, and modifications of Greek ideas by thinkers from Aquinas to Hegel. "Must" reading for anyone interested in the history of Western thought. Index. Chronological Table of Events. 2 Appendixes. xxiv + 560pp. 5⅜ x 8.   T521 Paperbound **$1.85**

THE IDEA OF PROGRESS, J. B. Bury. Practically unknown before the Reformation, the idea of progress has since become one of the central concepts of western civilization. Prof. Bury analyzes its evolution in the thought of Greece, Rome, the Middle Ages, the Renaissance, to its flowering in all branches of science, religion, philosophy, industry, art, and literature, during and following the 16th century. Introduction by Charles Beard. Index. xl + 357pp. 5⅜ x 8.   T40 Paperbound **$2.00**

THE ANCIENT GREEK HISTORIANS, J. B. Bury. This well known, easily read work covers the entire field of classical historians from the early writers to Herodotus, Thucydides, Xenophon, through Poseidonius and such Romans as Tacitus, Cato, Caesar, Livy. Scores of writers are studied biographically, in style, sources, accuracy, structure, historical concepts, and influences. Recent discoveries such as the Oxyrhinchus papyri are referred to, as well as such great scholars as Nissen, Gomperz, Cornford, etc. "Totally unblemished by pedantry." Outlook. "The best account in English," Dutcher, A Guide to Historical Lit. Bibliography, Index. x + 281pp. 5⅜ x 8.   T397 Paperbound **$1.50**

HISTORY OF THE LATER ROMAN EMPIRE, J. B. Bury. This standard work by the leading Byzantine scholar of our time discusses the later Roman and early Byzantine empires from 395 A.D. through the death of Justinian in 565, in their political, social, cultural, theological, and military aspects. Contemporary documents are quoted in full, making this the most complete reconstruction of the period and a fit successor to Gibbon's "Decline and Fall." "Most unlikely that it will ever be superseded," Glanville Downey, Dumbarton Oaks Research Lib. Geneological tables. 5 maps. Bibliography. Index. 2 volumes total of 965pp. 5⅜ x 8.
T398, 399 Two volume set, Paperbound **$4.00**

A HISTORY OF ANCIENT GEOGRAPHY, E. H. Bunbury. Standard study, in English, of ancient geography; never equalled for scope, detail. First full account of history of geography from Greeks' first world picture based on mariners, through Ptolemy. Discusses every important map, discovery, figure, travel expedition, war, conjecture, narrative, bearing on subject. Chapters on Homeric geography, Herodotus, Alexander expedition, Strabo, Pliny, Ptolemy, would stand alone as exhaustive monographs. Includes minor geographers, men not usually regarded in this context: Hecataeus, Pytheas, Hipparchus, Artemidorus, Marinus of Tyre, etc. Uses information gleaned from military campaigns such as Punic Wars, Hannibal's passage of Alps, campaigns of Lucullus, Pompey, Caesar's wars, the Trojan War. New introduction by W. H. Stahl, Brooklyn College. Bibliography. Index. 20 maps. 1426pp. 5⅜ x 8.
T570-1, clothbound, 2-volume set **$12.50**

POLITICAL PARTIES, Robert Michels. Classic of social science, reference point for all later work, deals with nature of leadership in social organization on government and trade union levels. Probing tendency of oligarchy to replace democracy, it studies need for leadership, desire for organization, psychological motivations, vested interests, hero worship, reaction of leaders to power, press relations, many other aspects. Trans. by E. & C. Paul. Introduction. 447pp. 5⅜ x 8.   T569 Paperbound **$2.00**

A HISTORY OF HISTORICAL WRITING, Harry Elmer Barnes. Virtually the only adequate survey of the whole course of historical writing in a single volume. Surveys developments from the beginnings of historiographies in the ancient Near East and the Classical World, up through the Cold War. Covers major historians in detail, shows interrelationship with cultural background, makes clear individual contributions, evaluates and estimates importance; also enormously rich upon minor authors and thinkers who are usually passed over. Packed with scholarship and learning, clear, easily written. Indispensable to every student of history. Revised and enlarged up to 1961. Index and bibliography. xv + 442pp. 5⅜ x 8½.
T104 Paperbound **$2.25**

Prices subject to change without notice.

Dover publishes books on art, music, philosophy, literature, languages, history, social sciences, psychology, handcrafts, orientalia, puzzles and entertainments, chess, pets and gardens, books explaining science, intermediate and higher mathematics, mathematical physics, engineering, biological sciences, earth sciences, classics of science, etc. Write to:

Dept. catrr.
Dover Publications, Inc.
180 Varick Street, N.Y. 14, N.Y.